Why Do Actors Train?

Embodiment for Theatre Makers and Thinkers

Brad Krumholz

methuen | drama
LONDON • NEW YORK • OXFORD • NEW DELHI • SYDNEY

METHUEN DRAMA
Bloomsbury Publishing Plc
50 Bedford Square, London, WC1B 3DP, UK
1385 Broadway, New York, NY 10018, USA
29 Earlsfort Terrace, Dublin 2, Ireland

BLOOMSBURY, METHUEN DRAMA and the Methuen Drama logo are trademarks of Bloomsbury Publishing Plc

First published in Great Britain 2023
Paperback edition published 2024

Copyright © Brad Krumholz, 2023, 2024

Brad Krumholz has asserted his right under the Copyright, Designs and Patents Act, 1988, to be identified as author of this work.

Cover design by Ben Anslow
Cover image: white and black abstract painting (© Luca Nicoletti / Unsplash)

All rights reserved. No part of this publication may be reproduced or transmitted in any form or by any means, electronic or mechanical, including photocopying, recording, or any information storage or retrieval system, without prior permission in writing from the publishers.

Bloomsbury Publishing Plc does not have any control over, or responsibility for, any third-party websites referred to or in this book. All internet addresses given in this book were correct at the time of going to press. The author and publisher regret any inconvenience caused if addresses have changed or sites have ceased to exist, but can accept no responsibility for any such changes.

A catalogue record for this book is available from the British Library.

Library of Congress Cataloging-in-Publication Data
Names: Krumholz, Brad, author.
Title: Why do actors train?: embodiment for theatre makers and thinkers / Brad Krumholz.
Description: London; New York: Methuen Drama, 2023. | Includes bibliographical references and index.
Identifiers: LCCN 2022043268 (print) | LCCN 2022043269 (ebook) |
ISBN 9781350236967 (hardback) | ISBN 9781350237001 (paperback) |
ISBN 9781350236974 (adobe pdf) | ISBN 9781350236981 (epub)
Subjects: LCSH: Acting--Study and teaching.
Classification: LCC PN2075 .K78 2023 (print) | LCC PN2075 (ebook) |
DDC 792.02/807–dc23/eng/20221014
LC record available at https://lccn.loc.gov/2022043268
LC ebook record available at https://lccn.loc.gov/2022043269

ISBN: HB: 978-1-3502-3696-7
PB: 978-1-3502-3700-1
ePDF: 978-1-3502-3697-4
eBook: 978-1-3502-3698-1

Typeset by Deanta Global Publishing Services, Chennai, India

To find out more about our authors and books visit www.bloomsbury.com and sign up for our newsletters.

"Some books might tell you that the body is important without going much beyond this slogan. This book tells you why! A sharp and careful analysis of the many ways theatre practice might be said to be embodied. Brad Krumholz expertly engages in some of the most recent contemporary philosophical theories and opens up a way for theatre scholars and practitioners to think differently."

—**Frédérique de Vignemont,** *CNRS Research Director, Jean Nicod Institute, Paris, France*

"How do the actions of everyday life change when they're performed under the eyes of an audience? Drawing on the growing field of embodied cognition and his own extensive experience in acting, directing, and actor training, Brad Krumholz answers this question with a rich account of acting—and actor training—as dynamic, relational, sensorimotor processes. Bristling with insights, this book is essential reading for anyone interested in why actors train and what this training accomplishes."

—**Stanton B. Garner Jr.,** *James Douglas Bruce Professor of English and Theatre, University of Tennessee, USA*

"*Why Do Actors Train?* is a thoroughly considered analysis of what is happening at the site of performance. I felt invited to encounter myself as a performer and a human being through a different lens, thus reconsidering myself onstage and off."

—**Jenn Kidwell,** *Performing Artist*

For the Survivors of the Ice Age

Contents

Overview		1
	What a Body Can Be: Defining Our Subject	2
	The Trouble with Mind/Body Dualism	4
	Embodied Cognition Defined	6
	Performance Philosophy: Contours of the Field	10
	Acting and Technique	13
	Performance Styles Considered	15
	Making Meaning through Acting	22
	My Methodology	23
	Structure of This Book	26
1	Action in Theory and Practice	33
	Introduction	33
	Training Exercises and the *Plastiques*	34
	Approaching Action through Wittgenstein	39
	What Is Intention?	44
	Principles of Scenic Behavior	49
	Mark Johnson and Image Schemas	51
	Maxine Sheets-Johnstone and Animate Forms	61
	Where Is Meaning Located?	63
	The Importance of Interaction	69
	Concluding Thoughts	72
2	Encountering Perception and Proprioception in the Actor's Craft	75
	Introduction: *The 3 Layers* Exercise	75
	Alva Noë and the Enactive View	79
	The Role of Attention	84
	Proprioception: Body Image and Body Schema	88
	Dynamic Space	94
	Competency and Presence	96
	Ways of Seeing	99
	Bodies Working Together	101
	Achieving Fluency	105
	Concluding Thoughts and the Fourth Layer	107

3	Approaching the Voice beyond the Word	109
	Introduction: *Vocal Action*	109
	Theorizing Sound and Voice	110
	Awakening the Resonators	113
	Kreiman and Sidtis: Voice and Voice Quality	117
	The Embodied Voice	119
	The Components of Prosody	123
	Listening	126
	Gesture and Speech, Connected	130
	Simulation and Vocal Production	135
	The Embodied Voice and Sociality	139
	Theatre as a Site of Engagement	145
	Concluding Thoughts	147

Afterthinking	149
Introduction	149
An Enactive Theory of Emotion	150
Imagination as an Embodied Process	154
Some Possible Concerns about This Book	160
Escaping the Dualistic Language Trap	166
The Proficiency Model: Real-life Benefits of Actor Training	168
Concluding Thoughts	172

Notes	175
Bibliography	194
Index	205

Overview

Acting is a mysterious craft. In some theatrical traditions, actors need to train from the time they are small children in order to master their art, while in others, it is possible for a person to become a star of the stage virtually overnight. As an actor, director, and teacher and scholar of theatre myself, the craft of acting has always held a deep fascination for me. In theatre, the action onstage is real, but it is also unreal; the pounding of a fist on a table is, indeed, a real fist colliding with solid wood, but it is also prearranged and contains meaning beyond itself as a facet of the developing story of relationships between characters. In many ways, the words uttered are just like the spontaneous words used in everyday speech; we recognize them, but they are the results of preparation and choice, pre-written, rehearsed, and stylized in their delivery. The actors themselves are simultaneously real people and constantly mutating objects of art.

This book is an attempt to understand how it is that actors live in the fictive reality of theatre. It asks, "What do actors do, and how do they do it?" It searches for answers to these questions by examining the tools that actors use to acquire and develop the abilities necessary to perform onstage. It is my contention that if we wish to answer these fundamental questions about the actor's craft, a good way to begin would be to analyze the tools that have proven successful over time at aiding in the formation of working actors. By looking at the component parts of actor-training exercises, we can see precisely how they function in the process of helping actors to develop particular techniques. This will, in turn, allow us to see why actors might need to develop such skills. In other words, through analyzing the tools, we can see their function, and in seeing their function, we can glean what the form of art requires and what defines it. Through the hammer and the saw, we can see the house.

In this book I present and analyze three distinct actor-training exercises primarily, but not exclusively, through the lens of the Embodied Cognition (EC) branch of contemporary philosophy. As I will make clear in the course of this introductory overview, EC attempts to frame human understanding as a fully embodied process of interaction with the environment. Drawing from neuroscience, psychology, linguistics, and other branches of philosophy, EC provides both an excellent set of strategies and a strong theoretical framework to help explain how people encounter meaning in life. I apply its unique perspectives to this philosophical account of the embodied actor as I analyze the various elements at play in actor-training praxis, which allows me to shed some light on both the mysterious craft of acting and on theatre itself.

Each of the exercises addressed in this book is geared toward developing different aspects of the actor's craft. As is often the case with such exercises, they are comprised of complicated sets of rules and guidelines, and their forms can be geared to operate within a range of applications and for actors at a variety of skill levels. It is not always apparent at first glance what skills these exercises are supposed to develop, mainly because the fundamental instrument and medium of the actor, namely the body, is made up of a vast array of simultaneously functioning elements and processes. So, before understanding the purpose of the exercises, it will be useful to consider the broad spectrum of components that are determined by what I am calling bodies and how they function.

What a Body Can Be: Defining Our Subject

At first glance it may seem fairly easy and intuitive to claim that actors have bodies and that those bodies are central to their work in the theatre. However, the question of "what is a body" is not only far from settled; it also brings with it complex and often divergent histories of how to formulate the concept of *body* (not to mention the complications that arise when considering bodily extensions, both material and digital, virtual and augmented reality, and a host of post-human notions of body, which I am not focusing on in this book). In the field of theatre studies alone there is a long and tortuous road of approaches to the subject. Joseph Roach, in *The Player's Passion*, lays out his "history of the theatricalization of the human body" by focusing on the question of emotion while tracing the dominant scientific paradigms of the ages, mainly in Europe. Roach begins by presenting various formulations of "the actor's body" in the sixteenth and seventeenth centuries, including one vivid example of a "large bag containing juice-filled sponges of various shapes and sizes," with the "humours" determining the functioning of the passions.[1] He moves on from there to the Cartesian vision of the body as mechanical animal guided by soul (or mind) in the later seventeenth century and beyond, and then to twentieth-century notions of the body as a social animal with guiding psychology, which was dominant during the time of Stanislavsky and Meyerhold (although each had his own unique interpretation of how the actor's body should function in performance). Roach ends with a brief discussion of Grotowski's vision of the "Holy Actor," in the context of "modernist concepts of mind-body monism, creative subconscious, and the conditioned ('canalized') stimulus and response" of the latter half of the twentieth century.[2] Throughout all of this, one gets a sense not only of how ideas about bodies change but also of how what bodies actually are changes. How we understand what a body is at a given place and time determines the body's reality.

This is, of course, only one way to see how "what the body is" changes over time. Simon Shepherd, in *Theatre, Body and Pleasure*, takes the reader down a different path of thinking about bodies, recounting "several stories [that] can be told about the causes of the contemporary interest in the body."[3] One of these stories begins in the 1960s with performance and "body art" as a point of departure and makes an argument that the appearance of the female body as a point of theatrical focus necessitated a reformulation of traditional masculinist ways of seeing bodies. "The feminist engagement," says Shepherd, "made the body into a key topic, politically and theoretically."[4] He locates the theories of theatre scholar Elizabeth Grosz at the center of this discussion. Critical to Grosz's project is the notion that there is no such thing as the "natural" or "real" body. All bodies, to her way of thinking, are socialized bodies, "inscribed" by the cultures in which they exist and defined by the ways in which they are conceived at a given time and place. "These representations and cultural inscriptions," she argues in *Volatile Bodies*, "quite literally constitute bodies and help to produce them as such."[5] She positions herself firmly against the assumptions of Cartesianism, which I will speak about shortly, and calls for a radical reenvisioning of how we understand all bodies, especially those of women. "We need an account which refuses reductionism," she says, "resists dualism, and remains suspicious of the holism and unity implied by monism—a notion of corporeality, that is, which avoids not only dualism but also the very problematic of dualism that makes alternatives to it and criticisms of it possible." Her work is part of the broader critical context of second-wave feminism, and in its attempt at an "inversion" of traditional conceptions of the individual, it succeeds in forming a new way of understanding what bodies might be.[6]

Shepherd's other "stories" include a critique of the "assumed (masculinist) separation of mind from body," from the philosophical perspective; projects aimed at healing bodies sick from "the alienation produced by modern and industrial life" in the therapeutic movement traditions of F. Matthias Alexander, Moshe Feldenkrais, and Rudolph Laban; and sociological perspectives of quotidian performance and performativity, such as those that connect back to Erving Goffman's seminal work *Presentation of the Self in Everyday Life* and the formulations of bodily performance presented in the theatre anthropologies of Victor Turner and Richard Schechner. He also touches upon some contemporary modes of conceiving of bodies in relation to today's fitness lifestyles and notions of beauty.[7] Again, all of these stories of bodies are told in tongues specific to a variety of disciplines, but what unites them is the fact that they are connected to a common concern, namely what "the body" is and how it functions in relation to "performance." Of course, there are a great many ways in which one can theorize bodies, both inside and alongside questions of performance. Entire edited volumes have been devoted to just that, and while this is not the place for a comprehensive review of the history of the body, it is safe to say that the "commonplace on which performers and spectators alike have readily agreed," and upon which Roach and many others base their analyses, namely that "the actor's body constitutes his instrument, his medium, his chief means of creative expression," is a far cry from easy reckoning.[8]

The Trouble with Mind/Body Dualism

A common component of stories of the body that applies directly to this book is the dismissal of the Cartensianist project of substance dualism.[9] Simply put, the problem of mental causation, which dates back to the correspondence between René Descartes and Princess Elisabeth of Bohemia over 350 years ago, hinges on the question of how it is possible, if the mind is understood to be a separate substance from the body, that bodily action can be instigated and directed by the mind.[10] More and more, general agreement is growing among contemporary philosophers that mind/body substance dualism cannot be maintained, and that idealist philosophies that posit a metaphysical realm of disembodied thought are all but insupportable.[11] Regardless, however much this may or may not continue to be a conceptual sticking point for philosophers, it presents a much deeper problem outside of philosophy proper. The tendency toward Cartesianism in the Western mindset writ large is so hegemonic that it finds its way into just about everything, from how we think about thinking to how our bodies act onstage.[12] So ingrained is the notion of thought and ideation as an abstract and symbolic process that happens in the disembodied space of the mind, on the one hand, and of action and physical processes as occurrences in the realm of the physical flesh of the body, on the other, that we can hardly imagine any other way of understanding our experience of being-in-the-world—thinking and processing meaning is assumed to occur separately from yet simultaneously alongside touching, eating, walking, moving, and so on.

If one believes, even without knowing that one believes it, that the process of engaging meaningfully with the world is independent of bodily existence, it stands to reason that one would not pay significant attention to the role of the body in consciousness and experience. In theatre, we can observe this lacuna in the structure of actor-training programs, which commonly separate out "movement" classes, Alexander Technique, Feldenkrais, and Yoga from classes focusing on "analysis" for what is generically called "psychological realism." As Nathan Stucky and Jessica Tomell-Presto make clear in their systematic review of actor-training programs in the United States, "the actor's training is typically divided into the training of the voice, body, and mind through coursework in voice, movement, and acting . . . classes in acting, through scene study, textual analysis, and character analysis, develop the mind."[13] Even so-called "sense memory" exercises frequently require actors to lie inertly on their backs with their eyes closed, locating the activity in some disembodied mind-space, where the faculty called "imagination" is supposed to live. As Roach bluntly and accusatorially asserts in his foreword to Ben Spatz's *What a Body Can Do*,

> as the most chicken-brained idea of Western metaphysics, "the separation of mind and body," still rules the roost . . . mind-body dualism also still constrains meaningful conversations across the hall between studio and study, even in institutions that should have left it behind long ago. Acing students are still told—I have heard it recently from teachers who ought to know better and almost certainly do—that actors need first of all "to get out of their heads," as if decapitation is a viable option as prerequisite to a course of study. Dance teachers are still told—I have heard it recently from administrators who don't know any better and probably never will—that students can't possibly be learning anything academically rigorous if they're on their feet and moving.[14]

What is more, if we conceive of the mind of the actor as functioning on purely symbolic and conceptual levels, the question arises as to how, exactly, the workings of the mind become meaningful and visible to an audience. There would have to be an additional step to get from thinking (with the mind) to doing (with the body), both on the philosophical level and on the practical level.

This book is an attempt to present an analysis of the actor's work that is solidly grounded in and framed by contemporary approaches to the body and mind that are in keeping with recent scientific discoveries and theories of sensorimotor interactionism and cognition. I present ways of understanding what actors do that rely upon particular approaches to what bodies are and how they function, and these approaches require a conception of the body that is radically different from that to which we have been accustomed throughout the bulk of the modern age. As I have already noted, in philosophy this non-dualistic approach is quite well accepted and developed, but in theatre, we are a little bit behind the curve, especially in the realm of practice. Part of the impulse for this book is to shed light on practice through theory, to bring to bear an understanding of these new modes in the theatre studio, so that the work being done there (and how it is spoken about) can reflect a way of thinking about bodies and what they do, both in and out of the theatre, that is in accordance with views that do not perpetuate outmoded conceptions of body that rely upon the entrenched yet false constructs implicit in mind/body dualism.

Embodied Cognition Defined

Of the various theoretical approaches to overcoming the difficulties posed by the persistence of dualism, the field of EC seems to be among the most direct and practicable and certainly the most applicable to the area of theatrical inquiry undertaken in this book. In this section I will make reference to several approaches to the field, leaving intact the often specialized theoretical language to emphasize the difficulty of settling on any one simple set of defining characteristics. Leading EC theorist Lawrence Shapiro offers a succinct encapsulation of the field, which he prefers to call a "research program," stating that "Embodied Cognition is an approach to cognition that departs from traditional cognitive science in its reluctance to conceive of cognition as computational and in its emphasis on the significance of an organism's body in how and what the organism thinks."[15] His insistence upon calling EC a research program, rather than a distinct discipline or school, results from the fact that there are so many, often contradictory, variations of approach to this central tenet that providing a true summary of its aims is nearly impossible. Shapiro organizes his broad analysis of EC into three "themes," which serve as a means to categorize the various approaches that currently exist. "The themes," he explains, "in no particular order of importance, are these":

1. *Conceptualization: The properties of an organism's body limit or constrain the concepts an organism can acquire.* That is, the concepts on which an

organism relies to understand its surrounding world depend on the kind of body that it has, so that were organisms to differ with respect to their bodies, they would differ as well in how they understand the world.

2. *Replacement: An organism's body in interaction with its environment replaces the need for representational processes thought to have been at the core of cognition.* Thus, cognition does not depend on algorithmic processes over symbolic representations. It can take place in systems that do not include representational states and can be explained without appeal to computational processes or representational states.

3. *Constitution: The body or world plays a constitutive rather than merely causal role in cognitive processing.* To illustrate this distinction in a different context, consider constitutive versus causal roles of oxygen. Oxygen is a constituent of water because water consists in atoms of oxygen conjoined with atoms of hydrogen. On the other hand, oxygen might be a cause of an explosion, because without the presence of oxygen, the fuse would not have ignited. Likewise, according to the Constitution claim, the body or world is a constituent of, and not merely a causal influence on, cognition.[16]

Shapiro's division of EC into these three themes is one useful way of organizing a basic understanding of the research program as a whole, but one would do well to keep in mind that the categories do not neatly align with one approach versus another; they frequently overlap and coexist within a given set of theoretical propositions.

Another useful way of separating out the various approaches of EC is presented by psychologist Margaret Wilson, who delineates six different "views" held by philosophers in the field, each based on a different claim:

1. *Cognition is situated.* Cognitive activity takes place in the context of a real-world environment, and it inherently involves perception and action.

2. *Cognition is time pressured.* We are "mind on the hoof" ... and cognition must be understood in terms of how it functions under the pressures of real-time interaction with the environment.

3. *We off-load cognitive work onto the environment.* Because of limits on our information-processing abilities (e.g., limits on attention and working memory), we exploit the environment to reduce the cognitive workload. We make the environment hold or even manipulate information for us, and we harvest that information only on a need-to-know basis.

4. *The environment is part of the cognitive system.* The information flow between mind and world is so dense and continuous that, for scientists studying the nature of cognitive activity, the mind alone is not a meaningful unit of analysis.
5. *Cognition is for action.* The function of the mind is to guide action, and cognitive mechanisms such as perception and memory must be understood in terms of their ultimate contribution to situation-appropriate behavior.
6. *Off-line cognition is body based.* Even when decoupled from the environment, the activity of the mind is grounded in mechanisms that evolved for interaction with the environment—that is, mechanisms of sensory processing and motor control.[17]

Again, while there is no single agreed-upon approach to EC, the overarching theme remains that, as Wilson summarizes, "the mind must be understood in the context of its relationship to a physical body that interacts with the world."[18] The various approaches to EC linked by this central thesis provide me with a set of scientifically based theoretical tools that aid substantially in my ability to analyze the process of the actor at work.

While it is true that I draw heavily from EC in this book, I do not, nor do I feel the need to commit wholesale to any one particular view. For example, while I tend to agree with certain approaches that would fall into Shapiro's second category of Replacement (e.g., that environmental interaction is central to cognition), my stance on the question of representationalism is still in progress. I do not necessarily subscribe to the "radical" view of EC proposed by Anthony Chemero and others, who believe that there simply are no mental representations, and that our encounter with the environment provides us with everything we need to process information and engage meaningfully with the world. As Chemero states unambiguously, "I hereby define radical embodied cognitive science as the scientific study of perception, cognition, and action as necessarily embodied phenomenon, using explanatory tools that do not posit mental representations."[19] For Chemero, traditional cognitive science has misconstrued cognition in a way that requires an unnecessary load of neural processing that, according to radical EC, can be explained "as the unfolding of a brain-body-environment system, and not as mental gymnastics." He bristles at the idea of any residual influence of "Cartesian extremism" and "the Cartesianism of early cognitive science," and he is committed to working toward a new science that "allow[s] that cognition is necessarily embodied."[20] Also, like Chemero, Mark Johnson considers the representational approach to be exceedingly problematic, calling it "one of the most dangerous dualistic traps of Western philosophy, namely, asking how something inside the 'mind' (i.e., ideas, thoughts, mathematical symbols) can represent the outside (i.e., the world)."[21] Johnson proposes a "nondualistic, nonrepresentational view of mind as a process of organism-environment interactions."[22] This *interactionist* view states that mind is not a static storehouse, nor is it disembodied in any way, but rather that "*cognition is action*, rather than mental mirroring of an external reality."[23] "The key to this reconciling of mind," says Johnson, "is to stop treating percepts, concepts, propositions, and thoughts as quasi-objects (mental entities or abstract structures) and to see them instead as patterns of experiential interaction."[24]

While I strongly agree with much of Johnson's perspective, and I sympathize with the general antagonism toward Cartesianism, I also remain unconvinced that, first, we can say that there are absolutely no mental representations involved in cognition, and that, second, there is even general agreement on the subject of what qualifies as a representation at all. Andy Clark, a philosopher whom Chemero admires and who is very much connected to Wilson's view number three, in which cognition is off-loaded into the environment, clearly states his opposition to what he calls "'objectivist' representations," defined as "sentence-like representations of the action-neutral environment in a language of thought," but he does allow for limited "action-oriented representations."[25] Alva Noë, in his "enactivist" approach (in line with Wilson's view number five), also eschews representationalism on the whole, but he is more in favor of a reassessment than an outright rejection, hoping that "'detailed internal world representations' can be demoted from their theoretical place of pride."[26] His work approaches cognition through the process of perception. According to his view, "to perceive something, you must understand it, and to understand it you must, in a way, already know it, you must have already made its acquaintance."[27] For Noë being-in-the-world is bound up with perception and cognition, and mind is an active process of making one's way in and through and with the world; it is the encounter, the interaction, that brings mind into being (see Chapter 2). Further, neurophilosopher Mark Rowlands, who is a situated cognition proponent (Wilson's view number one) in favor of representation, goes so far as to state that to have a representation is to act.[28]

For my current purposes it is less important to stake a claim in this philosophical debate than it is to provide for the reader a sense of the conversation comprehensive and clear enough to understand the various points of view involved, and to mobilize those that are strong enough claims to aid in theorizing what processes might be at play in the actor's encounter with craft. In other words, EC provides some very useful tools to understand what an actor's body is and how it can be said to function in the context of theatrical practice. In the following chapters I draw heavily upon the research of Johnson and Noë (in particular, but not solely), because even if their positions on representationalism might cause certain philosophical problems, I find the majority of their claims exceedingly useful and resistant to convincing criticism.

Performance Philosophy: Contours of the Field

While theatre studies has engaged with philosophical thinkers—from Aristotle to Žižek—throughout its existence, in recent years there has been a tremendous surge of interest in philosophy within the field. At the center of this trend is Performance Philosophy, a loosely affiliated network of philosophically inclined performance scholars and theatrically oriented philosophers, which has been actively increasing its membership since it was officially founded on September 3, 2012. The group, which has an interactive website (performance philosophy.org) with a membership at this writing of over 3,500 and includes an online, peer-reviewed, open-access journal devoted to the field, hosts stand-alone conferences and publishes a book series in conjunction with Palgrave Macmillan.[29] Scholars active in this field examine philosophical questions surrounding phenomenology, ethics, politics, bio-politics, erotics, and fashion and engage with the thinking of important figures such as Butler, Wittgenstein, Lacan, Deleuze, Guattari, Adorno, Bergson, Marx, and many more. The field is vast, and it continues to expand quickly and with great energy.

The majority of interest in this broad field tends to favor intertextual analysis. Those among the most well-known scholars in Performance Philosophy— Will Daddario, Laura Cull Ó Maoilearca, Alice Lagaay, and Freddie Rokem— approach dramatic texts, performance experiences, and general theatrical theory in conversation with the writings of major philosophers. The *Performance Philosophy Bibliography* posted on an early version of the website, for example, was tellingly divided alphabetically into categories such as "Agamben and Performance," "Althusser and Performance," "Aristotle and Performance," "Badiou and Performance," "Beckett and Philosophy," "Brecht and Philosophy," and so on. The Performance Philosophy project continues to center the application of the thinking of particular philosophers toward the elucidation of a variety of dramatic and theatrical concerns, and vice versa. Working groups in the field that focus on the practical work of the actor do exist, though, sometimes through the teachings of major directors who write theoretically about their own practical work (i.e., Grotowski, Barba, Suzuki, Bogart, and others), and sometimes as direct analysis of performances and theatre methodologies. It is with scholars that turn a philosophical eye toward the work process of the actor that I find myself in conversation most directly.

Of particular interest is the research of John Lutterbie and Rick Kemp, who, each in his own way, engage in a serious consideration of the connections between cognitive neuroscience and the practice of the actor. Lutterbie, in *Toward a General Theory of Acting*, applies the scientific model of Dynamic Systems Theory (DST) to the actor's creative process. He applies the basic premise of DST that "a dynamic system is always in a state of relative instability and subject to perturbations or disruptions that give rise to patterns that are responsive to the disturbance" to the processes by which actors engage with technique, improvisation, and creating a performance score through the use of "movement, gesture, language, memory, intention, and executive control."[30] While his research is thorough and compelling, and while I find common ground with Lutterbie in what he calls "the primary tenet" of his book, namely "that ignoring the body is not only wrongheadedness, it is simply wrong," I find that his attempts to theorize the actor's work in ways that fit neatly within the bounds of DST end up limiting the conclusions that a bit more theoretical freedom would enhance.[31] For example, in order to adhere to the language of DST, Lutterbie must frame the "perturbations" in the system of the actor's score as being akin to "mistakes." While this makes a certain amount of sense in the model of DST, it ultimately limits the scope of dynamicism that he is ultimately trying to expand, since variations in the actor's body-in-life are not necessarily mistakes. More often than not, subtle changes in thought and action are a vital part of the actor's creative process, and it would be better to have the freedom to refer to them as "developments," or some similarly productive term, rather than feeling pressured to frame them as errors. This may seem to be a small complaint, but the problem ultimately diminishes the appeal of his entire approach.

Rick Kemp's point of view in *Embodied Acting: What Neuroscience Tells Us about Performance* is closer to my own than is Lutterbie's. His project is "to explore the implications that recent findings in cognitive science have for the theory and practice of acting in the West," and he refers to many of the same figures and concepts with whom I engage in my own research.[32] He is among the few theatre scholars that focus on the actor-in-training, and he is deeply concerned by the limitations placed on the work of the actor that result from a theoretical separation between mind and body:

> The mainstream view of training that is primarily physically oriented, such as that of Grotowski and Lecoq, is that it is exotic and ties to a particular style of non-realist performance. Training methods that stress psychology tend to neglect the mechanics of expression beyond vocal work in the belief that these will take care of themselves, and that "technical" training will lead to non-naturalistic behavior in performance. I propose that the two approaches, rather than being mutually exclusive or necessarily oppositional, are more like two parts of the same river that flow into one another. Training that foregrounds the body does not necessarily neglect the mental activities generally termed "psychological." Instead, it grounds them in action. Physically-based work can stimulate the imagination to create performances of subtlety and nuance in both behavioral and linguistic expression. Training that focuses on mental processes also incorporates physical processes, but often without explicitly acknowledging them.[33]

These concerns I share almost to the letter (especially given my connection to the lineage of Grotowski, which I will discuss shortly), but again, as it often happens in research that attempts to explain art through science, Kemp's efforts to apply the theory to actual examples from the actor's repertoire result in the appearance of a certain amount of rigidity. As hard as he tries to handle the science loosely yet delicately and to place it in service of an accurate analysis of practice, it still tends to feel more often than not like a conceptual constraint.

I am keenly aware that similar dangers to those that I am critiquing exist in my own research. I am not trained as a scientist, and yet I am engaging with some complex scientific material; I am not a trained philosopher, but I am referring to the writings of philosophers and developing some philosophical propositions of my own. In *Staging Philosophy: Intersections of Theater, Performance, and Philosophy*, published well before Performance Philosophy acquired an official name, David Krasner and David Z. Saltz raise an important question regarding the theatre scholar's relationship to philosophy, namely, whether one is *using* philosophy to analyze performance or *doing* philosophy in its own right. Laura Cull Ó Maoilearca echoes the same question in her chapter in *Encounters in Performance Philosophy*, critiquing this *transcendence* versus *immanence* binary, as she calls it, by stating that all efforts to write Performance Philosophy must be made up of some combination of using and doing philosophy.[34] Both of these foundational works for the field, however separated by time, do make a plea in favor of doing, of "advanc[ing] original and thoughtful philosophical arguments about issues in the theater and performance," as Krasner and Saltz put it, or as Cull Ó Maoilearca would have it, of "increasing the tendency for concepts to *come from* performance," rather than maintaining the "tendency towards application or illustration [that] has been the historically more dominant of the two."[35]

As will become evident in my approach throughout the following pages, while the majority of references in this book will be from philosophical thinkers and writers, I do not adhere to any one school, nor even to any one time period. I give myself permission to interact with the philosophies of Wittgenstein and Mark Johnson when they provide me with ways of understanding action as readily as I make reference to American Pragmatist John Dewey and Dance Phenomenologist Maxine Sheets-Johnstone when they can help me to understand complex processes of human interaction. There are times when I draw directly from neuroscience or linguistics, as the need arises, and at other times I rely on the interpretations of this scientific data by scholars in other fields. At times I use philosophy (transcendence) as an aid to understanding the various actor-training exercises that I present, and quite frequently I engage in my own philosophical excursions (immanence) to shed light upon both the processes undertaken by actors and the significance of those undertakings. It is my hope that the breadth of freedom I am affording myself through this methodological approach will protect me from the dangers to which I allude earlier, which result from the constraints encountered when adhering strictly to a single scientifically inflected model. At the same time, I am also aware of the dangers of dilettantism inherent in multidisciplinary approaches such as this one, and I take pains to fight against it by being rigorous and precise in my usage of theories from disciplines that are not entirely my own. Ultimately, there is space for this sort of exploration in the expansive sphere of Performance Philosophy, which at its core is concerned with the connection between performance and philosophy, and not with which discipline is in charge at any given moment.

Acting and Technique

When we talk about what actors do and learn to do, we are speaking of *technique*. In *What a Body Can Do*, theatre theorist-practitioner Ben Spatz offers a useful definition of technique as "knowledge that structures practice."[36] He clarifies that we must draw a distinction between what a body is and what a body does when we are discussing learned behaviors. "The object of research in embodied technique," he says, "is not 'the body' or even 'embodiment' as an abstraction, but technique itself. Such research assumes no ideal body, although it must always work through particular bodies in order to discover possibilities that may then travel beyond them. . . . Knowing how to walk with one's legs is not the same as asserting that one needs legs to walk."[37] Spatz defines *practice* as a particular instantiation of applied bodily knowledge at a given time and place—for instance, a certain person walking at a certain moment and location, in accordance with the way that person has learned to walk, with all of the social and cultural forces at play in that instance of learning. Technique, however, is defined as more broadly functioning over time, according to the four following characteristics: "(1) Technique is knowledge; it is acquired and not easy to unlearn. (2) Technique is transmissible; it travels across time and space and is always hybrid and mixed. (3) Technique is a compromise between 'nature' and 'humanity.' (4) Technique can be embodied in the sense that it may work with and through the materiality of bodies as distinct from technologies."[38] Practice is applied technique.

Actor-training exercises are developed primarily according to their ability to help actors develop their technique—the knowledge that structures their practice. In the context of the theatre studio, whether or not these exercises "work" is determined by practical application in a given form or style of theatre. What works in one context may not work in another, and what works for one person may not be effective for someone else. Even so, exercises come into being and are transmitted according to their ability to work across more than one instance, which means that they must contain a structure that is flexible enough to answer to the needs of individual differences while being precise enough to be useful toward a particular end. In other words, each exercise has its own form, rules, and guiding principles that allow it to serve as a tool toward the proper development of particular elements of craft. Just as a fork, for example, is better suited to carry solid food to the mouth for eating than, say, a hammer is, particular exercises are designed to perform different pedagogical functions. This seems fairly obvious, but if we follow this thinking a little further, we run into a somewhat difficult question. The fork takes part in culturally determined practices of eating; its primary purpose is clear. What, though, is the purpose of the tool known as the acting exercise? To the development of what, precisely, does it contribute? Put more simply, what is it for?

To answer this question, we need to understand its utility in relation to the culturally determined practice of acting, which means we first need to answer the question, "What does an actor need to be able to do?" Only when we have a clear sense of what actors need to be able to do can we figure out how they might be assisted in learning how to do it, and then we can determine the effectiveness of a particular training tool or exercise. That understanding—of what actors need to be able to do—is, however, more frequently possessed through practice than via an ability to articulate it verbally. The best acting teachers get results by doing, not by offering up detailed analyses; in the studio, a primacy is placed on getting results, regardless of how clearly formulated the theories are. In other words, acting teachers know what their students need to be able to do, but they are not required to offer up articulate analyses of those processes or outcomes. As a result, we are left in the unfortunate situation in which those who are best able to understand the craft of acting are not inclined to take pains to explain it, if for no other reason than that it might well be seen as a waste of time to do so.

According to Spatz's view, those in the position of transmitting technique in the theatre, namely acting teachers, are in possession of knowledge on the deep level of embodied ability, but this transmission does not require the possession of any understanding beyond the technique itself, with the exception of the knowledge of how it might best be taught. We can call the technique of transmitting technique "pedagogy," and as its own technique, it takes the form of exercises meant to teach. One can certainly argue that there is a big difference between being able to teach an acting exercise and being able to act; however, successful teachers rely upon their technique in moments of pedagogical practice, and such moments are shaped by how well the teacher in question has mastered the ability to use the exercise to guide the student toward ends which are known, even if only on an unconscious level.

Performance Styles Considered

To repeat, in order for pedagogical technique to function, the instructor must possess the knowledge of how the actor-training exercises lead to the development of practicable technique for use in the performance context on the part of the student. As I mentioned, all exercises are designed to work some elements of craft more than others. In addition, the way an exercise may become useful to actors also depends on the theatrical style in which the actors ultimately find themselves working. Certain actor-training techniques will aid primarily in the development of a particular set of usable skills. For example, in Japanese Noh theatre training, a great amount of time and attention is spent on learning the correct way of moving the feet, and in Indian Kathakali training, students must learn how to embody and perform entire systems of traditional hand gestures (*mudras*) and movements of the facial muscles and eyes. The purpose of the training exercises in these traditions is, first and foremost, to aid in the ability of the young performers to embody these particular techniques toward incorporation into their life-long craft.

The training exercises I am discussing in this book have their origins in the very particular laboratory theatre work developed under the guidance of Jerzy Grotowski in Poland starting in the late 1950s. Since that time, the exercises have been developed and transformed in a variety of contexts, and they have come to be useful in developing for actors techniques that can be put into practice across a broad spectrum of performance contexts, and they are taught as an integral part of "movement" classes in actor-training programs across the globe. They are flexible enough to serve a variety of contemporary theatre and performance styles, rather than being designed to teach the codified forms of the types of performance traditions mentioned earlier. Similarly, much of my analysis, because it relies on embodied techniques that are, as Spatz says, "a compromise between 'nature' and 'humanity,'" can find useful application to a wide variety of performance forms, which likewise are comprised of human bodies engaging in culturally determined acts.

To understand this point a bit better, let us imagine two separate performances of a well-known play, Henrik Ibsen's *A Doll House*, produced in two distinct styles. The first hypothetical performance is a "realistic" play, set in a living room, staged in a proscenium theatre. The second is staged more along the lines of a "physical theatre" piece, or what is sometimes called dance or movement theatre. This version is highly abstracted. It takes place in the round in a black box theatre, the characters rarely, if ever, face each other, the text is fragmented and delivered via chant-like vocalizing, and the set pieces are a series of colorful, angular cutouts, none of which immediately resemble any object that might normally be found in a living room.

For the sake of this discussion, I will focus on one moment of the unfolding action in the fictive reality of the stage: the moment when Nora, after her argument with Krogstad, shows Christine the letter waiting in the mailbox to be discovered by Torvald. Before we look at what the actors are doing, let us first imagine that this scene was not a stage play, but actually happening in real life in a real house, inhabited by real people named Nora, Krogstad, Christine, Torvald, etc. Nora, unlike Christine, lives in this house, and she is familiar with it through her daily interaction with it. When Nora goes to look out the window to the hallway, she knows she will be able to see the mailbox. She also may, consciously or unconsciously, feel an association with looking out that same window, say, each time a package were to arrive, for which she excitedly waits. Neither that window nor the view through it means the same thing to Christine. It is the same window, and on one basic level, that is a shared unit of meaning between the two people, but beyond that, they each have their own separate world of private associations and history with it. The window is constituted contextually and differently by each person who encounters it at a moment in time.

Also, the behavior of these two people is bound by the context and the rules that govern that context. Christine may well be able to discern some of Nora's initial reactions to the presence of the letter, but there is also a world of hidden processes and feelings contained by Nora. For instance, Christine may understand Nora's panic on some significant level, but she will likely not sense (or know that she is sensing) the remainder of her looking-out-that-particular-window associations and feelings. It is also possible that the social conventions would not even permit Nora to reveal the full scope of her panic in that moment, in that context. And when they speak, they are speaking only to each other, communicating only so that something (perhaps quite complex) might be understood between them both—specifically them.

As we move from this *real* context to that of the *realistic* performance context, what changes? The first important difference to note is that Nora is actually an actor, and she has her own particular life history and defining characteristics. She has no long-standing associations with that living room, nor with a man named Torvald or a woman named Christine (who are themselves played by actors, with their own histories and characteristics). Also, this particular window does not actually open, since it is only a set piece constructed to look like a real window but not work like one. There is no mailbox there at all, nor is it surrounded by bookcases, a hallway, or anything of the sort; rather, when the actor playing Nora looks offstage right at the supposed mailbox, she actually sees a wooden stool with a curtain behind it. Sometimes, perhaps the stool is not there, or a stagehand may be sitting on it. The wall of the living room is only painted on one side, can hardly support any weight, and meets the upstage wall at about a 120-degree angle, not the 90-angle one would expect in an actual living room, in order to accommodate the needs of the staging and sightlines. The words this woman must say to these other people have been decided upon by a translator, based upon words written by a man named Henrik Ibsen over a century ago, and she has committed them to memory, as have the other actors. As a matter of fact, she knows, with a high degree of detail, exactly what she is going to be doing before, during, and after every moment and every word spoken over the course of the two hours she spends every night on this stage.

In order for the actor to be able to perform effectively, she needs first to be aware of her tasks, and second to be aware of the rules governing the fictive reality she encounters onstage. When Stanislavsky developed his System to deal with the realistic plays being written during the early part of the twentieth century, he understood that an effective performance would have to simulate certain key components of everyday behavior, *as if* they were real. His famous "magic if," however, is not simply regarding the plot and characters being portrayed.[39] Acting well is not, for example, just a matter of pretending you are a woman named Nora, who is involved in a life-altering deception, in Norway in 1789. The actor also needs to engage creatively and effectively with all the other elements of the fictive reality, as well, including, but not limited to, the view out the window into the wings mentioned in the example earlier.

This work is difficult, but it is still not all the actor must do. She cannot simply act imaginatively "in any old way"; she must make specific choices about exactly how the things she is doing are going to signify for the attending audience. She is engaged in an *acting for*—for an audience, and for a purpose. She must not only speak loudly enough for the audience to hear, but she must also deftly manage the desire to communicate to an onlooker in a way that works seamlessly with her embodied interaction with the fictive context. To do this, the actor needs skills, and those skills can be developed through training.

Through her training, she learns both how to be and how to be meaningful onstage. She must move to look out the window in exactly the right way each and every time. This means that she needs to know how to embody a reaction to an imaginary stimulus in a fictive setting that, by the nature of its formal and stylistic rules, bases its codes of meaning on those found in real life. A quick turn away from someone followed by a hurried walk toward and sudden stop at a window, followed by a wistful and anxious look, must mean something specific in real life in order to be represented onstage in a meaningful way. Using a sharp tone of voice must likewise mean something specific. The onstage action is different in multiple and significant ways from the real one, but it is designed to communicate a meaning based on its real-life analog. It is rehearsed and fine-tuned in order to become acceptable on the levels of meaning and convention.

We can see how a realistic stage performance is thus based on an extension of how meaning is experienced and constructed in real life. However interesting they may be, these are far from novel observations. The original impulse leading to the advent of realism onstage was to present a heightened yet believable version of "real life" onstage for the audience to observe and scrutinize for particularly crafted meaning. What about the second, nonrealistic example, though? In this production, Nora's moment with Christine appears quite differently. Here, Nora slithers to the floor while chanting in a deadpan manner, "the letter, the letter, the letter. . . ." She makes a barking sound, crawls on hands and knees around Christine, and then without warning jumps to a tip-toe position and takes quick, tiny steps over to face the audience, gazing at each of the faces there as she begins to tremor and cry silently, her tears streaking the mascara down her face, which is painted with faint, clown-white makeup. Although this (admittedly far-fetched) scene appears to be radically dissimilar from the realistic one described just before, from the perspective of the actor's craft, the primary functional distinction between the two is that the rules governing the fictive reality are different. In both cases, there are strict rules, and in both cases, meaning is connected to a basic understanding of embodied interaction with a real-life context.

It is essential here to acknowledge that I am not proposing that there is anything like a universal experience of embodied meaning. Standing on tiptoes might mean one thing in one culture and something completely different in another; a certain color of makeup, for instance, might signify one thing in one place at one time and other things in other places and times (a painted black face in Peking opera signifies an honorable character, while in Kathakali it signifies that the character is a demon). What *is* the same from context to context is the fact that humans engage with meaning through embodied interaction with their environment. Each culture reflects this in its own way. In the culture of which I am a part, an actor barking would call to mind dog-like behavior, and the specific mode of its execution might be designed to make me laugh, or it might make me feel upset for her. The point is that each action she does is crafted (on some level, be it conscious or not) to evoke a specific range of meaning based on the common cultural context of embodied environmental interaction derived from real-life experience. The bark means dog for me, but what dog means is ultimately culturally determined; I have experienced through my embodied life what a dog is and does, but in another place and time, the network of associations that connect to dog might be completely different. It would be the sign of an unsuccessful performance in my culture if the actor playing Nora were trying to make the audience call to mind the image of a playful puppy by barking ferociously, just as it would be an ineffective choice for her to attempt to evoke a feeling of heaviness by tiptoeing lightly and briskly, or for that matter, for her to attempt to evoke tenderness by yelling sharply at Christine.

Likewise, the ability to create meaning for an onlooker—*acting for* the audience—is rooted in the actor's own foundational experiences of play and performance. The actors playing the two Noras may have had to train in order to learn how to navigate successfully the rules of their respective performance contexts, but that learning is not disconnected from the common practice of "acting things out" or even simply showing things to another person. We watch each other perform actions all the time, and we are familiar with the difficulties sometimes inherent in such experiences. This becomes clear as soon as we call to mind, for example, the common experience of "I could do this before, but now that I'm being watched, I can't seem to do it anymore." The process of the actor must take this into account, just as it must take into account a whole set of foundational embodied experiences. For some actors, being watched does not interfere with their ability to perform, while for others it creates a major impediment to their acting. Some actors are able to effect believable behavior onstage with little to no formal training, while others require years of intense study to master their craft. Actor-training exercises, as I mentioned earlier, are designed to transmit particular elements of technique to actors, and if they are good exercises, they are flexible enough to address the particular needs of a wide variety of students with their own individual characteristics and challenges.

By looking at actor-training exercises through the lens of EC, whereby, to repeat Wilson's formulation, "the mind must be understood in the context of its relationship to a physical body that interacts with the world," we can begin to understand the techniques required by the theatre as embodied practices. When the actor playing realistic Nora looks out the window, she calls into being a series of fully embodied processes of mind, which are determined partly through her craft-imagination and partly through her ability to communicate to a third party (the audience), all under the influence of the operative theatrical conventions. Her onstage actions are designed to communicate, for example, a combination of the character's fear of the current circumstance, her desire not to appear pathetic to her friend, and also her attempt to convince Christine to help her. An audience ignorant of the local theatrical rules and conventions would miss this. While in this book I am going to avoid entering into a discussion of the field of spectatorship, which is dedicated to exploring what an audience is and does in the theatre, it is essential for my argument at least to acknowledge that effective actors are always "geared into" the world, as Maurice Merleau-Ponty might say, which includes the audience observer.[40]

Somehow, perhaps through training exercises, the actor playing Nora has learned the technique of how to activate a whole bodily network of small neural processes connected to muscles large and small in a way that corresponds to what will communicate to an audience within a certain set of behavioral conventions. Her process is not one of first thinking and then doing. She does not activate the mental representation first and then translate that into bodily action second. She activates the entire system all at once. However, because the acting process is "artificial" (i.e., auto-generated), rather than being simply part of the way that the organism has learned to exist over the course of its entire life in the context of being-in-the-world, such an entire-system activation can be very tricky to pull off. The fact that this type of "play acting" is based on real-world aspects of play acting does not mean it is a simple matter to act effectively in the theatrical context. To bring into being such a full-body-brain-environment system is exceedingly difficult and complex, and many things can get in the way (including trying too hard, trying the wrong way, being "out of touch" with the body, pushing emotion, overacting, "mugging," underplaying, mumbling or imprecision, breaking the rules without realizing it, choosing the wrong intended outcomes, etc.).

As I have already suggested, the processes of the actors playing the two Noras are more or less identical in structure, if not in content, with the exception that the "avant-garde" Nora engages with a context that is, in all likelihood, less regulated than is realistic theatre. What is acceptable scenic behavior in an "experimental theatre" context has often not yet been historically defined, but rather it is likely still in the process of being determined. Some elements of this new style of stage behavior may be recognizably associated with other various performance traditions, for example, and some may be entirely new or unfamiliar. This is perhaps one reason why audiences at such performances can sometimes be heard complaining of "not getting it." Others, though, who are comfortable with extreme abstraction (whether abstracted from their experience of everyday behavior or from established realistic conventions) or who are able to make the connection to new scenic behaviors to which they have already gained exposure, do "get it," and so the surprising and effective abstraction sheds new light on some aspect of human social behavior. "Not getting it" can also be based on unmet expectations that create cognitive dissonance in the observer. In such cases the audience might say something like, "the actor's performance was cold and formalistic," which could simply be indicative of an adverse reaction to a stylistic choice *not* to engage in scenic behavior that communicates "hot" emotion. What is important for our discussion here is not that one set of theatrical conventions is better or easier to navigate than another, but that the human actor's process is always fully embodied, regardless of the stylistic choices that guide the creative process.

Making Meaning through Acting

"Getting it" implies that there is an *it* to *get*. This *it* is the meaning of the performance. As I have already made clear, my aim in this book is primarily to analyze actor-training exercises to see what particular techniques they are designed to develop or transmit. I have also discussed how determining the functions of these techniques can reveal something important about the theatrical context in which they are put into practice. The performance event exists for one central reason, and that is to create a particular encounter with meaning in the artificial theatrical environment. I want to make clear that when I say *meaning* here, I am not simply referring to the "message" of the play, although this is surely a part of the meaning. I am not referring even to meaning in the classical semiotic sense, as the composite assemblage of signs that make up the semantic fabric of a performance text. I am speaking of meaning here in a very broad sense, such that every element onstage—from the most basic object identification ("that object is supposed to be a window") to the significance of those objects ("that window represents the view to a world outside the confines of the home") to the impassioned behavior of the actors' bodies ("those characters are saying things with intention and nuance as they move in ways that convey both obvious and subliminal information")—participates in a world complex beyond conscious apprehension, created as it unfolds according to the interactions of the embodied minds that inhabit and enact it. Every element of this expanse of scenic meaning is constructed, usually under the oversight of the director, but most of it operates unconsciously. I am interested in trying to understand how it is that actors can learn to become meaningful beyond themselves, as it were. What does an actor need to learn to do successfully in order to become replete with meaning in a way that contributes to the larger meaning of the performance event?

In the example of the two Noras, both actors need to find a way to communicate specific meanings to an audience, and those meanings are reliant on commonly held notions about what means what in the real world. However, it is not enough for them simply "to act naturally," because acting naturally has come about through experiential learning in the real world, which is populated with real objects, real people, and unpredictable occurrences and which does not normally include the scrutiny of an audience (at least not in the sense of a theatre audience and its particular expectations and behavior). In other words, actors somehow learn to embody an excess of associations through action (which, as I shall address later, includes speech) in order to communicate specific meaning in a fictive context. It is not enough for the actor to stand next to the fake window and think "I am trapped." She must find a way to communicate to the people in the furthest reaches of the theatre, through her fully embodied scenic behavior, that the house her character, Nora (who is her but not her, somehow), finds herself in, namely Torvald's home, is a very specific flavor of claustrophobic and life-threatening, all in a single moment, amid an ever-changing series of pre-crafted, scripted moments that make up the totality of the two-hour performance. The actors playing the two Noras learned the real world once, when they were growing up, but they had to learn a whole new set of rules at some point regarding how to be onstage meaningfully.

The example of these two hypothetical performances of *A Doll House* serves as a stand-in for the "theatre" for which actors train. As I move through the ensuing chapters, each moment of analysis of a particular element of an exercise is guided by a knowledge of the type of circumstances in which actors will eventually find themselves. In this way, the process of analysis is determined by the known use-factor of a given exercise. If I were examining, as I eventually do, the actor's relationship to the practice of walking, my path of inquiry would take a very different turn if I knew the actor would eventually be performing, say, underwater in scuba gear. I would, in that case, be compelled to elucidate how the exercise might function to help the actor do that better (assuming, of course, that it could). My guiding assumptions are rooted in a certain set of expectations determined by likelihood of practical application. In other words, my understanding of the eventual performance context shapes the process by which I analyze the exercise elements, and my observations of how the component parts function lead me, in turn, to new realizations about the nature of the performance context, and so on.

My Methodology

While this book is largely theoretical in nature, I attempt to ground my claims in examples drawn from my own practical experience in the theatre. Since 1991, I have been consistently engaged as a professional actor, director, and teacher in the field of ensemble, devised, experimental theatre. In 1997 I cofounded North American Cultural Laboratory (NACL Theatre), and I continue to serve as its executive artistic director. As a director of performances and as leader of the daily physical and vocal actor training of the company—in New York City, at the company's upstate NY theatre center, and elsewhere—I have developed a series of exercises aimed at addressing the various issues of technique that continually arise in the theatre laboratory setting. As I alluded to earlier, some of these exercises are rooted in the research of Jerzy Grotowski, who was a teacher to my primary teachers during various phases of the performance research that spanned his professional career. My first point of contact with his work lineage came when I visited Eugenio Barba's Odin Teatret in 1991, and the second came in 1994 when I began to train with a group of students from his Objective Drama period at UC Irvine in California. The exercises to which I refer in this study emerged in one way or another from the daily exploratory work with which I engaged first in these early settings and then after that, over the course of many years, sometimes as an actor-participant and more frequently as a director-leader.

In addition to the context of my own theatre laboratory, I have also taught a great number of workshops for actors in a variety of contexts. Some of the actors in these work encounters came from their own "experimental" ensembles, while others made their livings in the more traditionally mainstream, generally realistic theatre. Furthermore, for a period of three years I taught Introduction to Acting courses at Hunter College in NYC, where I currently hold the title of assistant professor in the Department of Theatre. In all of these pedagogical contexts, I have made continued use of all of the exercises about which I speak herein, and that experience has convinced me of their usefulness across boundaries of theatrical style.

My methodological approach in this book draws partly upon a model of performance ethnography developed by Gay McAuley under the influence of Clifford Geertz's notion of "thick description."[41] Whereas Geertz's approach begins with a finely honed description of a particular custom (as in the famous case of his account of a Balinese cock fight), and then expands to an analysis of the component parts, discussing what they reveal about the culture in which they are embedded, McAuley begins her "thick description" in the rehearsal room and expands outward from there.[42] She describes the relationship between Geertz's methodology and her own by saying that "applying the idea [of thick description] to rehearsal means broadening the focus from concentrating on the materiality of the performance signifiers being created to greater awareness of the social and professional networks relating the participants in the rehearsal room to each other, and attempting to establish the nature of the social field within which the work is occurring."[43] Starting with detailed observations of small, local moments, she sends out tendrils of analysis into the wider world in which the rehearsal event is embedded, thus illuminating a host of theoretical implications that resonate on a more global, cultural level.

Like McAuley, I base my own ethnographic work, such as it is, on countless encounters with the training exercises in a great variety of "in the field" circumstances. While the people with whom I have worked, and the places in which we trained, were not always the same, the consistency of the core elements of the exercises themselves holds my practical research together and has allowed it to form into a systematic whole of transmissible technique. Taking these remembered experiences as a body of knowledge from which I can draw specific examples, I first describe the basic elements of the exercises in detail. Then, after having established that foundation, I focus on the minute particulars of the work, teasing out observations that reveal connections between the tasks presented to the doer and the theoretical considerations upon which a given chapter hinges. Rather than positing social or broadly cultural implications based upon my observations as an ethnographer such as Macaulay might, I focus my attention on the questions that arise in relation to theatre as a culture with its own limiting factors. Frequently, such moments of "expanding out" into theory occur at the nodes of difficulty presented by the exercise. Such moments, when actors tend to have trouble performing a given task successfully, reveal the challenges built in to the exercise for the purpose of encouraging the discovery of new ways of doing. Once the actor figures out how to perform the difficult task, the obstacle more or less vanishes, and the technique can be said to have been learned, at least on some basic level. These moments on the road to mastery help us to see the purposes of an exercise. They provide a window of insight not only regarding the use of the tool but also about the essential theatrical component that the tool has been designed to help build. We can learn about theatre as an art form, and also the larger culture in which it is embedded, by examining the small, momentary instances of actors encountering technique in the studio.

Throughout the many forays into philosophy I make over the course of this book, I always attempt to provide support for my assertions from the relevant literature, primarily from theatre studies and philosophy but also from psychology, linguistics, and neuroscience, as well. Although I try as much as possible to follow a path of logic in my analysis, it must be said up front that, in the end, I am speaking of art and concerning such matters there is certainly likely to be a fair amount of disagreement. A good deal of what follows is held together by intuition; however, I must have faith that my intuition can be sufficiently supported by my lived, practical experience working in the studio for over thirty years.

In addition, inasmuch as I strive to connect my thinking to the most contemporary scientific and philosophical developments, it is no secret that the state of knowledge in these areas tends to change no matter how advanced the experts in a given field believe themselves to be. Changes in science, like changes in art, are par for the course throughout history, and their development is affected by any number of forces, not least among them sociopolitical ones. As Catherine Malabou argues persuasively in *What Should We Do with Our Brain?*, even the language used to describe science is by no means pure; rather, our vision of how bodies and brains work is under the direct and powerful influence of contemporary modes of thought and structures of power. At one moment in history, we think of brains as machines, while at another, we see them as computers. "We can thus affirm," claims Malabou, "that there is no scientific study of the modalities of cerebral power that does not by the same token—implicitly and usually unconsciously—adopt a stance with respect to the contemporary power of the very study within which it operates."[44] The very metaphors we use to contain our so-called scientifically based beliefs reflect the dominant ideology and the spirit of the age, and it would be foolish to think that anything I can say will be potent enough to fight against that current. This text presents a snapshot, as it were, of how new ways of talking about what bodies are, what they can be, and what they can do are gradually finding their way into the vernacular. We can be certain that the science will evolve and new metaphors will take hold over time; the task at hand is to engage thoughtfully as they develop and to help usher them in meaningful new directions now.

Structure of This Book

The body of this book is comprised of three main chapters. Each is written around one actor-training exercise, with which I have had sufficient experience, both as a doer and as a leader, to enable me to understand its internal workings and to be familiar with the tendencies of those that engage with them. My choice of which exercise to focus on for which chapter is somewhat arbitrary, in that there are a number of exercises from among which I might have chosen that could be fruitfully mined for their pedagogical and theoretical use value. I decided upon these three partly because I find their form and content particularly suited to an exploration of the philosophical concepts to which I am drawn here, and partly because I have worked with them for so long and know them so intimately. Of course, there are always surprises, and one can always discover new ways of articulating the fundamental principles of craft addressed by the exercises. Just as no single exercise can apply to every aspect of the actor's technique, it is also true that no single mode of pedagogy works for every student. To anyone who has ever taught any subject, this is obviously the case, and every instance of teaching is made up of a subtle, dynamic interplay between teacher and student that allows for each participant to engage with the material according to his or her strengths, weaknesses, abilities, characteristics, proclivities, and even momentary moods and reactions. The studio and the classroom are living laboratories of learning that manage, through the guiding principles of technique, to channel the attention and action of those present into the creation of new bodies of knowledge. My hope is that the assertions I make, drawn from the memories of past experiences that now inhabit my body as technique, will translate into new forms of understanding in the reader, even as we inhabit separate spaces and times at this moment.

Chapter 1 begins with a detailed account of the *plastiques*, a well-known exercise developed by Grotowski, subsequently practiced and elaborated upon by many of his artistic descendants. This exercise can be used in many different contexts toward any number of various ends, depending on who is teaching it and the goals of the particular pedagogical moment, but applied in the way that I present it here, it develops actors' abilities to encounter the component parts of action. The chapter is divided into six basic sections. The first introduces the basic elements of the exercise and its historical lineage. The second uses the "ordinary language" philosophy of Wittgenstein to dissect the concept of action, in order to elucidate the role of *intention* in the context of the actor's work and also the crucial difference between movement and action. The third section explores the concept of theatrical principles and how they are worked by the *plastiques*. It also mobilizes Mark Johnson's notion of *image schemas* to show how these principles, because of their connection to the ways in which we encounter meaning through fully embodied interactions with our environment, enable actors to develop a particular set of skills for use in the fictive realm of theatre. The next section draws from the work of Maxine Sheets-Johnstone, applying her concept of *animation* to see how meaningful action onstage is connected to the ways in which consciousness itself is rooted in an organism's interactions with environment. The section after that revisits Johnson's notion of *image schemas* to discuss how the *plastiques* make it possible for actors to engage with the metaphors that undergird meaning beyond the isolated mechanics of physical action. The final section makes reference to the pragmatic philosophy of John Dewey, particularly his ideas about cooperative action as the basis for communication, in order to understand certain interactive components of the *plastiques*. Throughout the chapter, I guide the reader through a close reading of the *plastiques* in order to arrive at an understanding of action, how it functions as the fundamental component of the actor's craft, and what a process of encountering action through technique might look like.

Actors do what no one else does. They isolate action, extrude it, break it down, and manipulate its elements to become more meaningful, to the doer and to the observer. Even how an actor moves from one place on the stage to another carries meaning. In the course of creating performance material, actors ultimately need to decide—consciously or not—which actions and moments will be chosen and set and, therefore, which meanings will be conveyed, even if this process of setting takes place in the "spontaneous" instant of an improvisation. To do this, actors must have the ability to explore and filter through many options in an effective manner, at will, and to make choices in a precise, and usually repeatable, way. This can only be done if the actor can successfully access and manipulate all the factors and components that a nonactor relies on unconsciously to engage meaningfully with the world in daily life. This includes not only elements of both coarse and fine motor control but also psychological and emotional channels, which, as we shall come to see in the course of this book, are also embodied processes. To accomplish all this requires skill and training; it requires effective technique.

I turn my attention from action to perception and proprioception in Chapter 2, presenting a description and analysis of an exercise called *The 3 Layers*, which I created in 2001 and have continued to develop since then. In *The 3 Layers* a group of actors moves around the space according to a particular set of rules, which the leader generally narrates as the exercise unfolds. As the work progresses, layers of attention are added. I describe the exercise in much greater detail later, but for now it will suffice to explain that the first layer requires the doers to place multimodal attention on the surrounding environment, the second layer directs the conscious attention inward to the joints of the actors' own bodies, and the third layer places the moving actors in an action-reaction relationship to one another. Because each instantiation of this exercise is necessarily different from all the rest, one can never execute it "perfectly"; however, by practicing it regularly, over time, actors develop an ability to juggle multiple levels of awareness at the same time. Simultaneously, their ability to move according to the rules of the game improves as their capacity of attention increases. *The 3 Layers* provides an excellent opportunity to uncover how perception and proprioception factor into the actor's work. My analysis of the exercise draws from enactive perception, neurophilosophy, EC, and phenomenology in order to put together a picture of how it is that actors have a sense of their own bodies, and how they can learn to embody new systems of conscious and unconscious awareness in action and interaction with other actors and the scenic environment.

Alva Noë, a key player in the field of enactive perception, or *enactivisim*, claims that our perceptual senses are functionally and constitutively bound up with our environment. According to enactivism we cannot claim that sight, for example, happens only in the body or the brain; rather, this and all perceptual activity must be said to exist in enactive relationship to the environment. With this theory as a starting point, I discuss the aspects of *The 3 Layers* exercise that focus on the relationship between the actor's sensory apparatus and its interaction with the perceivable environment. After clarifying the difference between perception and attention, and a discussion of why that distinction matters, I move on to a consideration of how the senses work in tandem with "internally directed" attention. For this, I turn to the exceptionally useful theories of *body image* and *body schema* developed by Shaun Gallagher. His particular formulations of these terms, which have come to be cited quite often in theatre studies research, are part of a larger conversation in neurophilosophy and EC regarding proprioception, which philosopher Brian O'Shaughnessy defines as "an immediate mode of feeling one's limbs to be present and disposed in a certain way."[45] The importance of proprioception for this chapter consists in the ways in which actors-in-training can learn (a) how to have improved knowledge of bodily positioning while acting and (b) how to develop alternate or "fictive" bodies as they embody a variety of possible scenic behaviors.

Having established a foundation of understanding regarding the basic components of perception and proprioception in the functioning of *The 3 Layers*, I move into some more advanced levels of the exercise. After examining the concept of "competency" in relation to performance practice, followed by an investigation of visual processes, I discuss the elements of technique being worked directly in the third layer, with particular focus on a practice that I call "schooling." Following the properties of *emergence* found, for example, in herds and flocks of animals, the actors work with each other to discover how they can move seamlessly from the role of group leader to follower, which illustrates the complex modes of interactivity present among bodies in space. Here, again, I refer to the important work of Maxine Sheets-Johnstone and other philosophers, who theorize the ways in which bodies move together as a way of perceiving and understanding both themselves and their environments. Throughout all of this, I explore how *The 3 Layers* allows for the formation of a simulacrum realm in which actors might explore, rediscover, remodel, and redirect unconscious processes of the body toward consciously guided use in the fictive space of the theatre. All of this work, as I take care to note at the end of the chapter, is intimately intertwined with the imaginative and emotional faculties that are also crucial to the actor's body of technique.

In Chapter 3 I attend to an exercise called *Vocal Action*, and in so doing, I provide a detailed account of how voice, speech production, and gesture factor into the training of the actor. I address those aspects of theatricality connected to emotion, intention, character, and inflectional meaning, which are all considered under the heading of prosody in contemporary linguistics and psychology. *Vocal Action* has its roots in the early work of Grotowski, and although I have continued to develop the particular elements of the exercise over the course of many years and many encounters with students, at its core it remains a way of working the voice that focuses more on vibration, tone, and the affective components of vocal sound than on the propositional meaning of spoken text. As such, it lends itself well to an examination of aspects of vocal meaning production that remain relatively unexamined in theatre studies. Much of my analysis of *Vocal Action* relies on the extraordinarily comprehensive research conducted by Jody Kreiman and Diana Sidtis in their book *Foundations of Voice Studies: An Interdisciplinary Approach to Voice Production and Perception*, especially with regard to the distinction they make between "voice" and "voice quality" as it pertains to the explorations of the actor during this exercise.

My discussion of how speech prosody factors into the work of the actor references Kreiman and Sidtis, in addition to a number of other linguists, neuroscientists, and psychologists working in the field. The primary claim in prosody studies is that there are aspects of speech production, namely "pitch, loudness, timing, and voice quality," by which listeners can ascertain an enormous amount of crucial information.[46] These prosodic elements are activated and altered spontaneously and generally in daily life, and I argue that an exercise such as *Vocal Action* allows for actors to focus specifically on those aspects as part of their developing body of technique. Built into any discussion of prosody must be a consideration of the role of the listener, since voice, as I define it in this chapter, has to be understood as a psychological process that takes place in relation to the listener rather than simply a mechanical process of phonation on the part of the vocalizer. Therefore, I discuss the role of the voice as a motivating force in the listener, both in the context of the *Vocal Action* exercise and in the space of theatrical performance practice. As is so often the case in this book on the whole, there is a great deal to be learned about how people function "in the world" by looking at the elements of craft as they are addressed by the actor-in-training for the stage.

The final section of Chapter 3 focuses on gesture. Here I outline the relationship between speech and gesture developed by linguists Adam Kendon and David McNeill and then move on to discuss the relationship between gesture and prosody in the actor's work. Essential to a consideration of gesture is the concept of *mental simulation*, which is the subject of an ongoing conversation in linguistics, psychology, and philosophy. The various theories I present here in connection to mental simulation center on the embodied nature of the speaker-listener relationship, both on the level of neurological activity and in sensorimotor activation on a larger scale. In particular, the aspects of voice connected to gesture, and also to affect and image-laden speech, are those that most activate simulative processes in and among speaker-listener groupings. Because of the ways in which speech and gesture are so essentially reliant upon sociality, I end the chapter by revisiting some thoughts about the importance of always considering social and cultural specificity when thinking about bodies in performance. Linguists committed to EC and interactionism, such as Jürgen Streeck, and theatre theorists engaging with contextual analyses of performance, such as Erika Fischer-Lichte, speak in similar ways about the necessity of understanding bodies in communication to be particular bodies at particular places and times, which are always both participating in culturally determined behaviors and expressing uniquely different identities and perspectives at the same time.

I end with a short concluding chapter, which I call "Afterthinking" in an effort to emphasize the extent to which my engagement with this material is active and ongoing. I begin this section by drawing connections between the theatrical principles addressed by the training exercises discussed in this book and the elements of technique they all work to develop. Each of these exercises comprises just one set of tools in the expansive toolkit available for actors to draw from in their search for mastery of theatrical craft. So, while each one focuses on distinct elements and principles, they would be ill conceived if they were not able to interact with each other and contribute to the creation of an integrated body of technique, which as a whole makes up the embodied practice of a particular actor. The questions raised in this book are by no means answered to completion; every point made carries with it a series of follow-up questions, some of which I address and some of which remain unresolved. With this in mind, I present some proposals for future areas of investigation, namely how we might understand more thoroughly both emotion and imagination as embodied processes. I also present some potential concerns that critical readers might hold about my approach in this book. While I feel that these concerns are easily dispelled, I still think it is important to raise them, if for no other reason than to demonstrate my conviction that science and empiricism can only go so far when trying to get at the ineffability of art. Finally, I offer some thoughts on the implications of the theories presented herein as they might pertain to the development of new approaches to theatre training and practice, grounded in an understanding of the embodied and interactive nature of the actor's craft.

1

Action in Theory and Practice

Introduction

Training exercises for actors come in many forms, but as a rule they are repeatable structures that contain in their design the possibility for actors to encounter specific principles of theatrical technique. Exercises are not the only way in which actors can learn how to act; in fact, many actors are able to become adept at their craft in very much the same way that an apprentice learns a trade or a child learns a language—by exposure and involvement. Through practice in improvisation and performance actors can learn by doing and become more and more proficient over time. Training exercises, however, provide us with an excellent opportunity to observe the component parts of the actor's craft, since by their very nature they are meant to focus on the elements of acting in distilled circumstances, removed from the more immersive experience of acting in the context of a scene, for example. This chapter is devoted to providing a detailed description and analysis of one particular actor-training exercise called the *plastiques*. I choose to focus on this exercise because it provides actors with an excellent way of developing their ability to engage with one of the primary components of the actor's craft—action. By looking closely at the *plastiques*, we can more deeply understand what action is, how to articulate the difference between movement and action, how to factor in the notion of *intention* to this theory of action, and what role interaction plays in the work of the actor.

The chapter is divided into six basic sections. In the first, I introduce the *plastiques* as an exercise defined by a set of precise characteristics that have been developed over its distinct historical lineage. In the second, I employ the "ordinary language" philosophy of Ludwig Wittgenstein as a tool to help understand what one might mean when one speaks about "action," and how that can help to understand why actors might benefit from working on the *plastiques*. In the third section, I make use of EC philosopher Mark Johnson's notion of *image schemas* in order to see how the theatrical principles developed through the *plastiques* lead to increased expressive and communicative capacity in the actor. In the next section, I focus on the concept of "fluency" in the actor's craft and draw upon Maxine Sheets-Johnstone's theory of *animation*. In the section after that, I circle back around to Johnson and his theory of aesthetic meaning to discuss how meaning appears and functions in theatre through action. In the final section I refer to the pragmatic philosophy of John Dewey to explore how the *plastiques* function in relation to the development of interactivity both between actors and with the audience, as well. As I have already suggested, at the heart of acting is action, and I have found that the ideas put forth by these particular theorists and philosophers provide an extraordinarily useful set of analytic tools when aimed at an elucidation of the actor's encounter with craft through the *plastiques*.

Training Exercises and the *Plastiques*

The *plastiques* is a well-known set of exercises, developed by Grotowski and his collaborators in an early period of exploration in Wroclaw, Poland, sometimes referred to as the Theatre of Productions phase (1957–69).[1] At this point, some fifty years after they were first developed, there are many variations of the exercise and its component parts. The version that I describe here was taught to me over the course of around three years, beginning in 1991, by actors from Eugenio Barba's Odin Teatret, who learned it from Ryczard Cieślak in the early 1970s. The Odin actors continued their relationship with this exercise not by way of rote repetition but as a dynamic tool that accommodated change over time, in conjunction with their own artistic development and with the formulation of Barba's research into theatrical principles. When I encountered the *plastiques* again subsequently, in the mid-1990s, from teachers who had learned them from Grotowski at a later point in his career, different aspects of the exercise were emphasized, while others seemed to be fairly similar. In this chapter I attempt to present an analysis of the *plastiques* neither for the purpose of teaching them nor to promote one particular version of them over another, but rather as a means to approach an understanding of how an exercise such as this might function in relation to the development of particular techniques in actors as they learn how to embody meaning in the theatrical context.

This exercise, however unique in form, is but one of many that actors may employ in their training. Every exercise offers a different experience, focuses on different principles and elements of craft, and some actors benefit more from some exercises than from others, if for no other reason than the fact that bodies, temperaments, and skill sets vary widely among actors. I am presenting this exercise because it stems from the theatrical tradition in which I was raised. I have worked on and developed it for many years, and over those years, as a doer and as an instructor, I have developed a strong sense of its potential, its breadth of variation, and its usefulness in a variety of contexts. The *plastiques* is perhaps the most well-known of the "Grotowski-based" exercises, and it is frequently employed in "movement" classes in both undergraduate and graduate actor-training programs. So, using it as the object of analysis here will also benefit from the fact that many readers will already be familiar with some version of it. That being said, another chapter on a different exercise would yield different opportunities for analysis, but I believe that all good actor-training exercises can be evaluated with regard to what skills or elements of craft they are best suited to develop and how well they accomplish that task. Among other things the *plastiques* are well suited to an analysis of how they develop the actor's ability to engage with meaningful action onstage.

The exercise, which on the surface seems quite simple, is comprised of a number of basic body part isolations, each with distinct rules of movement. For example, the shoulder *plastique* requires that actors move their shoulders, one at a time, in only one of six ways—up, down, forward, backward, in a forward rotating circle, and in a backward rotating circle. For the head *plastique*, the head may be moved forward-straight (the nose remains at the same level), forward-down (the head bends at the top of the spine), backward-straight (again, the nose stays level), backward-down (the head bends at the top of the spine, being careful not to pinch or strain), side-straight, either left or right (the ear stays on the same level), side-down, either left or right (the head bends down at the top of the spine, again being careful not to pinch or strain), or in a circle, either clockwise and counterclockwise (creating a circular motion that touches the extreme points of the "down" elements of the head *plastique*). Described in this way, the exercise seems fairly straightforward. However, the execution of even these basic physical details must be demonstrated by someone who already knows how to do the exercise, in order for it to be learned correctly. Through this process of embodied transmission the student also learns the other *plastiques*, which isolate other body parts—fingers, hands, wrists, elbows, chest, hips, and legs—with at least one set of governing rules for each. (There are a few versions of *plastiques* that engage the legs, which I will not have cause to elaborate here.) Once the actor has demonstrated a basic proficiency for the basic moves, the real focus of the exercise can be explored. From this starting point, the actor is to "use" the various *plastiques*—and those only—in order to move and act in the space, either alone or in relation to the other participant actors.

The process of learning the elements of the exercise varies. In some settings, led by some teachers, the actors are provided with detailed, hands-on guidance with each element before trying to do them fully in the space. Other teachers employ a "do as I do" approach, in which they just do the exercise one bit at a time and expect the students to follow by imitation. The teacher may provide verbal instruction while doing the exercise components, but sometimes they are done in complete silence. In all cases, though, the actors will, at some point, encounter difficulty, whether with simply being able to get a particular body part to respond readily and smoothly (many actors have a hard time doing the head-side *plastique* without tilting the ear downward, for example) or with their ability to move a particular body part past its current physical range, and so on. Through the actors' encounters with the various difficulties that arise in the process of learning and working with this exercise, both the habitual components of behavior that inhere in the actor are revealed and new building blocks of action are developed.

One of the more physically complex elements of the exercise is the hand *plastique* (often called the "fish hand"). In order to be done properly, the joints of the hand and fingers must be manipulated in a precise way, and many actors tend to find it quite difficult to manage when they first attempt it. Here is what must happen on the most basic, technical level for the exercise to be done correctly (I employ the anatomical terminology for the sake of explanatory precision; the actors do not think of what they are doing in these terms, nor are they required to learn them): first the Metacarpophalangeal (MCP) joints (commonly known as the knuckles) move in the direction of the palm as the Proximal Interphalangeal (PIP) joints (the next ones down from the knuckles) move in the opposite direction, while forming the fingers into something of a claw shape. Then the PIP joints are pushed in the direction of the palm as the Distal Interphalangeal (DIP) joints (the ones closest to the fingernails) move in the opposite direction. Finally, the MCP joints move in the opposite direction, the PIP and DIP joints relax back in the direction of the palm, and the fingers curve around to begin the cycle over again. The visual effect of this is reminiscent of the movement of a fish's tail, hence the nickname. Again, the doing is generally learned by imitation and hands-on instruction concerning the totality of the movement, not an anatomical breakdown of the component parts.

In general, when actors first begin to learn this exercise, they may find themselves experiencing a sense of frustration if the hand does not easily conform fully to the requirements of the task; the right combination of concentration, exertion, and relaxation is required for the actor to master the basic movement. As is the case when learning a musical instrument, for example, new patterns of movement need to be practiced before they can feel like "second nature," just as abilities that we already have under our control (using a knife and fork to eat, for example, or how to eat with chopsticks) needed to be learned and practiced in the context of the "everyday" world we inhabited as we grew up.[2] The object being used in the *plastiques*, though, is not an outside instrument or tool but, rather, the actor's body itself. The purpose of becoming proficient at the basic elements of the *plastiques* is to be able to use them as a tool for expanding the actor's capacity of expression through physical action. To answer the question of why this might be necessary and how it functions in relation to the totality of the actor's craft, as well as what we might mean by the term "expression," it will be helpful to have a clear sense of what, exactly, we mean when we speak of "action," not only in the theatrical context but also in everyday life.

It certainly seems logical that, in order to figure out what human actors are doing onstage, it would be useful to start with an investigation into what action is in everyday life, but can we apply the conclusions from such an analysis to the fictive theatrical environment? One might argue that observations about human behavior that occur in the context of everyday life do not just automatically apply to what trained actors do in the artificial world of the stage. This objection might easily be bolstered by the simple fact that being an actor is something that one often needs to train for in order to be able to do, so it is precisely not something that all people can do as part of their everyday socialization. I would argue, however, that, on a crucial level, there can actually be no distinct categorical separation between action onstage and offstage, and that the difference between the two is a matter of degree, rather than of class.

According to John Dewey's "principle of continuity," just as there can be no rupture in the continuum of existence that runs from early childhood development to the fully grown human, there can also be no break in the continuum that begins with the basic meaning-making processes of early life and those that come later in life, namely complex thought and abstract reasoning. As Dewey puts it,

> childhood and adulthood are phases of a continuity, in which just because it is a history, the later cannot exist until the earlier exists . . . ; and in which the later

makes use of the registered and cumulative outcome of the earlier—or, more strictly, is its utilization. . . . The real existence is the history in its entirety, the history as just what it is. The operations of splitting it up into two parts and then having to unite them again by appeal to causative power are equally arbitrary and gratuitous. Childhood is the childhood *of* and *in* a certain serial process of changes which is just what it is, and so is maturity. To give the traits of either phase a kind of independent existence, and then to use the form selected to account for or explain the rest of the process is a silly reduplication; reduplication because we have after all only parts of one and the same original history; silly because we fancy that we have accounted for the history on the basis of an arbitrary selection of part of itself.[3]

Mark Johnson, taking his lead from Dewey, applies the principle of continuity from the forms of learning engaged during early, preverbal development and the underpinnings of verbal language to later, more abstract forms such as poetry, art, and even mathematics. Johnson summarizes Dewey succinctly: "the 'higher' develops from the 'lower,' without introducing from the outside any new metaphysical kinds."[4] If we accept this general principle on the basis of its logic, then it follows that the way people engage meaningfully with the world through action in everyday life must somehow be continuous with the way people act onstage; even if theatrical behavior is stylized or abstract, the fact remains that the humans onstage have particular ways of acting in the world that is theirs and that is connected to the rest of their lives in a continuous, if circuitous, path.

People move through the world, acting in and upon it, all the while flowing through an experiential chain of meaning. The subject-environment context of interaction, which is essential and productive, is situated in what one might call "reality," the place wherein one might experience any and all facets of human existence, including perception of phenomena, interaction with objects, and navigation of living relationships, and ranging from love to death, pain to pleasure, and so on. In the fictive world of the stage, all of this appears to change. The scenic environment exists not for just "any old use," in the way that reality is simply available to be interacted with at will, but it is crafted for a specific use. The objects may be real, but then again, they may just be hollowed out props. Even in a "realistic" set (as in the *Doll's House* example provided in the Overview section), the walls may or may not support weight, the light switches do not necessarily work, the angles are mainly obtuse, there is usually no ceiling, and the windows do not look out into the world outside. The people one meets in this fictive reality are also both who and not who they are, and they will usually only behave and respond in preconditioned ways. The whole thing is a lie, a world nested inside a fabricated circumstance, which one cannot really call "reality," and yet, still, there is something real in its basic materiality, or as theatre phenomenologist Bert O. States might say, "a world within the world itself."[5] It is a realm of real fiction, a fictive reality.

The things that actors do (and also the things they say, which I will address in Chapter 3) in this fictive reality are meaningful, but again, not just in "any old way." In this realm there are rules and conventions, just as there are rules in the real, everyday social context, and actors must adhere to them. Why is it, we might wonder, that some actors may convey only a certain amount of meaning, while others somehow manage to give the impression that meaning is veritably emanating from them, as if naturally and without effort? Such actors are functioning seamlessly in the particular theatrical context, playing by the rules, as it were, so proficiently that it is as if they have become one with the world onstage and have themselves become equally fictive to match the surrounding scenic reality so that they do not stand out. Nothing they do is out of place, and everything they do participates in the fabric of the totality of the performance event. They have been subsumed into it. They are at home. They live there.[6]

In order to understand how this happens, and how an actor can develop the skills necessary to be able to play by the rules that inhere in a particular scenic reality, we first need to have a working theory of action, which, as I have indicated, is at the heart of acting. To gain clarity on the question of how action is experienced, how it communicates, and how one might learn to construct it successfully for use in the scenic context, I will need to deconstruct the concept and analyze its component parts and see how they function and in what they consist. Having done that, I can provide an account of how it is possible for actors to be absorbed so effectively and completely into the fictive world in which they labor.

Approaching Action through Wittgenstein

To this end I draw upon the philosophy of Ludwig Wittgenstein, who famously pulls apart our habitual understanding of things and reveals their complexity through a deceptively simple process of "ordinary language" philosophy. According to this approach, it is possible to learn everything we wish to know about how the world works by looking closely at the rules of human communication, at the "grammar" of what Wittgenstein calls "language games" (§7).[7] If one wishes to understand what action is, for example, one can begin by looking at how it functions in the context of its "ordinary" use. Then, having a sense of the contours of and limitations around the "language game" of action, one can be better situated to approach an understanding of how action functions in other contexts, such as that of theatre performance.

Wittgenstein's writing is notoriously difficult to grasp, mainly because of his aphoristic and fragmented approach to developing "proofs," which often read more like poetry than logic, but also because his early work in the *Tractatus Logico-Philosophicus* is frequently seen to contradict many of the ideas contained in his later writings, namely the *Philosophical Investigations*. I find, however, that this later work—partly thanks to the fact that it is so porous, and partly because it manages to address fundamental aspects of human action and interaction so profoundly—provides an excellent conceptual opening through which we might glimpse some very useful insights about action and how it functions both in everyday life and in artistic practice.

His treatment of will, intention, and action in the *Philosophical Investigations* is unique and provocative, but again, because of its incomplete and somewhat puzzling nature, it has tended to raise more questions than it has answered. In a sense, this is perhaps exactly what the philosopher would have wanted, since he is less interested in providing blanket solutions to philosophical problems than in stimulating people to think about the world they live in as an ever-changing network of socially, culturally, and linguistically connected "forms of life" (§19). To understand the world, according to Wittgenstein, is to engage with it as a *form of life*, a dynamic and situation-specific process of communication through language. Language, for Wittgenstein, consists not only in verbal constructions but of "grammar" in a more general sense, including all actions, interactions, and even nonverbal vocal gestures. His musings on action have inspired psychologists, philosophers, political scientists, linguists, and thinkers across disciplinary boundaries to shake off the dust of old assumptions and see what they might learn from what is now commonly called "ordinary language" philosophy.

Wittgenstein begins his line of inquiry into action in the *Philosophical Investigations* at §612 mainly as a means to investigate the concept of will, or volition, and at §621 he posits his famous conundrum, "when 'I raise my arm,' my arm goes up . . . what is left over if I subtract the fact that my arm goes up from the fact that I raise my arm?" This simple but dense question creates a prompt to consider the apparent gap between action and agency, and throughout this section Wittgenstein touches upon, in a relatively short amount of text, essential concepts contained by the broad notion of action, namely will, intention, sensation, autonomic bodily function, feeling, self-awareness, and memory. Wittgenstein's distinction between voluntary and involuntary action is somewhat perplexing, but taking the time now to consider it will lead later to a better understanding of how action operates in the realm of theatre, where action seems to inhabit an impossible zone made simultaneously of both spontaneity and predetermination.

To this end, the example of raising the arm can be useful as a point of entry into an analysis of the relationship of will to action. Wittgenstein points out that when one raises one's arm there seems to be some connection to the will, but it is difficult to understand in what exactly the will consists. It does not appear that the will can be said to precede the action, even though the action is voluntary (i.e., willful—"I raise my arm"), because the action just seems to happen ("my arm goes up"). It is true that sometimes we can decide ahead of time that we are going to do something, like raise an arm, but many times, or even most times in everyday life, we perform all sorts of actions and gestures without any prior conscious planning whatsoever. If that is the case, then, it could be that the will still operates prior to action, but it does so unconsciously. An irresolvable problem arises here, though. Whatever this mental occurrence called "will" is, it must itself be either voluntary or involuntary. If it is voluntary, we enter into the dilemma of eternal recurrence, in that, as Wittgenstein puts it, "it makes no sense to speak of willing willing," since the will that is doing the willing would need something to will it, and so on, forever (§613). If the mental occurrence is involuntary, then that makes no sense either, since it would not be consistent with our experience for the cause of our actions to be involuntary, since the whole idea of will in the first place is that it forms the basis (practically and etymologically) for voluntary action. This would seem to indicate that the will is not a mental occurrence at all but is rather something else entirely.[8]

For Wittgenstein it seems there can be no will without action, that doing something is itself somehow the will. In §620 he provides us with a statement that seems to be the closest we are going to get to anything definitive on the subject from him: "Doing itself seems not to have any volume of experience. It seems like an extensionless point, the point of a needle. This point seems to be the real agent. And the phenomenal happenings only to be consequences of this acting. 'I do . . .' seems to have a definite sense, separate from all experience." Action, in its most basic sense of "to do something," can be either a simultaneous experience of/with the will itself or a physiological reaction to an internal or external force or agent, or put more simply, it can be either voluntary or involuntary. In everyday life we experience both of these types of action, often simultaneously, on a regular basis.

In his short and incomplete treatment of the subject, Wittgenstein does not address any of the complexities that might arise regarding how the voluntary and involuntary can become interactive and intertwined, but we can consider the question briefly here. To take a somewhat gory example, what happens if I raise that same arm, and unbeknownst to me, there is a sharp metal fan above me? Perhaps my finger gets chopped off. Then what? The raising of my arm will hypothetically have led (minimally) to (1) a quick retraction of my arm from the raised position, (2) the movement of my other arm as it goes to grab my injured hand, (3) my vocal apparatus (including facial muscles, vocal cords, etc.) forming a scream, (4) an experience of overwhelming pain, and (5) a series of autonomic responses in my body. The voluntary, which Wittgenstein says, is known to us as being "marked by the absence of surprise," and the involuntary become implicated in the entire experience, in the immediate moment, and in those that follow (§628). It may be useful on the most basic philosophical level to use action to come to an understanding of will, but real-life experience shows that action is rarely, if ever, disentangled from a complex network of other bodies, acting and reacting in the never-ending stream of life.[9]

If the only thing we learn from Wittgenstein about the relationship between will and action is that sometimes action can be voluntary and sometimes involuntary, then what is the point of engaging with him on the question at all? While it may seem counterproductive to spend so much time theorizing the concept of will's relation to action only to discover that action can either be willed or not willed, it is an important point to realize as we consider how actors need to orient themselves as they labor to create scenic lives made up of action. Action's fluid relationship to will—the fact that it can be approached both directly and indirectly—makes it possible for actors to learn how to use it as a tool in the studio and ultimately employ it effectively onstage. Through Wittgenstein's musings, we come to see that whether or not an actor wills a particular action or set of actions is not the crucial point of concern. One of the central challenges of the actor is to perform actions that have been previously crafted, not only in a way that reads and does not disrupt the fictive reality onstage but also many times over. How, we might ask, is it possible for an actor to perform an action "naturally" if it has been put together first?

Near the end of his discussion of the will and voluntary action, Wittgenstein asks us to consider a specific example of a language game: "Someone gives someone else the order to make particular movements with his arm, or to assume particular bodily positions (gymnastics instructor and pupil). And here is a variation of this language-game: the pupil gives himself orders and then carries them out" (§630). In typical form he does not explicate this scenario further, but its significance in the context of his argument concerns the ability to know what one is going to do before one does it, through one's *intention*. Wittgenstein signals his awareness of the difference between when a person (the gymnast, in his example) just raises his arm in the course of living and when he does so as part of a preplanned course of action or in response to a command. The point is not that the doer who has already decided to act performs the action any differently from someone who is acting spontaneously, but simply that it is quite common for people to be able to act "naturally" when they know what they are about to do. It is easy to think of any number of instances from the course of everyday life in which preplanned action still manages to be spontaneous. We can give ourselves the command (consciously or not), as it were, to brush our teeth, or hammer a nail, or even juggle, but the way in which we accomplish those tasks in the moment is subject to any number of spontaneous and subtle variations each time we do them. Spontaneity is not a factor in the determination of whether or not an action is voluntary.

The example of the gymnast comes just after a rumination on why, when we raise our hand to ring a bell at a pre-ordained time, we do not exclaim, "'See, my arm is going up!'" (§627). Wittgenstein is right, of course, that we do not observe our actions in this way, but this is the case only in the context of ordinary life. Onstage, when each action is being watched and is so overburdened with import, it can take an immense amount of training for actors to be able to lift their arms and not say (to themselves, but this is what Wittgenstein is implying, anyway), "See, my arm is going up!" This training can occur partly in the course of everyday life, but often it happens in the actor-training studio.

Returning to the *plastiques* exercise, once the basic elements are learned formally, they can then be explored. Again, the procedures and goals of a particular instance of training will vary according to both context and lineage; however, whenever I have encountered the *plastiques*, as a doer or as an observer, certain core components have been consistently applied. For example, the *plastiques* are generally done quite vigorously over an extended period of time. Whether the actor is focusing on one body part at a time or on many in succession, the *plastiques* are to be executed in a constant flow. The reason for the insistence upon this component is twofold: first, it discourages the doer from taking even small breaks between actions to stop and think; second, it tends to make the doer quite tired, and as the level of exhaustion increases, the level of conscious involvement in the exercise decreases. This encourages a "fluency" on the part of the actor, similar to the process of learning a language through immersion, in which students progress from the need to "stop and think" about what they are going to say to being able to respond "without thinking." In these moments of "not thinking," conscious intentional control of action gives way to the doer's ability to allow other nonconscious intentional processes to activate more fully.

Also, it is not the case that actors simply stand in one place flapping their hands around during the exercise; rather, the *plastiques* can be said to lead the actors through space. The fish hand, for example, moves up, down, forward, backward, quickly, slowly, throughout the space, and although the actors are the agents of this movement, it is also true that certain movements cause the actors to respond. For example, if in a certain moment an actor causes the fish hand to move very quickly from one side of the room to the other, it becomes necessary to run after the hand in order to avoid falling down. In fact, it frequently happens that actors do fall to the ground unexpectedly, at which point they are faced with an unforeseen moment of unplanned (and spontaneous) physical reaction, which itself leads to the next movement of the hand, and so on. It should be clear that the *plastiques*, when given the requisite time and space, can present a very real challenge to the actor's strength, stamina, concentration, and balance.

While these challenges are important in their own ways (it is obviously essential for actors to be able to perform their roles without constantly battling exhaustion, distraction, loss of bodily control, etc.), they are not the central purpose of working the *plastiques*. In their notes from a workshop led by Grotowski in New York City in 1969, actors Tom Crawley and Jerry Mayer documented the instructions presented to them as they learned the exercises. They repeatedly stress that, while the "technique" of the movements is important to perform correctly, the true focus of the exercise is on the actors' "associations," which they clarify as being "images, moods, emotional tones ... personal images and experiences."[10] The importance of this balance between technique and associative elements cannot be overstated, and it needs to be understood if we are to comprehend what is going on in this exercise regarding the development of the actor's ability to embody meaning in the theatrical context.

What Is Intention?

The relationship between technique and association in this particular training exercise points to the broader difference between movement and action. If actors do the *plastiques* focusing, for example, on the technical form, or on the kinesthetic feeling of the body part in motion, or simply on moving it for its own sake, this will be apparent; it will not have a built-in connection to any real or imagined external object, and it will be read first and foremost as abstract movement. In order to be action, the isolation must contain *intention*, which, as I just addressed in my discussion of Wittgenstein's arm raising, does not necessarily need to form itself consciously in thought.

For all of its importance in the systems of actor training based on Stanislavsky, the concept of *intention* in the theatre tends to be rather mysterious. Sometimes the term is used in connection with a general "inner" desire of a character to bring about a certain outcome—such as Hamlet's intention to avenge the murder of his father—and it is seen as having an equally general effect on the overall behavior of the actor throughout the play. At other times, it is connected to more specific acts of the body or of speech—such as Hamlet's intention to kill Claudius as he mistakenly stabs Polonius—imbuing them with a certain quality and force on a moment-to-moment basis. In either case, the common thread pertains to action—what the actors are doing, physically and/or vocally, to achieve their aims, which some systems refer to as objectives and others as tasks. Broadly, the Stanislavskian use of intention allows action to be complex, just as in "real life" a person can do one thing in any number of ways. The way that something is done reveals the intention, and conversely, the intention determines the exact quality of an action.

Applying Wittgenstein's treatment of action and will to this discussion adds an important component that illuminates how intention operates. Without considering the concept of intention, the action of raising one's arm to ring a bell is simply and flatly that. However, in life, it is never such a two-dimensional affair. We always do things for reasons, in contexts—we ring the bell to raise the alert of fire, to call the kids in for dinner, to hear the pleasing tone of the bell, etc. In life, the intention determines an entire network of small but perceptible micro-actions and expressive details that read as how we raise our arm to ring that bell in that unique moment. Even raising one's arm "just to ring the bell" cannot be seen as simply neutral, as it brings into being its own set of meanings and implications. In ordinary life, all of this happens without effort. Onstage, however, each action must be a choice, and so it must be preplanned, crafted, and rehearsed.

Why rehearsed? Because the only way (or the best way, at least) to ensure that an action, which must be repeated on cue, contains the required components of meaning, life, and the appearance of spontaneity (and lack of surprise) is to practice it so many times that it becomes what is commonly called, as I mentioned earlier, "second nature." One of the central paradoxes of the actor's craft is apparent here, in that an action that appears to be "alive" is usually one that has been "rehearsed to death," as the expression goes. As reflected in the research of neuroscientist Elisabeth Pacherie, this fact is not odd at all. In her article, "Towards a dynamic theory of intentions," she describes the connection between conscious control of action through what she calls "present-directed" or "P-intentions" and the execution of difficult tasks. She observes that "well-practiced actions require little online control by P[resent-directed]-intentions. In contrast, novel or difficult actions are typically much more closely controlled by P-intentions." The freedom from the need to exercise "online control" allows "conscious agency" to be replaced by a complex of unconscious processes.[11]

It is important to realize here that it is not the mechanics that are being rehearsed by the actor, not the small muscular components of action, but rather the intention. The action itself can be said to reside in the intention, or at least to arise from it. Wittgensteinian theorist P. M. S. Hacker deals with this exact issue in his treatment of the will when he puts forth the following series of questions:

> If I want to pick up a glass, and will to do so, how does that affect my hand? Must I not have some idea of which movement to execute? Do I need to think of the requisite movement? It might seem that I do not merely have to think of the movement, but I must further have it in mind to innervate specific muscles, for in order to move my hand, such-and-such muscles must be contracted. If the will brings about these movements, must it not know where to catch hold, as it were? But even if it does "know where to catch hold," how is that supposed to help? Is the act of will the cause of the contraction of the relevant muscles? Do I then make the muscles in my arm contract by willing? Is acting then a form of psycho-kinesis?[12]

What is missing from this line of thinking is intention. It is not just that the actor is picking up a glass, but he is picking it up for a reason, in a context, and this determines the exact physical (and affective) nature of the action.

Wittgenstein, however, is firmly set against the idea of intention as "'inner experience,'" and he goes to great lengths to eliminate this way of thinking, just as Mark Johnson rails against any and all suggestions of the possibility of "disembodied thought" (§645).[13] He challenges the very notion that intention is something that happens inside, as distinct from action, and provides a clear example of how "the most explicit expression of intention is by itself insufficient evidence of intention" (§641). In his efforts to dispel the idea that intention is internal, Wittgenstein provides us with an account that is supremely useful for the theatre practitioner. He even employs surprisingly theatrical terms to make his case:

> "At that moment I hated him."—What happened here? Didn't it consist in thoughts, feelings, and actions? And if I were to rehearse that moment to myself I should assume a particular expression, think of certain happenings, breathe in a particular way, arouse certain feelings in myself. I might think up a conversation, a whole scene in which that hatred flared up. And I might play this scene through with feelings approximating to those of a real occasion. That I have actually experienced something of the sort will naturally help me to do so. (§642)

This description of the process whereby action, rooted in memory, yields an emotionally laden physiological response could easily have come from the notebooks of Stanislavsky, especially from his later work, in which he developed what is now known as the "Method of Physical Actions."[14]

As he developed his System, Stanislavsky came to realize that although, as Wittgenstein observes, simply calling to mind thoughts and feelings as a way of bringing about emotional states can be partially effective, such a practice is unreliable in the theatre, and even can be somewhat harmful to the actor's psychological well-being. Far more effective and useful to the actor is the component of action. By performing a certain action, Stanislavsky found, an actor can "arouse certain feelings" onstage, just as Wittgenstein proposes, but again, this process is not simply a matter of mechanics. We must take into consideration the intention of the action, not in the internal, mental sense but as a component part of it. As Wittgenstein urges with great clarity, "What is the natural expression of an intention?—Look at a cat when it stalks a bird; or a beast when it wants to escape" (§647). One might even say that this mode of experiencing intention as inseparable from action is precisely what actors draw upon in their creation of a role onstage.

By using a basic "vocabulary" of actions (as it is often called in the studio) in the *plastiques*, any number of different intentions can be embodied and put into effect. For example, the "same" basic element (the shoulder, the hand, the head, etc.) can hit or caress, slide, nudge, press, or any number of intentionally inflected actions. In this way, the intention informs the action and is inseparable from it. At a certain moment in the exercise—especially after working for close to, say, an hour and experiencing physical exhaustion—the conscious connection to the actions begins to slough off, and the actor comes close to being like Wittgenstein's cat stalking the bird—a creature of fully focused and embodied intention.

At this point we can see a connection between the work of the actor and Wittgenstein's scenario in §613, in which he speaks about bringing about actions and even bringing about an "act of willing to swim by jumping into the water." In ordinary life a person can perform an action that has will as its result, but can he bring about an involuntary action, like "the fact that the violent thudding of my heart will subside" (§612)? Through the rehearsal process, an actor learns how to do just that, finding the precise action that proves to be a trigger for a usually uncontrollable involuntary action, and learning how to repeat it, to make it happen at will.

In the theatre studio actors develop a working knowledge of how to build into each action of their "performance score" an intention that both functions and reads. This latter quality, being readable, is perhaps the most important to learn, since the actor's work is always for the purpose of being experienced by an audience. The audience, made up of people who can understand others in normal, ordinary life conditions only inasmuch as they are able, given limiting factors such as context, attention, distraction, clarity of signals, and the like, must be made to understand and believe every moment, every action, through every prefabricated intention upon immediate exposure. In part two of the *Philosophical Investigations*, Wittgenstein has this to say about knowing "what is going on in" another person:

> We also say of some people that they are transparent to us. It is, however, important as regards this observation that one human being can be a complete enigma to another. We learn this when we come into a strange country with entirely strange traditions; and what is more, even given a mastery of the country's language. We do not understand the people. (And not because of not knowing what they are saying to themselves.) We cannot find our feet with them. (§223)

The theatre is a different kind of strange country, in which we expect to understand the people we encounter. To be sure, we do not wish to understand consciously every single impulse and thought of the character, but even if the performance is experimenting with forms with which the audience is wholly unfamiliar, the artists must still craft their work in a way that is received the way they want it to be received. It must communicate fully in the desired registers, given what they know of what the audience "knows how to do," as Wittgenstein puts it, which is based on social, cultural, and aesthetic parameters and conventions (§31). The actors are not only illuminating how society works through their drama; they are, in the practice of their artistic craft, engaged in a study of human will, intention, and action in and through their living bodies. By examining action in everyday life, we can learn about action in the theatre, and the reverse is also true: the art and practice of theatre, both in the studio and onstage, provide us with a deeper understanding of how will, intention, and action function in ordinary life. Thus, we can see theatre as its own sort of philosophical investigation.

Principles of Scenic Behavior

Again, the *plastiques* is an exercise that has been utilized in countless ways by any number of theatre practitioners, from experimental settings to the mainstream of commercial theatre. Perhaps because its origin can be traced back to that paragon of theatrical esoterica, Jerzy Grotowski, it is an unfortunate reality that those who learn the exercise often maintain a rather dogmatic adoration of their own theatrical gospel; I have found that those who learn it tend to believe that their way is *the* way. My own point of view is that, if any exercise is used in the studio, it should serve a clear purpose, and that purpose should be to advance the craft of the actor in some way. Which way, in particular, is of little importance, so long as it "works."

My approach to the exercise, as I alluded to earlier, derives predominantly from the actors who taught it to me, Roberta Carerri and Richard Fowler, both of whom work or worked closely with Eugenio Barba's Odin Teatret, in Holstebro, Denmark. While I have encountered the *plastiques* in other studio settings, I find Barba's version most useful to my current theoretical account of actor training because his company uses the exercise in conjunction with a set of clearly articulated theatrical *principles*. While these principles are themselves derived from Barba's work with his International School of Theatre Anthropology (ISTA), which has been the focus of much criticism regarding its tendencies to universalize and appropriate from global cultures in allegedly problematic ways, their use in the *plastiques* exercise seems to me fairly free from those concerns. It is also an exercise that I find myself returning to again and again, because it is flexible enough to be useful in a great variety of training circumstances.

One of the core principles utilized in this tradition is *balance*. Barba noticed that performers from a number of cultures around the world all had what he refers to as an *extra-daily* sense of balance built into their variously trained bodies.[15] Part of his attempt to understand the significance of this fact was to incorporate exercises that play with balance as a component of his own actors' training exercises. So, while they sprang from observations of multicultural performance forms, the principles themselves are not reliant upon any particular form or tradition. Other such principles include *resistance, speed/ tempo, level, direction, introversion/extroversion, focus of the eyes, use of the feet, orientation of the spine, action preparation* (*sats*), and more. Some focus on particular parts of the body, and some focus on more general fields of inquiry, which can be applied broadly across any number of exercises. While all of these can be applied to the *plastiques*, I will place my attention mainly on the latter, more general kind.

The principles serve to focus the work of actors on a particular element of craft during a given session. Actors working with the fishhand *plastique*, for example, may choose to address the principle of *balance* for a period of time, and a bit later they may shift to working on another principle. While working *balance* at a given moment amid the complex and ongoing flow of the exercise, an actor can choose to move from a point of steady balance—body weight evenly distributed between the feet, which are spread about shoulder distance apart from each other—to a different part of the space a few feet to the side. In order to get to that spot, the actor will need to "follow the hand" to it. The hand alone moves at first, leading the rest of the body, and when it gets far enough away from the torso, the balance will be tested. At a certain moment, the actor has a choice: either take a step or not. Stepping will move the rest of the body in the direction of the hand, thus allowing the torso to "catch up" to the moving hand. Keeping the feet planted on the spot, thus allowing the continuation of the hand to move away from the rest of the body, will result in a fall to the floor. This fall can be interrupted either by one or both hands catching the weight of the body or by allowing a saving step to occur at the last moment. Actors can learn to play with this point of balance, sometimes working with it, sometimes working against it. They can extend the moment prior to falling, moving their feet quickly before giving in to gravity completely, thus allowing the energy of what would have been a fall to transform into a run, or they can experiment with different instantiations of actual falling and recovery.

One very effective way to formulate what actors are doing by engaging with the exercise in this way—what elements of craft they are actually developing and why they might wish to develop them—is through the use of Mark Johnson's concept of *image schemas*.

Mark Johnson and Image Schemas

With his book *The Body in the Mind: The Bodily Basis of Meaning, Imagination, and Reason*, Mark Johnson began to develop the concept of the image schema as a means of understanding the process by which human beings make sense of the world in which they exist. The concept, explored even more deeply in his subsequent book, *The Meaning of the Body*, relies on a view of meaning as being grounded experientially in a fully felt, embodied process of interaction with environment (or material reality). From their earliest living days, people explore their environment in whatever way their particular body allows, in ways constrained by the exigencies and limitations of the world in which they find themselves. Johnson's claim is that all humans make use of image schemas in order to make sense of their surroundings, even if those surroundings (which include every conceivable element of situational specificity—language, custom, convention, topography, technology, etc.) differ widely according to time and location. For example, we can say that all humans have experienced in some way the process of bodily growth, of their own body and of those bodies around them, whether consciously or not. They may process the significance of that growth in ways that are culturally variable, and their own particular process of growth will be unique, to be sure, but in every instance there is a *feeling* of what growth is, even if it is not consciously formulated. It can also be said that objects appear and disappear from perception for us in the course of living, that some objects fit inside other objects, that there are objects overhead and underfoot, in front of us and behind us, and that certain things occupy one's attention variously in both central and peripheral ways. Each of these, and more, are encountered by unique individuals with different abilities and within specific landscapes of experience and consciousness.

Each of the abovementioned examples also corresponds with one of Johnson's image schemas. The process of bodily growth, for example, is tied to the *scale* image schema, by which varying levels of intensity and size (force, mass, speed, volume, height, vibration, sensation, etc.) are processed. A small piece of food, for example, will satisfy hunger less than a larger piece; thus, in relation to food, a whole array of feelings becomes associated with and through the image schema of scale. Perhaps the thought of a small amount of food can arouse anxiety or even panic or can connect to a memory of lack, or can lead to the creation of a strategy to get more food, just as the idea of abundance may bring about happiness or contentment, etc. At first, this all happens on the level of physical interactive experience, and over time, the knowledge borne from this physical relationship is learned and eventually comes to exist on a more abstract, conceptual level, including but not limited to verbal linguistic formations.[16] However, it is essential to realize that the "conceptual" knowledge of the scalar significance of food quantity is never disconnected from the bodily experience upon which it is based. The same is true for one's awareness of bodily growth, tree height, car speed, cake density, stereo volume, etc. Again, according to Dewey's principle of continuity, what is considered abstract knowledge must necessarily be connected with the previous, "lower order" bodily knowledge upon which it is built.

In the environment in which I grew up (and it is of paramount importance always to remember that each circumstance is molded by different sociocultural factors, particular bodies with particular abilities, etc.), I was given a very common child's toy to play with, which was made up of a stick affixed to a base and a series of multicolored, donut-shaped pieces of plastic (similar to the more advanced "Tower of Hanoi problem" frequently presented to subjects in a whole range of psychological studies of motor function, gesture, spatial awareness, etc.).[17] The goal of the game was to place the donuts on the stick, with the biggest one at the bottom and the smallest on top. I had to learn how to do this, and if I was anything like the various children I have seen playing the same game during my later life, I was not able to succeed consistently for a while. Through practice, though, the task became simple, "second nature" even, and in this way, over time and by encountering many similar experiential challenges in my environmental interactions, I learned (how) to arrange my world to a certain extent according to the image schema of scale. The donut game was part of my preparation to understand later in life more complex systems of scale, like counting, by which each number stands in abstractly for an amount of something that increases according to a particular scale; I know through my feeling body how it is that two is larger than one and smaller than three.

I provide this simple memory from childhood in order to make as clear as possible the way image schemas function in the learning process, and how they connect, both practically and affectively, to more abstract processes and actions later in development. Having established this rudimentary understanding of how image schemas function in ordinary life, I can turn my attention to how they are connected to the theory of action I outlined earlier. I have discussed how in order for an action to be more than simply a movement, it must contain intention. I have also indicated how, in ordinary life, actions are organized meaningfully by image schemas. The string of actions that comprises putting the donuts on the stick is colored at every instant by the intention of arranging them in scalar order. Therefore, the image schema of scale can be said to run like an underground stream of "know-how" beneath the action. My mastery of the donut toy depends in part upon my mastery of a certain notion of the scalar relationships between objects.

Now, imagine that a child wishes to show his parents what a good job he can do at arranging the plastic donuts in order on the stick. His intention during the demonstration will continue to rely on his mastery of the toy, and thus the image schema of scale, but a new element will have been added. He also intends to show what he is doing to an onlooker. It is in moments such as this that we can catch a glimpse of the "language game" of performance. In ordinary life, we develop a certain knowledge of performance as part of our relationship to the people that surround us. I am not claiming that learning to demonstrate is equivalent to actor training; however, I am proposing that *showing* or *doing for another* is something we learn how to do and how to notice, and this knowledge is connected, in Dewey's sense of *continuity*, to what actors learn in the theatre studio. Furthermore, it is already within our grasp, for some more than for others, to be sure, to carry out an action with a primary intention while simultaneously engaging in some level of demonstration; the two intentions can coexist quite harmoniously, even at the most basic, ordinary life level.

Part of what I experience when I perform an action that is connected to a certain image schema is the underground stream that connects that action with other similar actions. When I am, for instance, arranging objects even in some complex order on a table, there are echoes of affect that connect to a whole history of similar actions. Just as I am able to connect value systems to scale (i.e., sometimes bigger is better, and in some instances, smaller is better, but in every case, some value is assigned according to the scalar relationship; in the culture in which I was raised, at least, we tend to ascribe feelings of value to scalar notions/relationships), my actions that are involved with the image schema of scale are never not felt. They contain hidden, and sometimes not-so-hidden, associations. So, in addition to the current situational context of any action, which will most certainly affect how the action is done, there is also an undercurrent of association. However, as soon as an action is performed outside of the context in which such actions are normally done, such as in the fictive realm onstage, it can often be the case that the action becomes instantly "hollowed out" of the associations that would normally accompany it.

One major task for actors is to find a way to awaken the subterranean connection to the world of association that normally "fills" such an action in a real-life context. Another is to be able to fill their actions with associations that may not normally accompany their actions in real life. In many instances, actors must fabricate not only the actions and the intentions but also the contours and details of the underground stream itself.

A similar underground stream of know-how and association exists in relation to the image schema of balance. I will now continue my investigation of the theatrical principle of *balance* by examining its connection to the image schema of the same name, in order to understand why actors-in-training might wish to focus on it during their work with the *plastiques*.[18] Johnson spends quite of bit of time discussing the balance image schema and uses it to explain the relationship of bodily experience to abstract metaphorical concepts. The core of his theory is that balance is an image-schematic structure that exists in one's experience of being-in-the-world, and that one's sense of bodily balance is a felt, preconceptual knowledge that one acquires early in life, as one learns how not to fall over or knock things over, for example. As with the other varieties of image schemas, it cannot be reduced to a set of rules, and even if it could, claims Johnson, those ex post facto rules would play no part in the lived actuality of bodily learning and the bodily understanding of balance. However, there is a set of characteristics particular to the balance image schema that allows it to work as a conceptual whole.

Johnson defines the "prototypical balance schema" as "consisting of force vectors . . . and some point or axis or plane in relation to which those forces are distributed. In every case, balance involves a symmetrical (or proportional) arrangement of forces around a point or axis."[19] As actors work on the theatrical principle of *balance* in the *plastiques*, the forces are the vectors of the moving body parts (in the case of the fishhand *plastique*, the primary vector is led by the hand, and the other forces are the various impulses of counterbalance in the rest of the body that are activated in the effort not to fall over, for example), and the point is variable, depending on how the actor is working. In general, the version of the *plastiques* to which I am presently referring requires that the body always be organized around a point called, in the studio, "the center." This is a common term in theatre training, in general, and as such it has many meanings, depending on context, system of thought, teaching lineage, etc. In the case of Barba's version of the *plastiques*, the *center* refers to a specific point in the center of the body, at the intersection of the line drawn between the tops of the hips and the line drawn between the center of the coccyx and a point about two inches below the navel. It is around this *center* point that all of the forces of the moving body are said to organize to find balance. So, by extending the hand beyond the sphere of the balanced body, the center is compelled to move if it is to regain its position as the organizing point of balance for the body. Another option in this particular exercise is to allow the *center* to exert its own force in an equal and opposite direction from the moving hand. As the hand moves to the right, for example, the center can move to the left. The result is that the hand becomes unable to draw the body off-balance.

According to Johnson, we have the ability to sense whether or not we are physically in balance ourselves, and based on that "internal" sense, we also have an "external" sense of *visual balance*, which occurs mainly in our perceptual relationship to the things we see. We learn to determine whether or not an image, for example, is "in balance" or "out of balance" as a component part of our ability to identify objects as distinct entities in the experiential and perceptual field. Referring to the paintings and writings of Vasily Kandinsky, Johnson speaks eloquently about both the experience of perceiving a work of art and also the theory behind achieving a sense of balance in the creation of a painting.

In his discussion of visual balance, Johnson refers to a study by psychologist Rudolf Arnheim, in which subjects are asked to comment on their perceived balance of some basic geometric shapes and patterns.[20] The study shows that subjects are consistently able to discern between images that are "in balance" and "out of balance." As Johnson notes, "Arnheim suggests that there is a large 'hidden structure' of tensions and forces present in all visual perception," and these tensions and forces do not exist objectively in the image itself, but in the act of perception.[21] The claim is not that one's ability to discern balance is innate but, rather, that this is something we learn to do, and that this ability is connected to our understanding of balance according to the image-schematic structure of our embodied experience in the world. As we move through the world, we learn how to sense balance in the various objects we encounter. We learn, for example, how to make a tower out of blocks, and we learn to sense not only when it is in danger of collapse but also what we need to do in order to counter that potentiality. We play on see-saws; we try to knock things over, and sometimes we succeed; we accidentally knock things over, and we learn how to avoid doing just that.

Both *bodily balance* and *visual balance* work together to form an embodied foundation for metaphoric concepts of balance, in general. As Johnson states, and as I will demonstrate in more detail shortly, "the several different senses of the term 'balance' are connected by metaphorical extensions of balance schemas."[22] As we are learning about the balance of the things that surround us in our world, we are also learning about our own sense of balance. Anyone who has watched for even a minute the act of a child learning how to stand can see not only when that child is in danger of falling down but also the complex of physical negotiations and adjustments and trial and error that goes along with that learning process. Standing, and walking for that matter, is for most people a pretty simple affair, but that is only because it is something they have already learned how to do. Even for people who require mechanical assistance to walk or are bound to a wheelchair, the encounter with balance is of undeniable significance. We master it, and as Wittgenstein describes what happens when we acquire any functioning ability, we learn "how to go on" (§154).

Why is it, we might ask, that theatre practitioners continue to encounter the age-old problem, most notably formulated by Stanislavsky, that untrained actors asked simply to stand or walk on stage often appear uncomfortable and suddenly feel like they do not know how to do that simplest of ordinary life tasks? The answer to this question lies in the fact that, as I have already discussed, actions in ordinary life occur in specific contexts and are part of the stream of life; as such, they have intention built into them. If a mother is called upon at a certain moment in the course of everyday life to show her son how to stand by offering up her own standing body as an example, she will likely have no problem doing that. Her intention in that life moment will be crystal clear, and even though she may be aware of being observed by onlookers, she is able to do and show and perform simultaneously and seamlessly. However, ask that same woman to go onstage and do nothing but stand there alone, and instantly she may become self-conscious and not know what to do with her body. She can do it, but she most likely cannot do it well, because she simply has not learned how. We can say that the ability to organize one's own body toward a task, in this case the task of standing, which could be referred to as "balancing on one's own two feet," is inextricably connected to intention and context. *Bodily balance*, therefore, is an image schema that is partially bound up with intention through action.

It is also true that, in the moment of going onstage, the woman has ceased to be engaging only with her own *bodily balance*. She has herself become an object of someone else's *visual balance* image schema, and she has not learned how to organize her parts to be reacted to by the onlooker's perceptual discernment, or to use Arnheim's terminology, the "'hidden structure' of tensions and forces." The doer in this example must employ a combination of the two abovementioned balance image schemas—both bodily and visual. In fact, because the actor is always simultaneously both the doer and the observed, we can say that the art of acting lies in how (well) actors manage to do *in order that* they be perceived in a particular way.

If we were to approach this concept by extending Johnson's use of visual art, we could imagine the actor as a living painting that had the ability to organize and reorganize itself constantly, with a deep working knowledge of exactly what effect each of its reconfigurations had on the person looking at it. I use the phrase "deep working knowledge" because, in the actor, it would not be a matter of making a series of actively conscious, puppet-like auto-manipulations of the body. Of course, such a choice is stylistically possible (the performance form of corporeal mime is one excellent example of this), but the training I am speaking of here is aimed at providing the actor with the ability to make these choices without having to spend much "online" conscious attention on each one. In other words, actors standing onstage need to learn how to do and be seen doing in the fictive context just as readily as "regular" people have learned to stand (and do) in the flow of their ordinary life context.

This is the purpose of the *plastiques*. Actors need to learn how to behave onstage with the same degree of facility that they already have in real-life behavior, and this means they need to be able to do and be seen doing in a way that has been preconstructed and set. Working with the principles in the context of this exercise is one way of allowing the actor to do just that, toward the eventual end of helping to generate effective performance behavior. The *plastiques* exercise turns balance into an action that can be created, scored, learned, and performed; it becomes an element that the actor can play with in the same way that a painter can play with balance in the composition of a painting.

The principles, of course, never exist simply on their own; they are always participating in the larger, complex context of multiple aesthetic categories that, according to Johnson, are connected to image schemas. Struck by the marvelous complexity of the processes involved in aesthetic labor, Johnson evocatively contemplates how visual art functions in relation to meaning and felt experience:

> It is enough to get a sense of just how many kinds of factors are involved in our meaningful grasp of the work as balanced, and thus to realize how unlikely it is that there could be any single unified literal concept of balance adequate to all cases. Arnheim gives a brief minimal list of factors that influence force and weight relations in a work and thus determine balance: (1) location in the plane, (2) spatial depth, (3) size, (4) intrinsic interest, (5) isolation, (6) shape, (7) knowledge, (8) color. Imagine the complex of forces that results from the interaction of these factors for each "element" within the work![23]

These factors are derived from a consideration of the function of balance in visual art. If the list were to be revised to apply to live performance, it would grow in complexity as it would have to answer to the liveness of all aspects of the event. If we consider my previous example of the simple but not so simple action of standing, we can see that whether or not the actor is "in balance" or "out of balance" or somewhere in between is a complicated matter. The task of this and all stage action is accomplished by the actor in order to be perceived by the spectator.

The choices involved in the creation of stage action can be made consciously, but it is important to note that this is not always the case; in fact, each choice is usually part of a series of choices that are made without being aware of the component parts. The actor and/or director is not always saying "stand with more balance in that moment" or "try to be more off-balance in that moment." It is far more likely that the director will ask the actors, if there is a sense that something is not quite working, to fix the problem of composition by some other more indirect means, which is more likely to be some sort of imagistic seed for action. For example, actors might be asked to act as if they heard something rustling in the leaves and were listening closely, in case they might need to run or attack, or perhaps they might simply be asked not to slouch, or not to shuffle their weight back and forth between their feet as they are standing in the background of a scene. The possible ways that balance comes into play in the course of a scene are infinite, but the balance of the actor is always engaged in one way or another, and as such, it functions as material of composition, expression, and communication.

To repeat, the reason why actors need to train in order to work balance in an effective way has to do with the context of performance and the intention that necessarily accompanies action and "fills it out." To be both a doing body and a seen body, in the artificial context of repeated, preconstructed action, the person must learn how to behave. The mother from the abovementioned example does not need to relearn how to stand *in general*, but how to stand *for the stage*, in a similar way that tennis players do not need to relearn how to stand *in general* when they are on the court, but how to stand in order to hit the ball effectively.

Grotowski, in his use of the term *via negativa* to describe actor training, is referring to this process, even if his terminology reveals certain problems with his approach. According to his view, actors must unlearn habitual modes of behavior in order to arrive at a more "natural" "organicity" of the body in action.[24] In light of our current conversation, however, we can see that actors are actually learning new ways of doing that are appropriate for their new theatrical context. It is simply not true that actors completely unlearn previous ways of doing. The bases for standing and walking have already been established during the learning experiences of early childhood, and those basic abilities remain. If they did actually disappear, actors would no longer be able to walk or stand at all, and this is patently not the case in any acting studio.

It also bears mentioning that the idea of a return to some original state of nature, unaffected by societal imprints, marks, and influences upon the active body, represents an unsupportable way of thinking. My contention that human subjects enter into meaningful relationship with reality through their embodied interactions with their environment includes within it the fact that that environment is a social one. We can hardly imagine a human being growing up completely out of society, and so the doings of that person will always already have been influenced by that basic environmental component.[25] As an imaginative aid to action in the studio, myths of natural states have no doubt proven somewhat useful, but one should be sure not to confuse language intended to inspire the working actor with language intended to describe accurately the nature of reality. "Learning how to behave" in life is accomplished under the guidance of structures of processing meaningful experience through interaction or image schemas.

Moving on, remember that the fact that there is a principle called *balance*, which is also the name of an image schema, is mostly a fortuitous coincidence. Image schemas are processes that are active without us necessarily being aware of them; principles are tools that actors may consciously use in order to explore the possibilities of scenic action and learn how to behave in the fictive realm of the stage. To see the difference a bit more clearly, I will look at a principle that does not correspond directly to one of Johnson's image schemas: the principle of *resistance*. Actors working the *plastiques* with the principle of *resistance* will often use some basic imagery in order to set themselves on a productive path. For instance, for some time they may choose to work with the image of "moving through quicksand" and experiment with how it is possible to alter the inner resistances of the body both to feel like this thick substance is acting upon their body, making it difficult to move, and to look like they are pushing against something dense. For another stretch of the *plastiques* session, they may play with the image of "moving through water," or even "moving through whipped cream." Each of these images causes the actors to behave in different ways over time, and the exercise can lead to a nuanced ability on the part of the actors to alter at will the apparent force acting upon their bodies in space.

There are both clear and obscure ways the principles can lead to effective stage behavior for the actor. It is easy to see how working on *resistance* can lead to the ability to make, say, an empty cardboard box onstage appears to be full and heavy. Perhaps less easy to perceive consciously would be the tense slowing of an actor's hand in the moments of reaching to pick up a teacup that is supposed to have a tarantula in it. In each of these instances, the actor is performing actions with clear intentions, and the ability to make those intentions "real" for the audience relies on the ability to "make believe" through preconstructed scenic behavior in the onstage fictive environment. The resonance of the meaning of these actions depends upon the actor's ability to do in order to be seen, and this relies on the structures of perception and interpretation of the audience that are based on the complex living network of image schemas.

As I said, there is no *resistance* image schema in Johnson's taxonomy; however, there are a good number of image schemas that are no doubt activated through working on this theatrical principle, including *blockage, compulsion, attraction, force, counterforce, matching,* and *restraint removal*. All of these image schemas are structures that exist in the human experience of interactive meaning-making with the environment. *Restraint removal* is something we learn about as we struggle, for example, to break free of our parents' grasp when we wish to do something that is, for whatever reason, forbidden. We experience it again in a different but connected way as we try to get out of the stroller or the car seat. Not being able to move in the way that we wish is a common experience, and it carries with it a world of significance, depending on the various elements of specificity that exist in a particular environment. The same is true for *blockage* (we wish to access an object, for example, but are blocked by something; we close the door and hold it shut against the efforts of the sibling who is attempting to enter the room), *attraction* (we move faster as we approach the bathroom when we seek to relieve ourselves; we experience the network of feelings associated with attempts to satisfy our physical and emotional desires), *force* (lifting and pushing heavy objects), *counterforce* (playing a game of tug-of-war), etc. We learn how the particularities of the world in which we exist operate, and we create deep and complex networks of association that have these image schemas at their roots.

Also at play, as I have already indicated, is the degree to which actors can be seen to be consciously manipulating their actions onstage. A mime pretending to lift an imaginary box can afford to "let the technique show" more than the realistic actor lifting the aforementioned cardboard box can. The core of the training is quite similar, even if the schools might be radically different. In each case—that of the mime and that of the realistic actor—the performer has learned how to do effectively for the scenic circumstance and style, and this has been accomplished by engaging in a rigorous retraining of putting intention into preconstructed scores of action. How the work is received by an audience is profoundly dependent upon its relationship to the particularities of the image-schematic culture in which it is developed and performed.[26]

Maxine Sheets-Johnstone and Animate Forms

The process of working on the *plastiques* can be difficult to describe, partly because a merely technical description of which body parts are moving where does not really capture the experience of doing them or seeing them in person, and partly because at any given moment there are a multitude of different things going on with the body, and these goings-on do not generally have clear stopping and starting points; rather, they occur continuously in what some practitioners refer to as a "river" of motion and action that flows from one moment seamlessly to the next.[27] To explain the importance of maintaining an awareness of the complex fluidity of the *plastiques*, a brief overview of Maxine Sheets-Johnstone's theory of *animation* will be extremely useful here. In *The Primacy of Movement* the core of the project is to theorize how the concept of "animate form" allows for an understanding of how the world is experienced and understood, not only by humans but also by all creatures with the ability to move, including single-celled organisms. "Animate form," she says, "captures what we actually experience when we experience our own bodies and the bodies of others: animation, aliveness, dynamically changing conformations and contours, qualitatively meaningful forms—and, by extension, a spatio-temporal world co-terminus with that experienced animation and aliveness, those dynamically changing contours, and so on."[28]

As she explores how animate forms live in and organize this dynamic and alive world, she draws upon examples from evolutionary biology, which show how certain epistemologies or "ways of knowing" appear even in simple organisms—how, for example, a single-celled organism is able to identify food or danger based upon its simple perceptual organs, which are tied into its own motility. As we move up the evolutionary chain, such perceptual, movement-based "knowings" become more complex, but they also form the foundation for the ability of conscious organisms, for example, both to make sense out of and within a complex environment and to communicate with other similarly conscious creatures. "Living creatures," says Sheets-Johnstone, "are sources of meaning and are primed for meaning; meaning is a dimension of both primal animation and primal bodily sensibilities. Interanimate meanings, and in turn species-specific semantics, are from this vantage point grounded in a fundamental and altogether natural propensity toward meaning."[29] In other words, as animate forms we are always in motion, and movement is the basis of all aspects of our conscious life, from the time we are born, through the developmental phases of early childhood and until we die. "Rather than speak of the period before language as the *pre-*

linguistic," she suggests, "we should speak of the advent of language as the *post-kinetic* . . . thinking in movement is our original mode of thinking. . . . The intelligence or logos is an elemental biological character of life."[30]

Referring to Wittgenstein's assertion about the origin of language that "in the beginning was the act," Sheets-Johnstone makes clear that she prefers the term "movement" to "act." I have already provided a different, acting studio-based set of definitions for these two terms, which can still function alongside her definitions, as long as we keep in mind the distinction in connotation. For her, an "act" carries with it the connotation of an isolated thing done for isolated reasons, like a task, which is seen as somehow bounded. In the context of the acting studio, this view of action is practically unproblematic. Sheets-Johnstone, however, prefers the term "movement" when discussing animation, because it connotes the more complex notion that kinetic forms are constantly in a stream of motion and reactivity. My distinction between action and movement focuses on the presence or absence of intention in scenic behavior, whereas hers is concerned more with fluidity and dynamic environmental interaction in the natural world. In her formulation, this flow of movement contains an intelligence; the flow of movement is the foundation of our consciousness and our cognition. "In lieu of 'act,' movement is the more appropriate term," she says, "'In the beginning was movement,' not a mere happening or doing, but a bodily-resonating event, and as such meaningful, meaningful not only to the moving creature itself but apperceptively meaningful to creatures perceiving the movement." Again, even though she uses the term "creature" rather than "human," her evolutionary biological perspective is wide and includes the human. Her interpretation of Wittgenstein's use of the terms "language" and "language games" is also broad and extends to include the totality of ways in which animation is at the foundation of all meaningful interaction with the world, for all creatures, and is inextricably linked evolutionarily to the process of communication between beings of the same species. She states quite succinctly that "inter-corporeal sense-making is not only an apperceptive phenomenon, but an evolutionary fact of life."[31] As Wittgenstein keenly observes, and as I have attempted to stress so far in this book, language games are composed of elements of dynamic meaning that exist always in relation to others, to society.

This point made by Sheets-Johnstone is quadruply significant: first, it acknowledges that "sense-making" is primordially movement-based, "that articulatory gestures were of primary semantic significance, which is to say the felt, moving body, the tactile-kinesthetic body, was the focal point of symbolization"; second, it makes clear that this same sense-making is always "inter-corporeal," placing the intersubjective relationship front and center in the process of environmentally interactive, embodied meaning-making; third, it allows us to understand this evolutionarily based process of embodied sense-making as contingent upon and informed by the multitude of variants contextually generated by society, culture, etc. at any given moment in space and time; and finally, it makes a claim that sense-making is always itself in motion and must be understood accordingly if it is to be understood at all.[32]

The first three of these observations pertain directly to a consideration of how the *plastiques* relate to essential characteristics of the process of meaning-making in the world-at-large. In other words, we make meaning in the world through movement, with and for others, and in a particular context, and the *plastiques* are one tool by which actors can learn to become meaningful onstage in front of an audience within a particular set of performance conventions. The fourth and last observation causes us to acknowledge how, while the *plastiques* are comprised of individual actions or tasks, it is the larger act of putting them together into a stream that allows them to achieve real effectiveness. This has already been addressed in my discussion of "fluency" and the flow of "associations" spoken about by Grotowski as he taught the exercise to actors in the workshop studio, but it points to the importance of remembering that the complex flow of movement, to use Sheets-Johnstone's term, is essential to the exercise.

Where Is Meaning Located?

The meaning of the actor's life onstage exists, as I have discussed, in the meeting point between the action and the reception of that action. This point is governed in part by the culturally determined space of interpretation based on image schemas. This space is quite wide, but it is not overly vague. There is precision there, and this precision moves from solid to abstract along a continuum of meaning. At base, we can say that the simple presence of the actor onstage, alongside familiar objects, etc., is a layer of meaning. As we move away from this solid layer of basic object identification, we enter more and more the space of metaphor.

Mark Johnson speaks in great detail about the relationship between image schemas and metaphor. He is particularly clear on this point with regard to balance, an image schema on which I have already spent some time. "The *meaning* of balance," he elaborates, "begins to emerge through our *acts* of balancing and through our *experience* of systemic processes and states within our bodies."³³ These embodied structures of organizing our world along lines of balance determine to a great extent how the world, and our experience in it, becomes meaningful to us on all levels, from the literal to the abstract. It is important to realize that these meanings are usually not occurring on the conscious level. "We are dealing," explains Johnson,

> with automatic, typically unconscious, operations that require no effort. But most of our understanding is, in fact, active at a level of which we are seldom reflectively aware. So, there is nothing unique about metaphorical understanding of this sort. . . . Metaphorical interpretations of various components of image schemas are structures in our *understanding and experience* of the world and, as such, are not ordinarily part of our *self-reflective* awareness, though they are part of our awareness. They can properly be called "structures of understanding" because they are patterns in terms of which we "have a world," which is what is meant by "understanding" in its broadest sense.³⁴

Through his description of how image schemas function on the deepest levels of meaning-making processes, we can begin to get a sense of how it is that the various elements of a work of art, such as a moment of theatre or the performance of an actor, can resonate with multiple levels of meaning, some of which can be grasped and articulated, and others of which affect us in particular ways, even if we are not quite aware how (or even *that*) it is happening.

As Johnson nicely sums up with regard to the image schema of balance,

> metaphorical projections move from the bodily sense (with its emergent schema) to the mental, epistemic, or logical domains. On this hypotheses, we should be able to see how it is that our experience of bodily balance, and of the perception of balance, is connected to our understanding of balanced personalities, balanced views, balanced systems, balanced equations, the balance of power, the balance of justice, and so on.³⁵

I will not provide a recap of the descriptions Johnson provides of how each of the points on this list of various types of balance functions in relation to image schemas. Suffice it to say that the list provides us with a glimpse of the multitude of possible reverberations of meaning connected to the work of the actor.

It would be simplistic and inaccurate to claim that there is a one-to-one relationship between individual moments of imbalance, say, in an actor's score and isolated meanings that relate to imbalance on a more abstract level. In other words, it is not the case that actors go around acting out of balance in the moments at which the play wishes to bring into focus, for example, an imbalance of power. Just as Johnson reminds us that these structures operate largely sub rosa, as it were, so too do the meanings built into theatrical action operate largely on a level just out of plain sight. This does not mean, however, that they are not there, nor does it mean that they cannot be (or are not) put there purposefully by the artist(s). In fact, in the process of creating a piece of theatre, the artists work together to form a whole that communicates, or "makes sense," as a totality, favoring certain points of view and interpretations over others, evoking this emotion and not that one, etc.

The choices that go into the construction of the "performance material," as it is often called, are clearly articulable by the artists on some levels, and on others, the choices can be made because "they just feel right" somehow. The fact that this distinction between the feeling of "yes, that works" and "no, that doesn't work, let's try something else" is such a commonplace in theatrical creation is further indication that there are structures at play, which allow the totality of meaning to cohere (even if that totality might be characterized in a particular performance by a purposeful lack of apparent coherence). These structures are image schemas, and to have the ability both to "act well"—to make choices that "work"—and to respond to requests for alterations in specific directions ("try this . . . no, more like that . . . ," etc.), actors must be able to embody these complex, and usually unconscious, layers of meaning at will.

I return to my discussion of the ways in which scales of value are connected to the image schema of scale. I already noted that, at least in the culture within which I am currently writing, it is frequently the case that values correspond to scalar image schemas. For example, in a certain context, more food is better and less is worse, or for one person, a bigger car is better than a small one, but for another person the smaller car is better—perhaps because it gets "better," that is to say *more*, gas mileage, etc. We even say that we like one thing "more" than another. Our very sense of value is interwoven with our sense of scalar relations, and these relations are based upon our bodily experiences in the world, which are structured in part by the image schema of *scale*.

One way to frame this phenomenon is to say, as I have just done, that the value in a given moment is determined by the specifics of context. However, it would be just as accurate, and also productive to the current investigation, to frame this in the reverse way, namely that the specifics of a given context, phenomenologically speaking, are determined by the process of evaluation. To continue with the example of cars, imagine the scenario of a car dealership. In this instance, the car I am hoping to buy exists in material reality alongside any number of other objects—the dealership, other cars, the road, etc. It is singled out, though, and put into meaningful relationship in accordance with a process of evaluation. I see the car, for example, and I compare it to one of a different size, and so the *meaning* of the moment of interaction with the car is determined by the functioning of my scalar image schema, and that is how that moment is experienced. This is, of course, not happening on its own. I am likely also engaging in meaning-making with regard to other aspects of the car, such as its mileage and its color, and also other non-car-related impressions, too, such as perhaps the grating voice of the car salesman, etc. The point is that even the voice of the salesman is factored into the overall experience in accordance with how I experience the totality of the moment, which is determined by the way I interact meaningfully with it. For another person, everything could be exactly the same on the level of the overall material reality of the scene, and yet on the phenomenological level the totality of the moment would be experienced quite differently, according to the processes of environmental interaction operative with that particular person.

This observation holds true in the theatre, as well, since as I have noted, the fictive reality of theatre is still real. The difference here, however, is that the scene—made up of objects and bodies and light and shadows and sound, and so on—is constructed in order to be meaningful to an audience within a specific range of probable interpretation. The character of "car salesman" in a play, for example, will have been designed to be received in pretty much the same way by everyone in the audience. In this hypothetical play he is annoying, pushy, and untrustworthy, and because he is the villain of the story, it is important that the efforts to portray him in this way be successful. The ways in which the audience evaluates this character are based on the ways they evaluate people in real life, namely via image schemas. At the same time, the ways in which the actor playing the car salesman creates the assemblage of qualities to be processed as meaningful by the audience are also based on image schemas, as I have already discussed in some detail. In short, the appropriate version of "car salesman" can only be brought into being night after night by an actor who has developed the ability to manage an entire body of image schemas in a scenically masterful manner.

Here, though, I am focusing on the question of "where the meaning is located" and, in particular, how metaphor and abstraction are embodied by the actor. When I observed how an actor might work in relation to the image schema of *balance* in the *plastiques*, I focused mainly on how the components of the exercise are mobilized to train the actor to put intention (along with associative elements) into physical form through action. I also noted how the actor is training both to do and to be seen, and how this doing in order to be seen is governed by culturally based systems of meaning-making through structures of image schemas. I have spoken mainly about the basic, most elementary levels of meaning (object identification, clarity of story, character traits, etc.), but a work of art is always more than the sum of its parts, and so far, I have not spoken about the abstract meaning of (a) performance. The meaning of a painting, for example, always resides in more than just the brushstrokes, color choices, and identifiable figures. The deeper meaning, that which one might say gives the work of art its durability and overall depth (and value), comes about *through* the assemblage of bits and also somehow *above* them. The same is true for theatre; the work of the actor both participates as a part of the larger whole and also stands in relief from it. Although the audience frequently evaluates the performance of an actor as if it were a stand-alone work of art, it never actually is; the actor's work can never be seen as separate from the context in which it lives. That context is present both visibly—in the surrounding material elements of the performance and the theatre—and invisibly—on the level of the cultural-historical moment in time and space in which the theatrical event is taking place. That being said, the fact that we are able to isolate conceptually the work of the actor provides us with an opportunity to hone in on the "deeper meaning" of the actor's craft, so that we might understand that component in the midst of all the others.

As I consider the complex functioning of the actor's work in the midst of the slippery field of meaning, it is important to be aware that what an actor is doing is not always what the audience is seeing. Take, for example, the famous performance of Ryszard Cieślak in Grotowski's production of *The Constant Prince*. During the central scene of his torture, to all appearances, Cieślak's Prince was the very embodiment of a suffering martyr, surrounded by his tormentors; however, Cieślak the actor was actually working with a series of pleasurable memories, "immune from every dark connotation," as he enacted this scene.[36] The actor's score took on a new meaning by being placed by the director into a well-crafted scenic environment. Cieślak was executing his actions, full of intention and association, in a way that was intense and repeatable, in relation to a host of other elements, which allowed them to become woven into the larger artistic whole, much like the way the lines of a Kandinsky painting interact (through both their own materiality and the gaze of the observer) with the surrounding shapes and colors of the canvas. His ability to perform actions in a way that felt so full of life in this context was made possible in part by his work with the *plastiques* (which, in fact, he helped to develop), and the *plastiques*, as we have seen, rely upon principles, which allow the actor to learn a scenic behavior that successfully draws upon the basic image schemas upon which we all rely in ordinary life for our embodied understanding of all facets of reality. In this theatrical instance, Grotowski's keen awareness of how the scenic components would be interpreted by his audience stemmed from an ability to understand and manipulate the various image schemas at play (onstage, in and through the actors' bodies, and in the body-minds of the prospective spectators) and put them into form through the performance (*per forma*).

In one way or another, this apparent discrepancy is always at play. I could just as easily apply the abovementioned analysis to any moment in which actors are drawing upon invisible undercurrents of association in their work, whether consciously or not. Whenever actors utilize the commonplace technique of "affective memory," for example, to fill a moment of their characters' lines of action with an association from their own personal life, the disconnect between the "inner life" and the scenic context is present. Sometimes, this "subtextual" element becomes a core component of the theatrical experience, while at other times it can function more broadly to imbue the overall scenic action with the factor of believability required for that particular style as dictated by cultural convention.

The "life of the mind" is never comprehensively transparent to the outside observer. Our words and actions can dole out small parcels of meaning to another, in any context, but there are and will always be immense realms of association and memory and feeling that cannot be directly and clearly communicated. However, the presence of these undercurrents informs in subtle but real ways every action we perform, as Maxine Sheets-Johnstone makes clear in her description of how "animation and aliveness" participate as inextricable elements of "animate form," as discussed earlier.

Sheets-Johnstone also elaborates upon this aspect of intersubjective communication through primatologist Stuart Altmann's concept of "comsigns." "Comsigns," she explains,

> refer to those behaviors of a group or species that are common to virtually all members in the group or species. . . . Though Altmann does not elaborate upon the concept of a comsign in bodily terms, it is obvious that comsigns could only arise on the basis of a common tactile-kinesthetic body, which is to say on the basis of *a common body of experience*. Short of an *experiencing body that is tactilely and kinesthetically common to all*, no language—verbal or nonverbal—could be standardized: there would be no honeybee dances, no alarm calls, no human speech.

She goes on to discuss the concept of "tactical deception," by which members of the same species are able to deceive one another, making clear that "it is because they are meaningful to all members of the group—*uniformly* meaningful to them—that the behaviors can be used by one individual in the group to deceive the other individuals in the group."[37] Sheets-Johnstone draws a direct and inextricable connection between the ability to communicate and the ability to deceive. The degree to which one is able to control the expression and reception of the undercurrent of intention and association of animate forms, then, determines one's success at both deception and truth-telling. The degree to which one can make this undercurrent felt and known, on all the various levels of perception and apprehension, depends upon the ability to communicate through action in a particular cultural context or, in the case of the current investigation, scenic environment.

The Importance of Interaction

As I have said, there are any number of potential variations on the *plastiques*. They can be done by one body part for an extended period of time, or a rule can be inserted into the exercise that a body part can only be activated once before moving on to a different body part, and so on, for a period of time or even for an entire session. They can be done to music, which helps actors to follow a flow of rhythm different from the one they might choose in silence, and which can also open the door to a new set of associations in the body-mind of the working actor. They can be explored as a story is being recited aloud by the leader, thus allowing actors to explore both the difference between associations generated "from the inside" and those that come "from the outside," and the relationship of words to their own abstract actions. Each of these variations can be analyzed using many of the tools and concepts I have discussed so far in this chapter. However, I have yet to discuss the importance of interaction among participants in the ongoing process of exploration of craft enabled by this exercise.

I have worked in studios for months on end where, no matter how many bodies were participating in the training, the *plastiques* were very much a solo activity. The actors focused on the principles that they needed to work on and simply shared the space with the other actors. The only interaction was embodied in the small effort it took not to bump into the others. There is great value in this work, to be sure, but in my experience there comes a time at which it is important for the actors to work together directly, first in pairs and then as a larger group. One way to begin partner work is to ask the actors to utilize individual *plastiques* in something like a physical call-and-response exchange.

A pair of actors starts by standing a few feet apart and facing each other. Then, one actor begins by activating one body part. The other actor responds with a single body part, either the same one or another, and they go back and forth in this way, trying to eliminate as much as possible any lag time between actions. While it is certainly possible to keep the exercise going in this way for quite some time, it is generally allowed to transform into a more fluid "conversation," in which one actor may offer up a "phrase" of *plastiques*, rather than limiting them to the one-at-a-time model, which can tend to feel like trying to speak with someone using only a staccato barrage of solitary "words." As the conversation continues, the actors are permitted to move around the space and in relation to each other as they wish (usually without making physical contact with each other, but this element can be played with), but it is of crucial importance always to focus the attention on the partner and to explore what it means to let the actions speak for themselves. In other words, actors are encouraged to see how it might be possible to use the *plastiques* as genuine carriers of some unconscious and abstract meaning in their own right, rather than letting them merely translate the ideas of the actor's conscious mind. For example, rather than thinking "I am swatting at you with my shoulder," or "I am soothing you with my hand," the actors should let the actions just appear through the call and response "spontaneously," in the course of conversation, as it were, rapidly and persistently, relegating as much as possible the conscious mind to the role of silent observer.

As I shall explore in greater detail in Chapter 3, in the section on listening, developing the capacity to fine tune the response to other people and to the environment itself is an important aspect of the actor's craft. In this exercise, actors are presented with an extended opportunity to focus on the ways in which bodies can interact with each other without focusing on the verbal component that is normally at the center of one's conscious awareness in conversation. As Rick Kemp notes, "50 percent (depending on context) of meaning in interpersonal interaction is communicated non-verbally," and language, which is made up of an intricate combination of word and gesture, is entirely grounded in the impulse to communicate with others.[38] Therefore, it is incumbent upon actors-in-training to attend not only to the ways in which actions express their own "inner lives" but also to how actions can effectively participate in the fundamental aspect of communication that is geared toward sharing thoughts, ideas, and desires with others. In everyday life it is, of course, possible to talk to oneself, but the language one uses to do that is based on the far more common occurrence of talking to other people. If, as I have already asserted, scenic life is grounded in the everyday, and if nonverbal communication is integrated fully into the act of intersubjective discourse, then actors must do what they can to develop their abilities to engage with action not just on their own but in active relation to other bodies.

An excellent example of how intersubjective human communication works is provided by John Dewey in *Experience and Nature*, as he describes the relationship between two people, one of whom, called A, points to a flower and asks the other, B, to get it for him. Dewey explains that, simply put, the indexical movement of A contains its meaning in B's ability to imagine himself in the position of A, and A's request contains its meaning in A's ability to imagine B being able to fulfill the request. The meanings of the actions, sounds, and objects involved in this transaction are the very stuff of communication through language. Like Wittgenstein, Dewey denies the need (or presence) of any "internal" mechanism of meaning-making; the process exists as an active cooperation between two subjects.[39] "The heart of language," he asserts, "is not 'expression' of something antecedent, much less expression of antecedent thought. It is communication; the establishment of cooperation in an activity in which there are partners, and in which the activity of each is modified and regulated by partnership."[40]

The step between this scenario and that of a performer onstage is not a difficult one to take. Using the partner *plastiques* as an example, it is a simple matter to understand (especially when witnessing the exercise in action) how "the activity of each is modified and regulated by partnership." Of course, the relationship can be expanded to include not only multiple partners but also the various scenic objects, some of which "speak" silently in their stillness through their own particular material qualities (i.e., a ratty couch downstage center will "interact" differently with an actor than will a brand new leather sofa; an old grandfather clock on the upstage wall will cause a different reaction than will a big, wall-mounted digital display, etc.), and some of which become akin to acting partners through their function as hand-held props, each with its own associative potential. The relationship can also be expanded to include the audience as a partner.

Even in the apparently complicated instance of Cieślak's performance in *The Constant Prince*, one can easily see how all of the preparation made by the actor in collaboration with the director was for the purpose of "the establishment of cooperation in an activity in which there are partners," where, in this case, partners A and B, say, are the actor and the audience members, respectively. A (in collaboration with the director, in this case) makes a request of B to think and feel something precise, knowing that B will need very specific cues if they are to respond in the hoped-for way, and B, in the position of active reception, finds a way to understand A, through their ability to "perceive the thing as it may function in A's experience, instead of just ego-centrically," just as Dewey describes.[41]

To be clear, A's experience here is importantly not the original stimulus he used to create his performance score; rather, it is the action as composed through its larger intention, crafted by multiple participants, to communicate to an audience a particular moment embedded in the performance. As Dewey suggests, Cieślak does not "express something antecedent" through his performance, but the preparation of that material has become an integral part of the "activity" of communication, nonetheless. The same is true for any actor, regardless of style. In any theatrical context, the performers' ability to put into form a line of action that successfully participates in the cooperative activity of actor-audience communication relies upon how well they are able to embody at will a complex network of meanings as dictated by the image schemas at play in that particular culturally determined space.

Concluding Thoughts

In this chapter I have attempted to elucidate the practical components of one particular actor-training exercise. In the process, I have found it necessary to consider how meaning is engaged in everyday life and how that process undergirds the abstract meaning-making of an actor in the fictive reality of the stage. An important part of this discussion has been directed toward how the theatrical act functions in relation to the audience. Viewing the practical effectiveness of the *plastiques* through the lens of Johnson's notion of image schemas, for example, has allowed me to show how the elements of the exercise aid actors to be clear and agile bodies of communication, and this necessitates an ability to work at the level of deep meaning at which the image schemas function. Again, the *plastiques* is just one set of exercises designed to train the actor. Even in the culture in which I live and create theatre, there are countless approaches to actor training and performance creation, not to mention those that exist throughout the many cultures of the world. The purpose of my exploration of the *plastiques* in this text is, as I have said, not to promote it as anything remotely resembling the only or even the best way for actors to learn to engage with meaning in the theatre. My contention is that if actors are to become meaningful onstage, the training in which they engage—whether this training be comprised of exercises or improvisation or scene-work or an apprenticeship model—must contain within it the means of enabling them to navigate the intricate web of abstract meaning-making, which I maintain relies upon a fully embodied interaction with the actual environment, along the lines described by Johnson and others.

This chapter has focused on action. Much of the discussion has stayed on phenomenological and epistemological levels, since the experience of the actor and the audience, along with their ability to make and understand meaning, can productively be viewed from these vantage points. There is more to the story, though. What is going on in the actor "below the surface," as it were? How is the actor's work influenced or guided by the limitations and capacities of, say, human perceptual systems? How does vision function in relation to how meaning is processed, and how might this be taken into account as we consider what an actor is and is not doing? How exactly is the actor keeping track of the body and all its various and complex movements, on a conscious or unconscious level? In the next chapter I take into consideration questions such as these by looking at some of the central arguments surrounding the field of EC as it exists in the field of contemporary philosophy. I demonstrate that much can be learned by applying neurophilosophical theories of perception and proprioception to the work of the actor. Even though there is a good deal of disagreement on some of these important questions, there has been a marked shift away from symbolic theories of mental representation over the past few decades, and toward a deeper acknowledgement of embodiment in the philosophical literature. It is crucial that theatre studies takes these trends into account as it wrestles with its own questions of the technique and practice of the human actor onstage.

2

Encountering Perception and Proprioception in the Actor's Craft

Introduction: *The 3 Layers* Exercise

In this chapter I offer an extended analysis of a training exercise called *The 3 Layers*, which I have been developing in a focused way over the past two decades. I have made use of it in various forms in a variety of pedagogical and studio contexts, from grade school drama classes to professional theatre training workshops, in the United States, Canada, England, and Eastern Europe. Its format is basic enough that it can be learned in a cursory way in a very short amount of time, although, as with many theatre training exercises and games, it rewards long-term exploration and practice. Like most exercises, and certainly those referred to in this book, it would be possible to examine it from any number of perspectives. The *plastiques* exercise discussed in the previous chapter, for instance, could have been looked at through the primary lens of its emotional and associative components, rather than as a way to lend focus to an analysis of the role of action in theatre vis-à-vis the actor-training studio. For reasons which I hope will become clear shortly, I believe the most fruitful exploration of *The 3 Layers* here would concentrate on what it can reveal about the role of perception and proprioception in the actor's work. To that end, and in keeping with the greater aim of this book to theorize the craft of the actor as a fully embodied process, I will engage in a description and analysis of the exercise that relies upon mainly contemporary philosophical thinking, predominantly in the fields of neurophilosophy, EC, enactive perception, and phenomenology. In this manner, I hope to make sense in theory of what has already proven useful in the arena of theatre praxis.

The specificity of the component parts of this training exercise makes it possible to observe in a rigorous and precise manner the encounter between actor and craft. As the chapter unfolds, I describe each element of the exercise in detail, starting with the rudiments and moving on to more advanced variations. Along the way, I attempt to understand both the underlying reasons for the existence of each part and the theoretical implications, as well. I should reiterate before continuing that not only is this exercise just one of many used in my own work with actors, but it is also one in a vast array of exercises that exist in the broader field of actor training at large. As with the other exercises presented in this book, it has its roots in the laboratory theatre tradition that can be traced back predominantly to Grotowski. In it, however, one will recognize features common to many other acting exercises, from this "experimental" lineage and also from training systems geared toward more traditional, realist forms of theatre. I have even been told that some of the elements of the exercise are reminiscent of other contemporary training systems, such as the Viewpoints developed by Mary Overlie and Anne Bogart, to which I have had virtually no direct exposure whatsoever. *The 3 Layers* grew out of my own theatrical explorations, both in the context of developing NACL Theatre's training regimen and through the great many encounters I have had as an actor, director, and teacher with other directors, actors, and teachers in various workshop settings and exchanges dating back to the late 1980s.

Some of the exercise's similarities to other techniques arise from direct influence, while others are coincidental and are likely the result of the fact that there are certain basic elements of craft that actors working at a given time and place need to develop. Actors working in both avant-garde and mainstream forms, at least in the contemporary United States, need to know how to stand and move around onstage, for example, without looking uncomfortable and awkward. Therefore, it is likely that exercises that focus on walking, breathing, core development, and specificity of physicalization will be a prominent part of any good training regimen. Also, an exercise from one tradition, if it is effective and flexible enough in its formal elements, can be made with a little effort to function quite well for actors training in other contexts, so the barriers that exist so clearly between performance styles onstage are not so important to observe in the training studio. Experienced teachers always have many tools at their disposal, and depending on their pedagogical aims in a given situation and the level of experience that the student possesses, they can avail themselves of whatever best suits the moment; the important thing is that it works. In the pages that follow, I speak about this particular exercise as it relates to the full range of stages in an actor's development—from the first, often awkward attempts of novices to learn the basics and assimilate new sensorimotor skills to expert execution by advanced practitioners.

As the name suggests, *The 3 Layers* is a training exercise divided into three basic sections or layers. I refer to the first of these as "the layer of the senses." Spread out evenly throughout the space (whenever possible, we work with bare feet in a sizable open studio with wood floors), the actors are instructed to begin by looking around, attempting to take in visually as many details as they can. These details might include the planks of wood on the floor, woodgrain patterns, the play of light across the ceiling tiles, the folds of a curtain, dust particles floating in the air, or whatever else one might see. The instructions stipulate that the actor's gaze should not fixate on any one object; rather, like a hummingbird, I sometimes like to say, it should flit around, stopping only for a moment to suck some vision-nectar before moving on to the next spot, and so on. Unlike what is often referred to in the training studio as "soft" or "general" focus, which encourages a panoramic view without letting single visual elements to come into clear focus, this way of seeing is intended to see many details in focus, one at a time and in quick succession. The actors are then instructed to add hearing into the mix, listening to everything, from the sounds of traffic outside to the hum of the electric lighting, the furnace, breathing, and what have you. Added to vision and hearing then is touch, as the actors are asked to feel the way the various items of clothing they are wearing feel against their skin and even the feel of the air in the room. Smell is the final component (and taste is not included at all). The challenge is for the actors to activate consciously all of these senses simultaneously, as fully as possible, without fixating on any one object for more than a moment or two at a time, and without letting attention to one modality inhibit, as it often does, the ability to attend to any of the others.

After some time has passed, when the actors feel like they would like to move, they are permitted to walk slowly in the space, taking into account new angles, perspectives, and stimuli. Some of the new elements the actors are asked to notice include the feeling of the bottoms of the feet on the floor, the movement of the clothing on the skin, and the feeling of air brushing the surface of the skin, all brought about by the act of stepping. While there are no additional instructions for the first layer, it is important to realize that the activation of perception called for so far is expected to continue with the same degree of intensity for the remainder of the exercise, hence the usefulness of the term "layer" rather than "section" or "part"; the three layers are intended to coexist, an important component to which I shall return in a moment.

Soon, the second layer, which I generally call "the layer of the joints," begins. Without stopping their sensory exploration of the space, the actors are instructed to become aware of the movements of the skeleton at the points of articulation as they step, starting with the joints of the toes, and very gradually working their way up the legs, the torso via the spine, to the head and then down the arms to end up at the fingers. During this exploration it can be useful to move the body part in question very slightly, only in order to make sure that the sense of feeling the joint is not merely imagined, since it can often be difficult to contact many of these points of articulation in any real way, especially for novice practitioners. In addition merely to becoming aware of the joints, the actor is also encouraged to release (let go of excess tension, but not totally relax, as this would result in limpness, which is not the aim) the muscles around them, to give the sense of opening and space between the bones. It is also important that, although the focus is on one joint at a time at the outset, the doers attempt to broaden their awareness to include as much of the skeleton as possible at any given moment.

This brings us to the third layer, "the layer of the space." Whereas the first layer concerns the activation of the externally directed senses and the second focuses more internally on the movement of the joints, the third layer involves the relationships between bodies in space. While still attempting to keep the first two layers alive, the actors are instructed to direct part of their attention to the other bodies in the room. While it is true that the senses are activated by this task, as in the first layer, the important element added by this new layer has to do with reactions to objects that are not fixed in place and are, thus, dynamic and unpredictable (and even potentially dangerous). Because of this infinitely multiple and constantly changing component, there are a number of options for establishing the operative rules, depending on the focus of training desired for a particular session.

For example, a common organizing principle of the third layer is "balancing the space." To balance the space effectively means that all of the bodies are moving in some sort of uniform rhythm and flow through the space, and they are all evenly spread out from each other at every moment. The image of a raft on the surface of the ocean can provide actors with a clear sense of how balancing the space might work. According to this prompt, the actors are encouraged to imagine that they are floating together on a big raft surrounded by water. They are also instructed that they are not permitted to stop moving. Therefore, if the raft is to be prevented from tipping over, the actors must constantly adjust to the ever-changing formation of bodies. If too many actors end up gathered on one side of the space, for example, the raft will tip and everyone will fall off into the sea. Furthermore, this balancing act is not merely a question of placement of bodies in the space. The actors are also asked to move as lightly and silently on the floor as possible, as too much frenetic energy in any one place can also result in an imbalance, and being too heavy on one's feet can also tip the raft. For this exercise to be successfully accomplished for any period of time, all actors must maintain a consistently high level of awareness of the entirety of the space as everybody moves around it. They must, for example, see where spaces are opening up, be ready to move to fill them, and also be ready to adjust and readjust when spaces that were just open become filled by other bodies, and so on.

As I shall demonstrate over the course of this chapter, the difficulties encountered in the execution of the various elements of this exercise open up opportunities for learning. The moments of clear inability reveal precisely what needs to be addressed if the actor is to overcome the obstacle that stands in the way of successful completion of the task at hand. These tend to show up for actors as they move through the sequential layering built in to the exercise, which is another reason for me to start from the beginning and work my way forward. Before I can get to an analysis of the lessons contained in the third layer, I will need to take a moment to account for what can be learned from the points of difficulty encountered in the first two.

Among the many challenges presented during the initial stages of *The 3 Layers*, the one reported over the years to be by far the biggest is the difficulty of maintaining the first and second layers simultaneously. Especially for the novice, whenever the attention is turned to the network of joints, the attention to the senses ceases, and the outside world virtually vanishes. The reverse is also true; placing the attention on external perceptual stimuli makes it difficult to attend to the functioning of the joints. This phenomenon can vary in duration, depending on the skill level of the doer. While it is hard to maintain simultaneous awareness of multiple senses at the same time without one stealing focus from the other, it is that much more difficult to keep conscious awareness of the externally directed senses while also focusing on the inside of the body, and vice versa.

Alva Noë and the Enactive View

When working with students with little to no acting experience whatsoever, it is almost universally the case that even keeping the eyes moving around the space while walking is a difficult task. New actors tend to do one of two things: they either drop the gaze to the floor in front of them as they walk or they look directly in front of them, but the eyes become fixed and relatively immobile. When given the direction to alter this behavior, either they do not change what they are doing or they make the change successfully, but it only lasts a few moments before reverting back to the original mode of the fixed gaze. As time moves on, however, the participants become better able to perform the assigned task. Over a period of days or weeks (depending on a number of factors, including size and quality of space, circumstance of pedagogy, number of bodies in motion, level of performance experience, etc.) they become able to move the eyes and head more and more freely, which in turn allows their progress through the space to become more varied and reactive, and less predictable. The ability to move more "freely" in this way is, of course, the result of attention being paid in practice to both of the first two layers—the joints of the body must be supple and responsive enough to react to the changes of visual orientation and the visual focus must be free enough to respond to alterations in body orientation, both large and small.

Why might it be important that an actor-in-training learn to execute this component of the exercise well? Alva Noë helps us to answer this question. Noë, a leading proponent of the philosophical branch of enactive perception (or enactivism), provides a useful starting point to understand why and how developing actors' perceptual faculties may be essential to an effective training toward the art of acting. So often, perception is understood to be something that happens in us, rather than "something we do."[1] According to the enactive view of bodily experience put forth by Noë and other philosophers of similar orientation, perception is not simply based on action, in the instrumental sense by which bodily activity is necessary for perceiving to occur, but it is, in fact, action itself.[2] The traditional model, whereby "perception is input from world to mind, action is output from mind to world, [and] thought is the mediating process," is referred to by Noë as "the input-output picture" (based on philosopher Susan Hurley's observation of the tendency to view "perception and action as separate input and output systems").[3] Against this model, Noë asserts not only that it is actually impossible "to disassociate capacities for perception, action, and thought" but also that "all perception . . . is intrinsically active . . . [and] intrinsically thoughtful."[4]

In *Action in Perception* (2004) Noë asserts that the perceived material world does not exist as content in the brain separate from action, but that active perception and the experience of content are mutually co-constitutive, meaning that each feeds into the existence and development of the other: the actions of perception create for us the world as we experience it and we, simultaneously, act in the world in accordance with the constraints and possibilities provided by (or afforded by) the material environment. This view is controversial, and many philosophers are positioned quite firmly against it.[5] For starters, while admitting that there is likely a causal relationship between action and perception, many are unwilling to go further and admit a constitutive relationship between the two. As Ned Block succinctly states, "This distinction between the claim that sensorimotor contingencies affect experience and the claim that experience is constituted by the exercise of sensorimotor know-how poses a major problem for many of Noë's arguments."[6] I will not take up a position in this complicated debate; whether or not I can accept Noë's premise that perception and action can be classified as truly co-constitutive, his insights provide a fresh way to understand what actors do when they engage in any of the wide range of training exercises that serve, overtly or not, to develop perceptual faculties in action.

I will move on to interrogate some of enactivism's core assumptions a bit further on, but first it will be important to establish why one might be interested in this philosophical view from the perspective of theatre studies. To my mind, the implications of the enactivist view are of tremendous import as we consider what actors are learning to do when they train for their craft. As I established in the previous chapter, action conveys meaning through a fully embodied, living network of associations and intentions, implemented and put to work through a painstaking practice of abstract composition. If it is true that, as Noë states, "for mere sensory stimulation to constitute perceptual experience—that is, for it to have genuine world-presenting content—the perceiver must possess and make use of *sensorimotor knowledge*," then our action can never be separated out from the world-making act of perceiving our surroundings. Therefore, what we perceive is bound up with what we do as much as what we do is bound up with what we perceive. For the actor, developing an ability not only to perceive keenly and freely but also to deepen the connection between action and perception opens the way for a wide assortment of performance practices grounded in finely tuned capacities of sensorimotor knowledge.

If one does not adopt the enactive model but instead accepts the traditional input-output picture, what would change (both on the level of understanding and on the level of practice)? To begin with, the "world out there," without any constitutive dependency on our active involvement with it, would have the possibility of existing as a "whole picture," on its own, unaffected by our interaction with it. It would not simply be the case that in order to see the table, for example, I would need to train my eyes upon it, but also that my sense of all the properties of the table would be held conceptually in my mind, and that all I would need to do to be conscious of them—that is, to be aware of how heavy it might be, or how the texture might feel, or even that there are parts of the table not available to my current visual perspective—would be to turn my thoughts to what I know about tables in that representational storehouse. Action would be confined to its own system, as would perception. Thus, there would be a processual disconnect between actor and environment. The important point for this investigation is not so much that the piece of scenery, for example, would not be affected by the actor's perception of it but, rather, that the actor would not be affected by the object. I could move around and in relation to the table, and how I would do that would not be fundamentally impacted by the material reality and qualities of the table. On this view, my actions would remain more or less the same, whether the table is round or rectangular, short or tall, wood or glass.

If the enactive view is correct, though, the small but important details of my actions in relation to the table are intimately tied to the specifics of the table as I encounter it in space. I move in relation to the table in accordance with my sensorimotor knowledge, or "know-how," and the more I am able to perceive the specifics of the table, the more I engage in a complex series of physical adjustments—on a spectrum from gross and noticeable to fine and imperceptible—and mental conceptions. Noë provides a simple example, which helps to understand why the "whole picture" way of thinking about perception does not actually correspond to phenomenological experience of the world. In his description of how one visually perceives a cube, he notes that from no vantage point is the entirety of this six-sided object visible to the onlooker; however, when we see a cube, we experience it as existing in three dimensions. Of course, it is always possible that the away-facing side has an unexpected feature—a mark or a protuberance, say—but in order to become aware of that aberration, the onlooker would need to move around the cube or pick it up and rotate it. Because of how we experience the world, we have a sense of the away-facing sides of things, and we even have a sense that they may contain certain surprises (and not others). So, "the *visual potential* of a cube (at least with respect to shape) is the way its aspect changes as a result of movement (of the cube itself, or of the perceiver around the cube)."[7] Perception of the cube is grounded in the knowledge of how to move in relation to it (even if one is currently unable to do so, for whatever reason).

Active perception is not just a matter of how an onlooker is positioned in relation to an object in space, though. A host of other factors play into this interactive system, as well. For example, one's relationship to objects and the visual perception of them, says Noë, has more processually in common with the sense of touch than with, say, taking a series of snapshots with the visual apparatus. He calls to mind the example of a bottle, the shape of which can be experienced by tactile exploration, and even with the eyes closed, "the bottle as a whole is present . . . by means of a temporally extended process of directed finger and hand movements." Making the connection between this process and the process of seeing, he proposes that

> vision acquires content in exactly this way. You aren't given the visual world all at once. You are *in* the world, and through skillful visual probing—what Merleau-Ponty called "palpation with the eyes"—you bring yourself into contact with it... . Like touch, vision is *active*. You perceive the scene not all at once, in a flash. You move your eyes around the scene the way you move your hands about the bottle. As in touch, the content of visual experience is not given all at once. We gain content by looking around just as we gain tactile content by moving our hands. You enact your perceptual content, through the activity of skillful looking.[8]

While it is more commonplace to conceive of vision in connection with photographic or filmic processes, we can see that our experience in the three-dimensional, phenomenal world does not conform well to that analogy. "We experience the world as unbounded and densely detailed because we do not inhabit a domain of visual snapshot-like fixations," observes Noë. "When we hold our gaze fixed in that way, we do not look around, and insofar as we do not look around, we do not see. Vision is active; it is an active exploration of the world."[9]

The combination of the first two layers of *The 3 Layers* exercise creates the conditions for actors to inhabit the fictive reality of the theatre not simply by learning how to perceive the world "out there," and not by developing the ability to move the body freely for its own sake, but by sharpening the ability of action and perception to function together. The necessity for this work can be seen quite easily if one notes how consistently young actors, who presumably have little trouble living a full life-in-action in their normal, daily environment, find it exceedingly difficult to allow action and perception to function together "properly" as soon as they find themselves inside the fabricated circumstances of the exercise.

Playing out this scenario a bit further, we can move from the circumstance of the training exercise to that of the stage. If, for example, I wish to give the impression that I am "at home" in relation to an object (or set piece, such as a table) onstage, I will need to bring into being an acceptable facsimile of the complex system of interactivity of action and perception that exists in everyday life. To do this, I engage both consciously and unconsciously the aforementioned gross and fine sensorimotor adjustments required to give the impression of a complete, "believable" set of reactions. If I do not, the deficiency will be perceived by the onlooker, who is accustomed to seeing not only the way people behave in relation to real objects in real life but also the way characters in a given style of theatre behave convincingly in that system of artistic convention. Regardless of style, my inability "to fire on all cylinders," as it were, will read as false, stilted—as bad acting.

The Role of Attention

The 3 Layers begins to accomplish its pedagogical task partly with the aid of *attention*. This is an important point to consider, because while perception and action function together to make the world appear for us, this happens to a large degree on a level that is inaccessible to cognition. As Ned Block proposes in his theory of phenomenal overflow, there is a richness to the content of phenomenal experience that exceeds what is available to the faculty of cognition.[10] So, while it may not be practical to ask actors to *perceive* something, it is quite reasonable to ask them to *pay attention* to something. I can say, "pay attention to the table" much more precisely and easily than I can say, "perceive the table"; when I say, "pay attention to the table," the actor has the opportunity to act in response to my request and will presumably perceive the table, if everything is functioning effectively. My claim here, though, is not that *The 3 Layers* is an exercise focused on developing the actors' ability to pay attention; rather, through the repeated practice of paying heightened attention, capacities of *perception-in-action* are opened up and expanded, and thus they become available to the actor as tools by which affective performance material might be crafted in the process of artistic creation.

A difficulty commonly experienced with the exercise can help to understand this point a bit better. As I mentioned earlier, when actors begin working on adding the second layer, the tendency is for the "attention to turn inward," as we say in the studio. When this happens, it is as if the phenomenal world disappears (visually, aurally, tactilely, etc.). Noë notes that this phenomenon of "inattentional blindness," whereby "if something occurs outside the scope of attention, even if it's perfectly visible (i.e., unobstructed, central, large), you won't see it," lends force to the idea that "vision is, to some substantial degree, attention-dependent."[11] Inattentional blindness is experienced by actors when they turn their attention to one of the layers to the exclusion of another. It is also noticeable to an onlooker. As soon as it happens, the face of the actor changes, and it is quite clear that, even though the eyes are open, they are no longer "really seeing." Often, in moments such as this, the pattern of movement in the space becomes mechanical and repetitive, and the number of collisions increases. The rigorous and consistent application of multi-directional attention called for by the exercise is a necessary step toward developing the actors' ability to perceive-in-action, and the more the actors gain in proficiency with the exercise, the less the attention needs to be willfully activated and managed in order to do it well.

So here I am in the first layer. I turn my attention to the shadow cast by a fleck of plaster on the wall and simultaneously hear the distinctive sound of a mourning dove's coo drifting in from outside. These things I perceive. But what about the door handle I was just looking at? It is still within the field of my vision, but it is now off to the periphery. Am I still perceiving it? According to Noë, the answer would be yes. "From the standpoint of the enactive approach," he says, "all perceptual representation, whether the result of dorsal [related to peripheral vision, for the guidance of action] or ventral [related to centrally focused vision, for identification] stream activity, depends on the perceiver's deployment of sensorimotor skills."[12] As objects flow through my visual field, I am perceiving them, and the way I am perceiving them changes according to how I am oriented and moving in relation to them. (Remember that it is crucial for the enactive view that we experience a phenomenon not as *out there* in the world of sense data to be processed by our brains; rather, we experience it as the something that it is in the *act* of perceiving it.) Therefore, we can say that an object is being perceived so long as it is in a position to be sensed. I hear a rumbling outside, and even though I do not know exactly what is causing it, I still perceive it as a rumbling. I see something out of the corner of my eye, and even though I do not know what it is, I perceive it as a something toward which I could direct my eyes and explore through action in more focused detail.

As Noë makes clear in his description of perceptual presence as "availability," we should "think of what is visible as what is *available from a place*. Perceptual presence is availability." Here he provides a detailed account of how this process functions:

> My sense of the presence of the detail in the room before me consists not in the fact that I represent it all in my consciousness in the way a picture might—all the detail spread out at once in sharp focus and high resolution. It does not even seem as if the detail is present in my mind in that way. It seems as if the detail is present in the world, out there, before me and around me. The detail shows up not as "represented in my mind," but as available to me. It shows up as present—and this is crucial—in that I understand, implicitly, practically, that

> by the merest movement of my eyes and head I can secure access to an element that now is obscured on the periphery of the visual field. It *now* shows up as present, but out of view, insofar as I understand that I am now related to it by familiar patterns of motor sensory dependence. It is my basic understanding of the way my movements produce sensory change given my situation that makes it the case, now, even before I've moved a jot, that elements outside of focus and attention can be perceptually present.[13]

Attention, or where and how I focus my perception, plays a role in the quality of my perceptual experience but does not absolutely limit it; I can perceive something without "paying attention," but I cannot "turn my attention" to something until and unless I perceive that it is there.

However, it is also true, according to Noë, that we only ever perceive the world in bits and pieces, anyway. Not only do we see only the side of the cube that we are facing at a given moment, but we also put together a virtual reality of our environment without perceiving every bit of it. We fill things in.[14] I might have the impression that I am seeing the trees outside my window, for example, but I can have that experience without perceiving every detail of every single leaf as it flutters around in the breeze at every single moment. Even so, my perception of the tree, regardless of how virtual it is, is bound up with my active relationship to it. Without the *doing*, there can be no *seeing*. Perceiving is a fully embodied act, and it stands to reason that, like any physical skill, it can be practiced, improved, and put to use. While it may be true that I do not need to see every detail of every tree in order to have the experience that I am seeing the forest, I do have the ability to focus my attention on details, and if I make a practice of activating that attention, I might perceive a previously unnoticed bird sitting on a branch somewhere. When I do, and if I have developed the interactive connection between my kinetic framework (joints, musculature, etc.) and my perceiving organs, my whole body reacts, even if that reaction might only be registered on a level inaccessible to conscious cognition.

The 3 Layers obviously requires a much more active implementation of attentional focus than is required in daily life. At first, as we have seen, this effort tends to be somewhat clunky, but over time it operates more smoothly. Something one begins to notice when the first and second layers start to function together without too much interference is that, as the joints achieve more freedom of movement, the activity of perception does have a noticeable physical effect on the movement of the body, which, as a whole, functions as a network of its various assembled parts working together to walk in space in a particular way.

At some point in the exercise, the direction can be given that there will soon be a sudden, sharp sound in the room. The actors' task is to react as if the sound were coming from directly behind them, and that they are to go toward it.[15] When the sound is heard, the eyes lead the head to turn 180 degrees from the direction in which they were previously walking. This starts a chain reaction from the head all the way down the spine to the feet, as the actors "turn on a dime," and their bodies are suddenly moving in a new direction. This "game" is repeated, but each time, the degree of directional change is diminished, first to 90 degrees, then 45, then 10, 5, and finally to 1 degree. The function of this sequence of decreasing magnitude is to show that even at 1 degree, the change of the direction of the eyes alters the network of joints throughout the body from head to toe, forming a clear and direct link between the eyes and the toes, and all points in between.

Not only does this procedure demonstrate a connection between vision (and audition, since the hearing of the sound provides the initial impulse to change direction) and bodily action, but the doer is also made aware that the flexibility of the joints and their readiness to respond *allows for* increased functioning of perception, that is, if the neck cannot turn, you cannot see what is to your left without twisting at the hips, etc. The motility of the neck—a series of vertebral joints—aids in the action of perception. Enhanced responsiveness and flexibility allows for enhanced perception, both focused and peripheral.[16] Over time, as the actors' ability to maintain both externally and internally focused attention in *The 3 Layers* improves, and what began as a struggle eventually becomes easier, a more elaborate base layer of active perception is established. It is important to note that this skill is not isolated only to one particular, familiar location, namely the unchanging environment of the studio to which the actors have become acclimated; in fact, in the actors' experience of the exercise, no such space can actually ever be said to exist. At every moment the actors are moving in space, so even if they were alone, the perspective and experience would be ever shifting and non-repeating. Add to this the fact that there are other bodies moving in ever-changing ways in and through the room, and it is easy to see how the space is in a constant state of dynamism. The ability, the sensorimotor skill or know-how, of the actors themselves is improving; the task is repetitive, but the experience is never the same twice, because the skill is one of reacting to an ever-mutating stream of stimuli according to a general rule of behavior that is being learned. The richness of the perceptual experience increases in proportion to the degree of proficiency achieved in the enactment.

Proprioception: Body Image and Body Schema

In my discussion of the first two layers, I have focused predominantly on how externally directed attention works to alter and enhance perception of the available environment. I have made frequent reference to "turning the attention inward" as something to avoid in this exercise, because it diminishes the effectiveness of the first layer exploration. Before moving on to a deeper consideration of the third layer, however, it would be fruitful to spend some time on what exactly is happening with actors as they attend to the second layer, and why it might be the case that the second layer so readily and persistently inhibits the functioning of the first. Understanding this process helps build a clearer picture of what is going on with the actor and provides a fuller sense of why and how an exercise such as *The 3 Layers* might be of use to the actor-in-training.

Philosopher Brian O'Shaughnessy formulates the concept of *proprioception* as "an immediate mode of feeling one's limbs to be present and disposed in a certain way."[17] While the term generally refers to one's internally directed sense of body position, the process by which it occurs, or even how its functioning is to be understood, is far from a settled issue. According to Jonathan Cole and Jacques Paillard, neuroscientists who believe that "position and movement sense or proprioception" is "possibly the most crucial of all our senses," the concept dates back to Charles Bell's 1833 research on "the consciousness of muscular exertion as being a sixth sense."[18] In this current investigation, I am predominantly concerned not with the neurological components of proprioception but, rather, with how it participates in our ability to have and maintain a sense of our own bodies. In other words, an analysis of how proprioception functions in the experience of embodiment clarifies what is happening when actors "turn their attention inward."

In recent research on the subject in theatre studies, the position of authority has been taken up de facto by philosopher Shaun Gallagher, whose work itself has recently made forays into the arena of theatre and performance studies.[19] Gallagher's alignment with enactivism and EC makes him an attractive theorist with whom theatre scholars might be in conversation, and he is widely cited for his detailed articulation of the concepts of *body image* and *body schema*. While his formulation of these ideas is certainly not the only one there is, it has achieved a degree of centrality thanks to its clarity and its usefulness across disciplinary boundaries. Not only has Gallagher developed useful definitions of body image and body schema, but he has also provided a way of clearing up some of the conceptual confusion that has surrounded these terms since they first entered the psychological discourse in 1920 as part of the research of Henry Head and subsequently became commonplace in the philosophical literature.[20] While a consideration of the history of usage of these important terms would be illuminating, as it would shed some light on some of Gallagher's more nuanced terminological distinctions, a general summary of how Gallagher himself prefers to use the terms will be sufficient for the purposes of this chapter.

Briefly, Gallagher defines *body image* as "either a conscious representation of the body or a set of beliefs about the body," which may be unconsciously held, as well. The sense of "having a body" is a function of the body image, which belongs to the "experiencing subject," but the consciousness of this body is almost always fragmentary, as "the body image often involves an abstract, partial, or articulated representation of the body insofar as conscious awareness typically attends to only one part or area of the body at a time."[21] As I move through the world, I am aware of having a body, and I have certain ideas and feelings about my body's shape. These subjective and mutable notions about my own body are in play as I think about myself, and they are connected to various parts of my body according to my conscious awareness in certain moments. I may think I am short or skinny or ugly, or I may choose, say, one size hat over another based on my belief about how it feels and looks on my head, or I may consciously direct my nondominant hand to pick up a bowling ball, but these points of focus have no bearing on my body's overall ability to function as it interacts with and navigates through its surroundings.

The *body schema*, on the other hand, being neither consciously accessible nor comprised of beliefs, is a "subconscious system," the primary function of which is "in monitoring and governing posture and movement." Also, the body schema is not experienced as personal; rather, it "functions in a subpersonal, unowned, anonymous way." The body schema is also to be distinguished from the body image in that the former functions as an entire system, "in a holistic way," and is frequently making "global adjustment[s] across a large number of muscle systems."[22] To take the above example of picking up a bowling ball, while my conscious mind is aware of the task I have decided to undertake, it is the body schema that manages the unconscious network of actions and adjustments that makes it possible for my body (hand, arm, spine, leg placement, the other body parts that work to keep me from falling over and ensure the proper leverage to lift the heavy object, all in coordination with the micro-movements of my eyes) to perform it and to act proficiently in the world in general. Every day, all day long, I engage in an immensely complex series of bodily movements, of which I have no awareness and over which I exert no conscious control.

For the current exploration, this last point is crucial. One of the key observations made by Gallagher regarding the difference between body image and body schema is that, unlike the body image, the body schema is "prenoetic," meaning that it functions unconsciously as we navigate through space over the course of our daily activity. Gallagher provides the example of a person walking, in this case, through the woods, in conversation. "The body schema," he says,

> allows a subject who is immersed in conversation, for instance, to walk beneath the low hung tree branch without bumping her head, or enables her to maneuver around objects in her path without having to think about what she is doing. . . . If we needed to depend solely on the body image to get around . . . our movements would be inexact and awkward. Just consider, for example, the prospect of having to *think through* every step of walking across a room.[23]

Focusing conscious attention on every body part involved in the stepping, and thus relying on the body image to do the work instead of the body schema, would result in a chaotic and confusing experience, and it might even lead to injury. The prenoetic functioning of the body schema allows us to function smoothly, without the interference that would necessarily result from having to pay conscious attention to all of the countless micro-movements made in the course of even the most incidental actions.

However, paying conscious attention to those functions normally overseen by the prenoetic body schema is precisely what is asked of the actor in the second layer of *The 3 Layers* exercise.[24] Why? Gallagher observes the importance of the body schema in daily activity, which he equates with "mindless" activity, in that there is simply no reason for one to pay conscious attention to certain routine activities at the expense of actions that do require more conscious control.[25] Remember, though, as discussed in the previous chapter, that the circumstance of theatre does not function in the same way as "everyday life," and as soon as actors find themselves onstage and under the watchful gaze of the audience, a level of self-consciousness enters the scene. It is as if, on some level, actors begin to see their own bodies from a distance, through the eyes of the spectators, as it were. Every movement is under the microscope, or could be under the microscope, and suddenly the usual unconscious functioning of the body schema is shifted into consciousness, the domain of the body image. What just a moment ago was accomplished easily and without thought is now exceedingly difficult, cumbersome, and awkward. To be clear, this is not the case for every actor in every circumstance, but it is common enough that measures must be taken in the actor-training studio either to preempt this problem or to remedy it should it arise.

Among the useful functions of *The 3 Layers* is that it provides the opportunity for the actor to have extended and repeated periods of exploration, in order to figure out how to move the body in the theatrical setting. By placing an overabundance of awareness on the activity of the joints, for example, it is as if the actor is replicating the mechanism of theatrical self-consciousness just described. However, the exercise never requires the actor to focus solely on the second layer; attention to the first layer is always required at the same time (not to mention the third layer, to which I will turn shortly). Therefore, while an "abnormal" degree of self-consciousness is being demanded, so is an excess of externally directed awareness. By retraining the relationship between the body image and body schema, actors become acclimated to the extraordinary forces at play in the theatrical environment.

Additionally, beyond the necessity of managing bodily processes in a simulacrum of daily-life behavior, it is often the case that the way an actor's body moves onstage is required to be markedly different from the way it normally moves. For example, in the case that actors are playing characters whose body postures, gaits, and mannerisms are fundamentally different from their own, they must construct these new systems of behavior quite consciously, paying attention to and preventing any unwanted movements, any discrepancies between the desired outcomes and the lingering habits of the daily-life bodies, etc. This conscious attention to postural details requires the body image to be in effect; but, as I have already made clear, going about one's business with complete conscious control is not something that one normally does, and when one does try to do it, one faces tremendous obstacles, and the result is generally awkward.

The 3 Layers prepares the actor for this set of challenges in a number of ways. First, it develops the ability of the actor to mobilize the body image readily. Of course, each time actors engage with the exercise they are not creating the behavior of a new character. Rather, the exercise improves the actors' ability to direct the body image toward functions normally reserved for the body schema, allowing work with conscious control of physical behavior to operate as a rudimentary skill set. In this way, when it does come time to create a character, for example, the actor will have the necessary foundation to be able to tackle the task at hand. Also, because the second layer demands a continual scanning of the entire body, thus creating a degree of sensitivity to body awareness that far exceeds the daily-life norm, the exercise helps to ensure that no part of the character's physicalization is omitted. Finally, and crucially, as actors become more proficient with the exercise, the more readily they can shift control of the new, character-based behaviors from the domain of the body image back to that of the body schema.

Eventually, the newly constructed "fictive body" can operate with the same lack of conscious attention that the body schema does in everyday life. With the help of *The 3 Layers*, actors can prepare themselves for the important task of fabricating new prenoetic body schemas as an integral component of their craft. As Gallagher makes clear regarding this process of "rehabituation," it is common for the body image to become involved in a restructuring of the body schema, especially during processes of new skill acquisition. He explains that although "the body image does not normally interfere with the performance of the body schema. . . . This does not mean that the body image cannot affect the body schema. For example, in cases of learning dance or athletic movements, focusing attention on specific body parts can alter the established postural schema."[26]

Making good use of Gallagher's theatre-friendly findings, performance scholar Gabriele Sofia refers to this constructed fictive body as a "performative body schema." The development of this "*art*-ificial construction," as he calls it, relies on the experimentally grounded notion that "the more a pattern of actions activates, the less effort is needed to activate it again," and "the frequent activation of the same pattern allows us to activate it without a conscious effort." To illustrate the process by which this works, Sofia uses the example of learning to drive a car. He begins by drawing our attention to the initial phase of body image engagement: "During the first attempts, the pattern of simultaneous activation of our limbs is activated by an explicit effort and through a quite complicated execution." As the process continues, he goes on to say,

> experience allows these patterns to activate with progressively less effort, until the actions are embodied as pre-reflexive mechanisms. At that point our conscious control is no longer engaged in "how to drive," but focused on "where to drive" or on the several other thoughts that constantly pass through our mind. Repeated experience adapts our body schema to the interaction with the car and the road.

Referring back to the work of the actor, Sofia asserts that "it is through rehearsals and his repeated and constant training, that—despite of [*sic*] the absence of any conscious access—the actor becomes able to *embody* a different body schema, that we can call a *performative body schema*."[27]

Sofia is speaking about the actual process of developing the performative body schema through rehearsal and repetition, whereas *The 3 Layers* is designed to ensure that the actor is ready to encounter this difficult task. He does not offer an example of the process by which an actor accomplishes this, nor does he specify what sort of training might be helpful toward the effort. As a matter of fact, the central focus of Sofia's observations is mainly limited to the actors' ability not to give away the surprise of what is to come—"to avoid the spectator's anticipation"—by giving the impression that, as in everyday life, each unfolding moment in the theatre is unexpected and happening for the first time.[28] However, regardless of the different object of study, the underlying principle of how actors function with regard to body image and schema is the same.

It would be a mistake to think that I am suggesting that, in the previous description of how actors go about creating a performative body schema, the process is in any way mechanical. The point of activating consciously the physical control of the body image is precisely to allow the control eventually to disappear, for the behavior to get reabsorbed back into the unconscious and generally automatic functioning of the body schema. This is how theatrical forms and stylized performance behavior are actually able to appear "life-like." As Gallagher says, "in all cases, prenoetic performances of the body schema influence intentionality."[29] This means that all the minute particulars of behavior and action, such as "automatic postural and motor adjustments," that spring from the performed intentions of the actor occur under the auspices of the body schema.[30]

The body schema is capable of being altered by conscious attention via the body image, but it remains active in the space between pure biology and sociality. It exists in (or as) the relationship between the complex and evolved human organism and the rules and conventions that accompany social existence. "The body schema reflects a practical attunement of the body to its environment," explains Gallagher. "Its development in the various social practices that lead to habitual dispositions—think here of jumping to catch [a] ball within the context of a game—involves it in relations to physical and social environments that, on the one hand, fall short of intentionality, that is, remain prenoetic, and, on the other, transcend neurophysiology."[31] This same relationship—between the biological capacity of the human body and its interactive relationship with the environment—is at the root of Mark Johnson's notion of the image schema, discussed at length in the previous chapter. In fact, one could assert that the project of establishing EC as a field is ideologically grounded in a view that conscientiously objects to biological essentialism in both the hard and social sciences.

The fact that body schemas are, in fact, living systems, that they are "not fixed photographs of bodily structure but are active, changing processes," has led Maxine Sheets-Johnstone to dispute Gallagher's own use of terminology.[32] She takes issue with the terms "body image" and "body schema," because they do not effectively communicate the dynamism of what they are intended to describe. "Reification," she points out, "concretizes the concepts 'body image' and 'body schema,' making each not just a spatial entity, but a spatial entity with no inherent temporal dimensions." For her, this is not just a matter of terminology; or rather, she maintains that the language we use to describe these processes needs to do what it can to work against a whole history of misguided thinking on the subject of embodiment. "Spatialization through reification," she continues,

> indeed conveniently evades the temporal, and happily so for reductionists, because the temporal destroys their cultivated ontology of perdurable objects or structures. Temporal dimensions would "kineticize" body image and body schema, forcing recognition of their foundational *impermanence*, and eliminate the possibility of conceiving them as fixed and durable material entities in the brain.[33]

In order to combat this dangerous reification and bring a crucial sense of animation and temporality to the concepts "body image" and "body schema," she recommends that they be replaced by "corporeal-kinetic intentionality" and "corporeal-kinetic patterning," respectively.[34]

In response to Sheets-Johnstone's critique, Gallagher simply maintains that there is no reason to assume that his terms necessarily exclude temporality, especially since his writings on the subject always make plain that both *body image* and *body schema* are active and ever-changing systems, rather than fixed entities. He is, however, willing "to embrace the general tenor that motivates her critique" and even concedes that perhaps the term "body schematic processes" might be useful.[35] Regardless of which terms we use and on which side of the dispute we land, the fact remains that it is of vital importance as we conceive of these processes that we do not fall into the trap of seeing them as merely spatial, atemporal structures. While working on *The 3 Layers*, it becomes quite clear that the actor's ability to perform effectively requires a readiness to mobilize animate networks of embodied experience—not reified and static structures—toward the creation of constructed systems of unconsciously activated, but consciously guided, behavior in the context of the theatrical environment.

Dynamic Space

Now that I have gone some distance in exploring the components of the first two layers, I can shift to a consideration of the third. To do so I return as always to the central question of this book: Why might proficiency in this exercise be useful to the actor-in-training? To begin with, perhaps the most important purpose of the addition of this layer concerns its relationship with the first two.

The third layer, of course, is to be enacted simultaneously with the other two layers. The actors must ensure that all perceptual faculties are open to as many details as possible in the quickly changing and active space, and they must also maintain a proprioceptive awareness of the functioning of the various moving parts of the body, with particular attention to disallowing any extra tension from entering the muscles surrounding the joints, from the toes to the head and the arms. As one might guess, adding this new complication to the overall exercise is exceedingly difficult; however, as with the other layers, the more one does it, the better one gets.

Prior to the addition of the third layer, the actors are required to see the other bodies in the space as they move around, but the focus remains intentionally disconnected from the various changes in posture, location, and direction made by the others. With the exception of the fact that alterations in course are made in order to avoid collisions, the attention is on perceiving the material environment and releasing the tension surrounding the joints of the body. Now, however, the actors must respond actively to each new changing element of the physical space as it happens. As I showed with the hand-clapping sound element described earlier, each alteration of the perceiving apparatus is immediately linked to a series of adjustments to the network of joints as the body moves through space. This occurs here in a way that is simultaneously active and reactive: it is active because the actors are moving according to their own volition; it is reactive because it is as if the choice about which direction to move at every moment does not originate from the will of the actors, but from outside, from the other bodies and the space itself.

To employ Sofia's example of driving a car, the actor is in the driver's seat and has decided upon the destination, but all of the various small reactions—moving around potholes, reacting to the unexpected swerving of a nearby car, avoiding collisions in general, following detours, etc.—occur spontaneously and, for the most part, unconsciously. (Certainly, the driver is aware of these occurrences writ large, but the network of subtle bodily actions remains unobserved and unguided.) Learning to drive is similar to learning to walk, in this regard. We master the act of walking at an early age, and from then on, we do not think about how we are doing it; it becomes "second nature." However, as I have already pointed out, walking "naturally" onstage is not so simple. It is as if actors must relearn the skill of walking all over again for use in the theatrical environment. The addition of the third layer creates the conditions for this "rehabituation" to occur by providing a simulacrum of the ever-changing "real world" for the actor to navigate, thus shifting the mental focus from the act of walking itself to an interaction with the environment.³⁶ Obviously, walking is not the only thing actors do onstage. However, the full-body awareness and activity practiced by *The 3 Layers* develops in the actor a substantial foundation of expertise upon which other, more specific, character-related behaviors may be built.

Competency and Presence

It is commonly understood that a crucial part of becoming an expert in a skill or craft is the doer's ability to perform the task at hand at a high level of proficiency without needing to pay conscious attention to the task itself. Rick Kemp refers to the "'conscious competency' model of assimilation," which originated in the business world in the 1970s.³⁷ According to this model, there are four stages of gaining competence in a particular skill, and each stage is designated by a shift in the subject's relationship to conscious awareness. As Kemp explains,

> In Stage 1, the student has no awareness of, or ability in the skill being taught. In Stage 2, the student is aware of the skill, but has not yet developed any ability. In Stage 3, the student is able to perform the skill, but needs to consciously think about it to execute it, while in Stage 4, the skill has become integrated to the point where it can be performed without conscious thought.³⁸

Shaun Gallagher presents a similar model, using five stages instead of four, developed by philosophers Dreyfus and Dreyfus in 1980 and grounded in the thinking of Merleau-Ponty. This model, based on notions of how bodies interact effectively with environment, starts with "Novice practitioner" and ends with "Expert practitioner." The former, according to Gallagher, is "characterised by 'rigid adherence to taught rules or plans,'" and the latter "transcends the rules and has an 'intuitive grasp of situations based on deep, tacit understanding.'"³⁹

While this model is frequently cited in the field of EC, not all theorists are entirely in agreement about its accuracy, especially regarding the ultimate absence of conscious thought in expert performance. For example, sports performance theorist John Sutton believes that "expert performance is not without some sort of reflection," and dance performance theorist Barbara Gail Montero asserts not only that conscious thought is often present in expert performance but also that some degree of "conscious monitoring" is essential to high-level performance ability.⁴⁰ Even if Sutton and Montero are correct, however, their positions should not be taken to endorse a view according to which conscious thought is applied to the minutia of the skillful activity; rather, the type of conscious thought discussed by these theorists has more to do with thoughtful contextual guidance, by which the performance can be focused and allow for the intelligence of the doer to engage with the task's overall accomplishment and quality. For Gallagher, in order for this to be possible, a substantial amount of control needs to be taken up unconsciously by the body schema. On his view, "the body schema is attuned by practice so that one can simply play 'from the body schema' in a way that allows one to forget about many details of the performance, thereby giving one freedom to focus on selective target control."[41]

While it is certainly the case that actors engaging with *The 3 Layers* are able to reach high levels of proficiency through extensive practice over time, it would be a mistake to equate an ability to perform this exercise well with having achieved expertise in the art of acting. However, if we accept the notion that expertise in acting, like expertise in other skill-based activities, involves the ability to do something well without the interference of conscious reflection (to the degree and with the caveats just mentioned), the question again arises: What is it, precisely, that the actor needs to learn to do well? Put another way, what mechanisms are being trained to be taken care of on an unconscious level by the body schema? Surely, the answer cannot be "the performance score of a particular role," since by that reasoning, an expert pianist would be considered an expert only in relation to particular pieces, rather than by being in possession of the ability to play more or less anything at a very high level of accomplishment. No, the actor no more becomes an expert by rehearsing a single role than a pianist does by practicing only a particular sonata. To continue along the lines of this analogy, we can say that pianists are considered to be experts when they are able to activate their bodily ability in the encounter with and performance of any particular piece (within a given style). The perceptual organs work in tandem with the motor coordination of the fingers (and the rest of the body, which is by no means passive in the playing); the body schema takes care of all that, and the pianist is able to "focus on selective target control," as Gallagher puts it, making subtle adjustments in dynamic, tempo, timbre, etc. Accordingly, actors perform expertly in their bodily encounters with the material, which means that their body schemas must somehow have learned to navigate the basics of the doing, thus allowing the conscious reflection to happen as necessary in relation to contextual guidance.

This is where *The 3 Layers* comes into play. I have already shown how the exercise opens the actor to a full-body receptivity to active encounters with environment. This occurs, though, not simply via the avenues already discussed. There is also an important aspect of the exercise that relates directly to the absence of conscious reflection I have been discussing. In order for actors to be ready for an encounter with the material, they must have the ability to be somewhat thoughtless (in the sense of body-schematic control I have been discussing). The thoughtlessness of the pianist lies in the bodily doing in relation to the tool of the trade: the object of the piano itself. In theatre, as I have touched on before, the object upon which actors act is their own body.[42] Therefore, if the doings, which taken together form a role, say, are to be successfully enacted (and received), they must contain within themselves the characteristic of what is sometimes referred to in the studio as "presence." While this term itself has undergone copious amounts of theoretical scrutiny in general—especially under the critical projects of Deconstruction and Postmodernism—and although it is often spoken of in theatre as a quasi-magical quality that appears in certain special performers, I would like to use it here in, as much as possible, its purely temporo-spatial sense, as in the "present" moment, or to be "present" in a particular place.[43] Especially when observing the encounter of inexperienced actors with the exercise, it is easy to see how frequently "the mind wanders." Especially in the early moments of the day's work, and especially after the novelty of the exercise has worn off (say after having done it for a few sessions already), an onlooker can easily see (and it is generally confirmed by the participants later on, in conversation) the difference between moments of "full engagement" with the tasks at hand and moments in which, like the moments of "turning inward" discussed earlier, it is as if the actor is no longer fully "present" inside of the action. As the exercise continues, however, this problem begins to subside.

By requiring the actors to engage with multiple difficult tasks simultaneously, the degree to which it is possible for the attention to wander is diminished. This is the direct result of what I call the *overload* factor of the exercise. In many popular training exercises, at the point at which a skill becomes too mastered or habitual, it is either removed from the training regimen or made more complicated. In this way, the learning of skills serves not as a final goal but as a pretext for placing the actor in a perpetual state of encountering things "as if for the first time." It is essential for actors to cultivate this orientation toward action, since their art requires exactly that at every moment—the ability to repeat an action over and over again without appearing to have ever done it before is central to the actor's work.

In this exercise, for instance, a frequent component of the third layer exploration of balancing the space is acceleration. The actors are instructed to increase their speed moving through the space gradually (i.e., over a period of anywhere from ten to thirty minutes or more, depending on the focus and span of the day's work), eventually culminating in an extended high-speed sprint through the space. There are to be no sharp or sudden changes of direction; rather, in order to maintain the speed and acceleration without stopping, while also attempting to balance the space, the actors must curve their paths gently as they run, negotiating other bodies, walls, and corners as they "flow" through the room. It is also against the rules to "get stuck" in repetitive patterns, in relation to both the path being cut through the space and the activation of the various body parts engaged by the act of running; one must be finding one's way spontaneously at every moment, in a series of complex, full-body reactions to the ever-changing configuration of moving object-bodies. During all of this it becomes increasingly difficult to avoid collisions. However, over time actors can become quite proficient at this part of the exercise. It is plain to see: experienced and proficient actors rarely, if ever, collide, even with novices; novices frequently collide with other novices.

The exercise, with its three simultaneously functioning layers of attention, in combination with a host of complicating elements such as acceleration, is training the actor to be temporally present, to "be in the here and now," as the cliché goes. This is useful not only because of the aforementioned necessity for the action to appear as if it is being performed "for the first time" each time but also because the actor's attention is actually one of the components of craft being observed (and evaluated) by the audience. The actor's attention is a core component of the artistic medium, and if it is true that expert performers must achieve a level of unconscious control over their work, then it follows that part of what actors must learn to control via the performative body schema is attention itself.

Ways of Seeing

Another important aspect of this training of attention in *The 3 Layers* concerns the discrepancy between the simultaneous functioning of central and peripheral perceptual focus. Sometimes, to provide one example, we incorporate a little game of "freeze" into the third layer, before the speed picks up too much. At a certain moment, one actor can make the choice to stop moving and freeze the body completely. The goal of the game is for the other actors to freeze, too. The last one to freeze is the "loser" (although the only thing that is lost is perhaps a little pride). The key to gaining proficiency at this game is to find the way to be sensitive and reactive to peripheral vision. One way to accomplish this is to practice (not necessarily during this game, but perhaps earlier in the exercise structure) switching back and forth between what we call in the studio "hard" focus and "soft" focus.[44] Hard focus more or less corresponds to the process by which the visual signal lands on the fovea, the central portion of the retina. Through conscious adjustment of the seeing apparatus, actors can learn to "soften" the visual focus, causing the center of the visual field to lose its definition, so that they are better able to attend to signals on the periphery.

Experimental evidence suggests that the role of central visual focus is operated by a different neural system from that of peripheral vision. The ventral stream, as it is called, takes care of identification of objects in the central field of visual focus and is quite receptive to conscious control. Referred to by Noë as the "'what' stream," it is "dedicated to perceptual representation, experience, and identification." The dorsal (or "'how'") stream, on the other hand, which handles visual signals on the outskirts of the visual field, is "dedicated to the visual guidance of action" and is connected to the normally unconscious operations of reflexes and navigation through the environment.[45] If the body is in a state of active readiness, spreading out the attention to span the entirety of the visual field allows the actors to be able to influence the functions controlled by the dorsal stream, which is not normally available to conscious control. To be clear, I am not claiming that the dorsal stream is being consciously controlled; rather, it is being given permission, as it were, to do what it normally does, except that the added attention allows it to function at a higher level of receptivity and acuity. When observing a group of experienced practitioners playing this game of freeze, even if there are some actors directly behind others (and thus technically "invisible" to them), it is often next to impossible to determine who was the first to freeze.

The importance of the actor's visual processes is elaborated by Kemp in his discussion of the function of the eyes in nonverbal communication. Referring to a series of experiments cited by psychologists Daniel Richardson, Rick Dale, and Michael Spivey who demonstrate the ways in which the eyes are involved in both cognitive and perceptual processes, Kemp proposes an exercise designed to maximize the potential of the eyes both to stimulate the imagination of the actor and to communicate to an audience.[46] Utilizing a process called "spatial indexing," Kemp's exercise asks the actors to activate intentionally and consciously the normally unintentional and unconscious functioning of the eyes. According to Kemp, controlling the movement of the eyes in this way provides actors with a double benefit: first, the focusing and refocusing of optical attention on the part of the actor is crucial to communicating subtle but important nonverbal information to the audience; second, the various shifts in visual focus stimulate "internal processes" of imagination and memory on the part of the actor, thus filling out the performance affectively in important ways.

Seen in the light of the discussion so far about the relationship between visual, spatial, and proprioceptive systems and how they are potentially mobilized by the actor, Kemp's view makes good sense. I would add, however, that Kemp's insistence on the actor's conscious control is overly limiting. "Given that eye movements are linked to so many mental processes, including memories, expectations, and goals," he says, "the ability to make voluntary choices about them gives the actor an invaluable tool, both in defining expression and in proprioceptively generating thoughts and emotions." He refers to a number of studies that indicate that the same neural pathways are activated in the brain whether objects are visually present to the perceiver or merely imagined, but while this particular point is supported by the research, I stop short at Kemp's connection of this research with his conclusion that *"voluntary control of eye movements can affect thought."*[47] While it is true that "voluntary choices" must always be made by the actor, an effective training regimen would make it possible for those choices to set in motion a network of nonvoluntary reactions and adjustments, throughout the entire body of the actor. Still, Kemp's exercise, as well as *The 3 Layers*, as we have seen, makes it possible for the actor to summon consciously those faculties normally under unconscious bodily control, in order to allow them to continue to act unconsciously, but in a way that suits the theatrical exigencies of the moment.

Bodies Working Together

Unlike the first and second layers, the third layer incorporates intersubjective relationships and reactivity. More often than not, actors are not alone onstage but occupy the space with other bodies, each of which is engaged in its own "score" of actions, intentions, behaviors, etc. Simply "acting alone" or "on your own track" is not an option; such a disconnection between actors will normally be noticed by the audience (and frowned upon by audience and scene partners alike). Therefore, it is essential that actors develop the ability "to listen with their whole bodies" to the other actors onstage, as is frequently said in the studio. Crucial to the actor's craft is the ability to be receptive to the nonverbal communication of the other actors and to respond to them in such a way that it appears to be just as unprepared and spontaneous as everyday life behavior does. Preparing this element of craft is an important part of the actor's work in the third layer.

In an article with far-reaching implications regarding the relationship between embodiment and culture, Tamer Soliman and Arthur M. Glenberg propose that close physical interactions between subjects involved in similar connected activities create what they call an "in group." The members of this "in group," or at least the dyads studied in their experiment, by engaging in a process of "sensorimotor tuning," form what the authors call a "joint body schema (JBS)," whereby "participants adapt their own body schemas to incorporate aspects of the partner in the service of effective coordination." The creation of a JBS inclines the members of the "in group" toward "strong empathic response" with each other and forms a foundation for the creation of culture, which the authors define as "a repertoire of bodily modes of interaction . . . in socio-physical ecologies."

It is easy to see how a group of actors, training together in the ways I have been discussing, are quite intentionally creating, in the "socio-physical ecology" of the theatre, just such a "repertoire of bodily modes of interaction." Not only are the actors working to become expert in the act of generating performative body schemas of their own, but they are also, according to Soliman and Glenberg's study, participating in a process of Joint Body Schema formation with their cohort. The third layer, with its focus on the interrelationship of bodies moving in space, and in conjunction with the perceptual component of the first layer and the proprioceptive element of the second, assures that the bodies-in-training are actually working together, not just arbitrarily co-occupying the space.[48]

Keep in mind that the actor is engaged in this process in order for the work to live and be legible onstage, not in the world of everyday life. Relationships between bodies (and between bodies and space) onstage are primary means of communicating meaning in the theatre. Drawing from psychologist Dale Leathers, Kemp divides the visually based system of nonverbal communication (nvc) into two subsystems: Kinesic communication and Proxemics. "Kinesic communication," he explains, "is made up of facial expression, eye behavior, gesture, and posture. Proxemics consists of the use of space, distance between individuals, and the idea of territory (the 'ownership' of spatial areas)."[49] We can observe the importance of Proxemics quite plainly, for example, in the proliferation of the use of end-of-scene *tableaux* in nineteenth-century melodrama, by means of which the audience could understand at a single glance the dynamics of the operative power struggles in the unfolding drama. While this technique is rarely in use today, one can still see without too much trouble how the use of "stage pictures" and blocking choices can communicate volumes to the audience by means of Proxemics. While many of these relational decisions are made by the director in today's theatre, it is also true that actors, too, have a substantial role to play in their development, implementation, and effectiveness. Of course, the particular meaning expressed by variations in spatial relationships between bodies onstage depends on the style of theatre and the various conventions inherent to it. However, the fact remains that Proxemics communicate meaning, and if actors are to exist onstage with skill and nuance in relation to that meaning, they will need to modulate not only their own bodily nonverbal communication but also that which results from their relationship to the other bodies onstage with them. The third layer allows for the development of precisely this aspect of theatrical meaning-making.

I have mentioned that there are many possible tasks that can be the focus of a given day's work on the third layer. Often, the focus is on balancing the space, in the way that I have described. Another possible configuration of the third layer, which can shed some light on Proxemics and the intersubjective relationship of bodies in space, is sometimes referred to as *schooling*. Drawing from the behavioral phenomenon of *emergence*, which allows large groups of fish (or flocks of birds or herds of buffalo, etc.) to move as if they were one single entity, this exercise element permits each individual actor to be both fully independent of and fully reactive to the movements of the other actors' bodies in and through space. Rather than following the directive of *balancing the space*, in which each actor is responsible for maintaining the even distribution of bodies throughout the entirety of the room, actors engaged in *schooling* are expected to move alongside each other as a group through the space. In order to keep track of this process, the actors must be able to see the shape of the entirety of the group as it moves and shifts as a unit.

To accomplish this, they must rely to a significant extent on their ability to maintain the wide visual focus mentioned just now in my discussion of the freeze game. As the group moves this way and that, each actor must follow either behind or alongside the others, taking care not to "go against the flow" of the whole. At the same time, however, it is the responsibility of the actors to maintain their impulses toward their own individual senses of flow. For example, if I am on the left side of the group toward the rear, to my right I can see the mass of bodies moving together, say, curving to the right. I must not destroy the sense of togetherness, but if I choose to, I may, instead of staying on the outside left, turn to the right with a somewhat more narrowly arced path than the others, thus moving through the other bodies and eventually ending up on the inside right of the curving group, I am still "in the flow," but I have shifted my location within the whole by following my own impulses. In this way each actor is simultaneously following and leading the group, very much like the fish in an actual school.

As actors work the third layer in this way, in continuing simultaneity with the first and second layers, their perception and proprioception become the faculties by which they enter into meaningful relationship with their fellow actors. Once again, if we look at Kemp's notion of Proxemics as a significant component of nvc, we can see how this exercise helps actors to develop full-body awareness and receptivity toward action, incorporated into the developing performative body schema through repeated training encounters, in such a way that takes into account the presence of stage partners. Again, this procedure is not a matter of moving bodies around like chess pieces, with each resulting position achieving some particular, bounded significance. Rather, the exercise serves as an opening to develop the kind of sensorimotor know-how described by Noë in his discussion of how subjects interact meaningfully with their surroundings in "everyday life." When acting onstage, or even while developing material for a scene, actors must be able to react to each other and their surroundings as readily as they would in everyday life, but they must simultaneously be able to mobilize a broad spectrum of meanings for a particular scenic space, the appropriate theatrical style, and the active set of conventions, including but not limited to those inherent in proxemic relationships.

In her discussion of *animation,* Maxine Sheets-Johnstone asserts that we come to understand the world through movement.[50] Our ability to act meaningfully and relationally with and among others is learned experientially from our earliest days, and it is the bodily exploration of our environment that serves as a foundation for all knowledge and understanding. "Consider, for example," she suggests,

> how keenly attuned we are to the slightest movements of others—a flickering of the eyes, a pulling in of lips, a waywardness of gaze, a tremoring of hands, a fleeting contraction in the torso, a sudden intake of breath, a softly beating foot. We are kinetically attuned to each other. . . . We are kinetically attuned to the world. No one teaches us how to be attuned. We teach ourselves—nonverbally. In a word, movement is our mother tongue.[51]

She then goes on to draw a connection between this everyday life kinetic attunement and how we extend it into the realm of performance, particularly dance. "What allows us to dance in the first place," she claims, "and in turn, to appreciate, analyze, and understand dance . . . is our common apprenticeship in learning our bodies and learning to move ourselves, and our common capacity to think in movement."[52] This "apprenticeship" is conducted through the building up of habits. In everyday life these habits are developed through trial and error in the context of our culturally specific surroundings. In the fictive realm of dance or theatre, specialized training is required to acquire the appropriate and necessary body of habits, which enables us to become fluent in the context of a particular form or style.

Achieving Fluency

Forming habits takes time and work, in the realm of both everyday life and artistic practice. In the theatre training studio actors encounter their own habits, allow for new ones to be ushered in, and open their awareness to the subtle habits and movements of others. Therefore, *The 3 Layers* and other training exercises need to be practiced frequently and consistently, rather than only occasionally. In order to be effective, or put another way, in order for them to lead to fluency on the part of the actor, they need to contribute to the development of a performative body schema, as I have already discussed. Considered in this light, we must conceive of training exercises as a way for actors to develop not a set of discrete skills, per se, but a fluency of sensorimotor know-how that, having become "second nature," spills over into phenomenal excess.

This is partially why it is also important not to see these exercises as completely separate from each other. (It also provides a glimpse into why it is so essential to integrate so-called movement classes into the core curriculum of any well-constructed actor-training program and not merely as supplementary "electives.") The fluency developed by *The 3 Layers* is not limited to the topics isolated and discussed here, just as the effectiveness of the *plastiques* is not limited simply to what was theorized in the previous chapter. The world of experience opened up by entering into long-term relationships with actor-training exercises is vast, and each exercise is like a doorway that leads to a network of experiential connections that forms a greater whole. As in everyday life, living through moments carries with it a great assortment of "unrelated" goings-on. The mind "wanders," and images, thoughts, and feelings seem to arise and appear from nowhere. One might even say that, according to the stages of expert learning outlined earlier, a clear sign of having attained a high degree of mastery in a field would be the (re)appearance of these "automatic" processes.

Important director-theorists have long acknowledged that the development of a fully functioning performative body schema is central to the actor's craft, even if the terms they use have varied. Sharon Carnicke, in her indispensable analysis of Stanislavsky's work, takes great pains to explain just how essential—and essentially misunderstood—is the concept of *perezhivanie* to the System. Translated as "experiencing" by Carnicke, *perezhivanie* is a complex term, as it contains the possibility of various interpretations, depending on context. On the whole, though, the term points to the moments onstage in which actors are both fully consumed by their roles and simultaneously in complete control of their performance. According to Carnicke, Stanislavsky's ideal actor had the ability "to improvise continually without changing a moment of blocking or a word of text"; or, in Stanislavsky's own words, *perezhivanie* could be described in a masterful performance (in this case by Michael Chekhov) as "'the improvisatory state of mind and body within the rigid framework of first-class dramatic material.'"[53] The work of the actor reaches its apogee in those moments when the whole of the various component parts of the role—the complex score of actions, including text and voice—becomes somehow greater than the sum of its parts, and the flow of conscious and unconscious processes becomes reactivated in the theatrical setting.

Carnicke is careful to remind us that the work of the actor developed by Stanislavsky must not be equated with any one particular style. "Recovering Stanislavsky's lost term, *perezhivanie*, unequivocally breaks the assumed but inaccurate link between the multivalent training System and the aesthetic style of Psychological Realism," she writes. "Stanislavsky's redefinition of truth as whatever happens during performance can take the contemporary actor into any dramatic style, including those yet to be invented."[54] A wide variety of training programs geared to a multiplicity of performance styles aims to achieve this very quality of mastery. In fact, a similar conceptual formulation can be found in the writings of the decidedly non-realist director, Eugenio Barba, who refers to the fully functioning life of the performer-in-action as "scenic *bios*." Through the rigorous training of performance behavior, Barba says, actors may undergo a process by which daily habitual behavior patterns make way for new, "extra-daily" scenic behaviors onstage:

> The more daily techniques are unconscious, the more functional they are. For this reason, we move, we sit, we carry things, we kiss, we agree and disagree with gestures which we believe to be natural but which are in fact culturally determined. Different cultures determine different body techniques according to whether people walk with or without shoes, whether they carry things on their heads or with their hands, whether they kiss with the lips or with the nose. The first step in discovering what the principles governing a performer's scenic

bios, or life, might be, lies in understanding that the body's daily techniques can be replaced by extra-daily techniques which do not respect the habitual conditionings of the use of the body.[55]

The concepts of experiencing, or *perezhivanie*, and scenic *bios* draw a similar trajectory for the actor-in-training, from the initial confrontation between old and new habits to the eventual embodiment of a seamless living role.

Concluding Thoughts and the Fourth Layer

In *The 3 Layers* it often happens (and even more frequently in the *plastiques*) that the actor begins to experience spontaneous feelings, images, and associations while engaged in the doing of the exercise. Interestingly, when I began to develop the exercise in the late 1990s, I initially called it *The 4 Layers*. This fourth layer, which I referred to as "the layer of the imagination," was initiated by the prompt that the actors should actively imagine that they were moving around a space other than the studio in which they were actually working—for example, a forest, or a beach, or a city street. The idea was to provide a way for actors to practice playing with the associative component of their craft in a fairly controlled setting. It ultimately became clear, however, that asking actors to turn their attention consciously to active imagination in the context of the exercise was ineffective, as the resulting behavior generally felt forced and stilted. While, as I said, associative elements do frequently appear in the course of working the first three layers, over time I came to understand that elements such as feelings and associations are best arrived at as the result—rather than as the cause or prompt—of effective intention-filled action. Setting up the circumstances that allow actors to live imaginatively and affectively inside the exercise (or role) turns out to be much more effective than forcing the actor to feel or to activate associations.

In the next chapter, as part of an investigation into the relationship between voice, gesture, and imagination, I look more deeply into why this might be the case, and why actors frequently find that "playing emotions" is a less effective approach to the craft of acting than "playing action." For the moment, we can simply acknowledge the fact that, in everyday life at least, associations come while we are in the midst of going about our business, and not because we seek them out directly. *The 3 Layers* creates a simulacrum realm in which the body learns how to allow those unconscious processes that function in daily life to be rediscovered or reactivated in the artificially constructed space of the theatre.

In the preceding pages, I have examined *The 3 Layers* exercise step by step. The first layer—the layer of perception—works both in tandem with and in opposition to the second layer—the layer of proprioception. In combination, they provide a foundation upon which the third layer—the layer of the space—is able to operate at maximum pedagogical potential. It bears repeating that, while my discussion of the exercises in this chapter is quite analytical, it should never be assumed that the doing of them is in any way sterile or "cold." The spontaneous appearance of the "fourth layer" of association is, as I have suggested, quite commonplace in the course of engaging with these exercises, and any attempt to keep it at bay would be a great disservice to the work of the actor-in-training. It shows up in *The 3 Layers*, and it appears perhaps even more frequently and profoundly in the *plastiques*. Even more than that, when working with the voice, the flow of associations activates so abundantly that it can almost be said to be a core component of vocal training exercises.

In the next chapter, as I examine the inner workings of an exercise called *Vocal Action*, I look more closely at the complex and often elusive relationship between physical action, voice, imagination, and emotion. It is worth restating that the effects of any one training exercise almost always overlap with the effects of others; they are all part of the holistic training of the unified actor. No single aspect or faculty can be truly isolated in practice; it is only possible to disassemble the process and treat its elements as singular in theory. That being said, there is still much to be gained by continued and meticulous analysis of the various components of the actor's work, and looking at it through the lens of contemporary philosophical approaches to embodiment proves particularly fruitful.

3

Approaching the Voice beyond the Word

Introduction: *Vocal Action*

This chapter is grounded in an analysis of an exercise called *Vocal Action*. In the previous chapters I investigated how actors function in praxis connected with the conceptual spaces of embodied action, perception, and proprioception. Now, by looking carefully at the *Vocal Action* exercise, I show how actors communicate emotion, intention, character, and meaning through another fully embodied process—speech production. I begin by providing a fairly complete overview of the exercise as it is encountered by actors at the entry level. Having done that, I turn my attention to an analysis of its inner workings, and after that, I move on to more advanced elements of the work and analyses of the processes involved in those, as well. Throughout the chapter, which always comes back to the notion of voice as essentially interactive, I place my thinking in direct and persistent conversation with what can sometimes seem like a cacophonous chorus of thinkers and researchers. I invite the reader to imagine, as much as possible, these participants to be present and engaged in active dialogue, as if seated together around a dinner table, for instance, rather than simply as a list of quotations assembled solely to prove a point or two. What they have to say is, in my view, at least as important as what I have to say, and it is my hope that their insights will inspire lines of thought in the reader leading beyond the bounds of this book.

Since a significant portion of contemporary scholarship theorizing the voice as an embodied process is in the fields of psychology and linguistics, I focus quite a bit on them in this chapter. As time moves on, each of these fields engages more and more with EC, so I, too, refer frequently to those contemporary philosophers writing on the subject, incorporating their observations systematically into each step of my analysis. For the most part, my inquiry focuses on the material processes involved in voice production. This necessitates covering research being undertaken in prosody and gesture studies, in addition to offering some thoughts on the process of listening and its relationship to voice, especially in the context of this particular training exercise. I finish the chapter with a few words regarding some largely theoretical considerations that place my materialist theory of voice in conversation with theories of sociality and ecology, which are a bit broader in scope, but without which an analysis of the actor's work with voice would not be complete. As I discuss throughout this book, it is my assertion that the insights provided by examining this particular exercise could be arrived at through a rigorous investigation into any of a number of time-tested vocal training exercises. I choose this one partly because I know it so well, and partly because it lends itself readily to an analysis of the connection of voice to embodiment. As I hope to have demonstrated by the end of the chapter, the voice needs to be reconceived as an embodied process embedded in the same conceptual framework and interactionist ecology as the exercises presented in the earlier chapters.

Theorizing Sound and Voice

A number of philosophers and sound theorists have recently addressed the dearth of scholarship on voice, especially in comparison to the extensive literature on vision. Adriana Cavarero is perhaps the most influential critic of this tendency. She interprets the theoretical preference for vision over voice as a "symptom of a problem that has to do with the philosophical affinity for an abstract and bodiless universality, and for the domain of a word that does not come out of any throat of flesh."[1] Likewise, Don Ihde understands the lack of attention to the sonic in general to be symptomatic of a greater problem of "reductionism in philosophy," noting that "not only are sounds, in the metaphysical tradition, secondary, but the inattention to the sounding of things has led to the gradual loss of understanding of whole ranges of phenomena that are there to be noted." He calls for a "turn to the *auditory dimension*" as a way to resuscitate philosophical inquiry into everyday phenomenology, which has illogically posited vision as somehow more precise and immediate than sound.[2] Taking this shift toward the auditory even further, musicologist Nina Sun Eidsheim calls for a mode of engaging with sound not as an ossified, independent, and static object—what she refers to as a "figure of sound"—but rather as a "practice of vibration," that is always relational, dynamic, and tactile.[3]

These thinkers outline the philosophical context within which the voice has been problematically theorized, when it has been approached at all. Not only is the lack of attention to voice symptomatic of a philosophical shortcoming, but it also results in a paucity of scholarship upon which disciplines such as theatre studies might draw in any concerted effort toward rigorous analysis. As Andrew M. Kimbrough notes,

> Until recently, theatre scholarship focused almost exclusively on the visual artifact: the body, the mise-en-scène, and the dramatic text. A handful of articles on the voice serve as exceptions, but the exceptions tend to suffer because, as a discipline, we have yet to create a critical language adequate to address the voice. Also, prior to this work we have not had a book-length study that has attempted to supply an overview of the issues, historical context, or theoretical parameters.[4]

Konstantinos Thomaidis and Ben Macpherson, in their edited volume devoted to voice studies, similarly note the relative absence of scholarship on voice. "Until now," they write, "there has been little concerted attempt to bring together the disparate disciplinary scholarship that effectively addresses voice, not merely as a theme, but as a discrete area or critical methodology."[5] The two works to which I have just referred are evidence of efforts of late that work toward a potential remediation of this problem.

Flloyd Kennedy, in her article entitled, "The Challenge of Theorizing the Voice in Performance," points to a further difficulty with regard to voice studies, discussing the conflict between practical application and transmission of vocal technique in the studio and theoretical analysis of voice. "The published, practical methodologies of voice trainers such as Patsy Rodenburg, Kristin Linklater, and Cicely Berry," she writes, referring to three of the most influential voice teachers in the field of the past generation, "offer imaginative processes for developing the physical power and flexibility of the voice but generally fall short of articulating the philosophical underpinnings of their theories in ways that can be challenged."[6] Linklater was, before her death in 2020, becoming more engaged with the literature in philosophy and neuroscience, making frequent reference to the work of Antonio Damasio, for example; that being said, it is still the case that, as Kennedy puts it, "recent developments in voice science support the notion that, while imagery is neither 'factually accurate' nor 'precise,' it is one of the most demonstrably useful tools in the process of facilitating healthy, dynamic, and effective choices."[7] Linklater herself acknowledges this split between the need for scientific accuracy and pedagogical effectiveness, admitting at one point in her text, "I have outlined the physical anatomy faithfully, but I have chosen to describe the voice by its perceivable features in metaphor and in analogy. This simplification may make the voice scientist quail, but it has proven to be the best approach for the voice user."[8]

Another important figure in contemporary voice training for actors, Arthur Lessac, makes similar efforts to ground his teachings in the hard sciences of anatomy and physics, but he also mobilizes the imagistic and evocative aspects of language toward the practical enrichment of the actor's voice in training.[9] "Before anyone sets out to train and develop the human voice and body, he or she should first develop an awareness of the body's bioneural physical principles and its energy precepts," writes Lessac. He goes on to describe what he sees as the relationship between two different epistemologies of the actor:

> the artist must have the *knowing* and the *feeling* of how the body's systems work and how its creative instrumentalities function. The artist must acquire this inner intelligence and experience with gutfelt and heartfelt awareness; he or she can have the technical knowledge of the fundamentals but can understand them organically and vitally only by physically *experiencing the feeling* while at the very same time behaviorally *feeling the experience*.[10]

While Lessac is committed to these two ways of knowing, his primary concern remains with the effective training of the actor, and the majority of his teaching freely explores metaphoric and poetic language toward that goal.

As Kennedy observes, the generally perceived necessity for theoretical rigor when exploring the voice is superseded by a desire for practical results in the training studio. So, even though, as she points out, "greater emphasis among voice trainers upon 'situating their methodologies within an intellectual framework' would also provide fertile ground for a more rigorous exchange between the practitioner and the scientific communities," the vast majority of voice teaching approaches continue to prioritize practical results over scientific accuracy or theoretical precision. We can see historical traces of this tendency toward terminological imprecision quite clearly, for example, in the words of Zygmunt Molik, one of Grotowski's main actors from the Polish Teatr Laboratorium: "I don't know how the larynx works technically, but it has a strong connection with the energy, also with the psyche, because the voice has different colours."[11] This sort of approach, because of its emphasis on the imagistic and its reliance on vague theatrical jargon, may perhaps be effective for working with individual actors in the studio setting, but it does not contribute meaningfully to scientifically grounded philosophical analysis.

The analytic method I follow in this chapter mirrors the way actors encounter *Vocal Action*. Since the exercise is composed of elements that grow in complexity over time, it must be learned sequentially; without proper grounding in the rudimentary components, it is inadvisable to move on to the increasingly more complex and demanding variations. Thus, its form in any given training session depends on the actor's level of ability and the particular skill being developed during that moment in the span of a carefully constructed course of pedagogy. This trajectory of learning allows me to focus theoretically on each part of the exercise on its own before moving on to the next. As the complexity of the exercise increases, so do the ways in which I can elucidate its inner workings and address its uses as a tool for developing technique. By the end, I hope to have presented a cumulative and comprehensive picture of both the practice and the theory. I also hope that my analysis of this exercise can be applied to other approaches to the voice for actors, thereby yielding the type of "deliberate decentering" encouraged by Ihde, Cavarero, and Eidsheim. Thus, "the *invisible* that poses a series of almost insurmountable problems for much contemporary philosophy" might come to be understood, in the case of human phonation, as fundamentally embodied and relational in nature.[12]

Awakening the Resonators

I first encountered the *Vocal Action* exercise while training in 1991 in Holstebro, Denmark, with Odin Teatret actor Roberta Carreri. Since that time, I have developed the exercise in many significant ways, but of all the exercises I learned around that time, it is probably the one that I have altered the least, even after fairly continuous usage. In order to understand *Vocal Action*, it is essential to address first its grounding in Grotowski's research into *vocal resonators*.[13] While different approaches to vocal training have their own ways of characterizing both the function and the usage of *resonators*, as they are widely known, they are generally understood to be chambers of sonic resonance that exist in the human body. The differentiation of vowel sounds produced by human speech, for example, depends upon the flexibility of the resonating chamber of the oral cavity. In English, the /u/ sound (as in the word "sue") can be made by forming the lips into a puckering position, whereas the /i/ sound (as in the word "see") can be made by forming the lips and teeth more or less into a smile. These oral forms (and others) create vocal spaces that allow for the creation of particular sounds.[14] The flesh of the inside of the mouth, plus the hard and soft palate, the alveolar ridge, the teeth, and even the hollows of the nostrils function together in such a way that the shape of the opening works in tandem with the substance of the walls to create a resonating chamber for the sound produced by the apparatus of the vocal chords, which I will discuss in more detail a bit later. Because the mouth and the nose and the sinuses and all of the bony components of the face often work more or less together, they are sometimes referred to collectively as the *facial mask resonator*. It is also entirely possible to alter the placement of the vibratory activation of the various parts of the facial mask resonator. For example, while making the /i/ sound, one can make subtle alterations whereby a vibration felt predominantly in the teeth can be relocated into the nasal cavity, or vice versa. In this way, we can speak of differentiating the *nasal resonator* from the *mouth resonator*.

Resonators are not only to be found in the face, however. Importantly, Grotowski found that it is within the actor's power to move the vibration of the voice to other centers of resonance in the human body. According to James Slowiak and Jairo Cuesta, Grotowski "identified at least twenty-four different resonators in the body," while Lessac identifies "the primary resonating structures" as "the teeth, hard palate, nasal bone, cheekbones, sinuses, forehead and cranium," adding that the "spinal vertebrae and rib cage" can conduct resonance, as well.[15] Linklater asserts that many of the various bodily components, including "bone, cartilage, membrane, and muscle," are able to conduct and amplify vibration, while also pointing out that

> the voice finds its most satisfying resonators where there are clearly defined hollows and empty tunnels in the architecture of the body, such as the pharynx, the mouth, the nose; but the bony structures of the chest, the cheekbones, the jawbone, the acoustically powerful sinus hollows, the skull, the cartilage of the larynx, and the vertebrae of the spine all demonstrably contribute resonance.[16]

While it is true that the various bony bodily structures and cavities function in subtle and complex ways very much as a whole, I isolate mainly eight particular resonators while working on *Vocal Action*: the facial mask, the nose, the crown of the head, the back of the head, the chest, the belly, the upper back, and the lower back. Some of these have proven quite simple to access for the beginning actor, even on the first try, but others, such as the belly and lower back, can be more difficult to activate. Also, as with the relocation of a sound from mouth to nose mentioned earlier, each resonator allows for the creation of its own particular qualities of tone, and so each one causes vocal vibrations to sound different. As Linklater elucidates,

> The pattern of resonating response to changing pitch can be observed as follows: the low sounds get resonance from the chest and lower throat (pharynx); the lower-middle part of the range is amplified from the back wall of the throat up through the soft palate, the teeth, the jawbone, and the hard palate; moving

upward through the middle voice, resonance comes in from the mid-sinuses, the cheekbones, the nose; finally the upper-middle and high voice resonate in the upper sinuses above the nose, and in the skull. All the pitches and resonance spill into one another's precincts, creating harmonics and overtones.[17]

The first step in *Vocal Action* occurs prior to the training session itself. Before beginning, the actors are instructed to choose and memorize a piece of text. Ultimately, it is unimportant which text is chosen, although I have found that poetry tends to work better for actors working on this exercise than does prose, for reasons I will expand upon shortly. The text can also be any length, but I generally recommend somewhere around ten lines of poetry or a paragraph of prose. It is important that the actors do whatever they can to memorize the text with as little attention to the meaning of the words as possible. Unlike an audition monologue, for example, the primary purpose of which will eventually be the communication of its interpreted meaning, the words of the text in this case are to be used first and foremost as containers of sound, as a unique combination of vowels and consonants strung together in a repeatable order, rather than for their propositional content.

Once the text is memorized so well that it can be rattled off at high speeds without stopping to remember what comes next, the *Vocal Action* exercise proper can begin. The first direction given to an actor working on *Vocal Action* is to stand in a starting "ready position," with arms engaged but not tense at the sides of the torso and with the knees slightly bent, thus engaging the muscles of the legs, but again, without allowing them to become rigid. When ready, the actor begins to recite the memorized text in a "basic speaking voice." This voice, of course, differs according to each doer's preexisting vocal quality and also according to the doer's interpretation of the instructions, but the general sense is that the words are being produced in a way that feels unforced and unimpeded. In order to keep the knees from reverting to a straight-legged standing position, and also to encourage the important component of lower-body engagement, actors are often instructed to walk slowly through the space while producing the vocalized text. After the actor begins to feel somewhat acclimated to the basic activity of the exercise, instruction is given to elongate the vowels into what is generally referred to as a steady stream or a river of sound.[18] When this begins to happen, the volume of the voice usually begins to increase, and it becomes possible to register the feelings of vibration on both the inner and outer surfaces of the mouth and face. From here, the actor is asked to intensify the amplitude of vibration, focusing not on the volume of the sound but, rather, on the tactile feelings of the affected parts of the face.

Just as each body part allows for a particular "family" of tonal qualities to be associated with it, every vowel and consonant combination has a different effect on the various resonators; also, the pitch of the vocal sounds in combination with the changing vowels can be felt more or less acutely depending on the location of the resonator. As noted by Linklater earlier, some sounds and tones more readily vibrate the nasal cavity or the teeth, for instance, but the aim is for the actor to achieve maximum vibration in the chosen resonator throughout the exploration. This requires attentiveness and sensitivity to the feelings of vibration as they shift from moment to moment, which Lessac refers to as "bioneural bone-conducted sensing," and the development of an ability to make small adjustments that encourage an expansion of the felt vibration.[19]

A beginning actor may stay focused for quite some time—five, ten, fifteen minutes, maybe more, depending on the aim of the training session—on a given resonator. After working with the facial mask, the actor may begin to explore moving the vibration to other resonators. Those resonators closest to the facial mask—the nasal cavity and the chest—are often the next logical steps in the progression of exploration, but it is also quite common for some actors to have an easier time feeling the vibration in the crown of the head or the back of the head, depending on the particularities of the actor in question. In any case, the primary goal of the exercise on its most basic level is to amplify the feelings of vibration generated by the voice in particular resonators, one at a time. The different sounds required by the text assist in this task by providing a variety of vowels, one of which might "strike a chord" in a particular resonator more than another, thus allowing the vocalizer to feel the localized vibration and expand upon it with the other, less immediately effective vowels. Linklater uses the image of a ladder, "big and broad at the base and gradually getting smaller and narrower toward the top," to illustrate the usual correspondence between the resonators and their accompanying tones.[20] Over time, not only does it become possible to feel strong vibrations in the various resonators with every different vowel, it also becomes possible to do so with a variety of tones, not simply those that cause the strongest initial vibration in a particular resonator. In other words, the doer becomes able to feel the vibration of higher tones in the chest and lower tones in the crown of the head, even though the opposite is more common.

Before moving on to more advanced levels and versions of the exercise, I will devote some time to approach the components I have discussed so far in a less descriptive and more analytical mode. The fundamental purpose of *Vocal Action* is not difficult to apprehend. On a basic level, the exercise functions in a similar way to a simple warm-up or stretch. Just as athletes can prepare for a game by performing a series of exercises that activate the muscles about to be used in their expert application to the sport, or as instrumental musicians may perhaps go through a series of finger exercises prior to playing a concert, actors can clearly benefit by warming up the tools of their trade. The voice is, similarly, comprised of series of muscles and processes that can be developed, fine-tuned, stretched, expanded, and applied in a great variety of ways. Training the vocal apparatus for speaking roles in realistic theatre is not the same as training it for opera, which is also not the same as training it for choral music or Japanese Noh theatre. The voice, because it is invisible, is often conceived of as a disembodied entity.[21] In fact, it is anything but, and if we are to understand how the voice functions in theatre and how actors might best train for its various uses, it will benefit us to develop a comprehensive understanding of its fundamentally embodied nature. In the following sections, I will parse the elements of *Vocal Action* described earlier, taking time to isolate and analyze some crucial elements of vocal production in order to build a clear picture of the forces at play as the actor trains what we generically call "the voice."

Kreiman and Sidtis: Voice and Voice Quality

In the opening chapters of their book, *Foundations of Voice Studies: An Interdisciplinary Approach to Voice Production and Perception*, Jody Kreiman and Diana Sidtis provide an excellent overview of the physical processes by which the voice is produced, on both the muscular level and the neurological level of brain activity. This groundbreaking text is perhaps the most thorough contemporary study of the vocal production process, and I rely heavily on the resource of their scholarship to elucidate my current investigation. Although in the following pages I cite their research frequently, I will not recapitulate here their point-by-point analysis of the various and complex elements of human voice production and perception. It will suffice for my current purposes simply to acknowledge that they make clear that the voice must be understood both as a physical process made up of many discrete anatomical elements functioning together and as a fully embodied process of situated interaction. This involves not only the production of an acoustic signal but also listening—on the part of both interlocutors and the speakers themselves—in addition to the overall social context in which the voice is produced.

Kreiman and Sidtis draw a definitional distinction between *voice*, on the one hand, and *voice quality*, on the other: "The term 'voice' has a physical and physiological base that refers to the acoustic signal (as generated by the voice production system), while 'voice quality' refers to the perceptual impression that occurs as a result of that signal, analogous to the distinction between 'frequency' (a physical property of vibration) and 'pitch' (a listener's sensation)."[22] *Voice*, in its narrow definition, refers to the sound produced by the vocal folds and surrounding apparatus and in its broader definition includes the chain of physiological resonance employed in the act of vocal sound production. *Voice quality*, however, refers to the broad array of components processed by listeners, including but not limited to "articulatory details, laryngeal settings, F0 and amplitude variations, and temporal patterning," which allow us to speak about voice in qualitative and not simply physiological or anatomical terms. Importantly, Kreiman and Sidtis add that voice and voice quality are "best considered as analogous to a two-sided coin, melding the production characteristics of one side to the perceptual characteristics of the other side."[23]

This important distinction reminds us to consider both of these aspects of vocal production as part of a larger process, known generally as the "speech chain." "According to the speech chain," the authors explain,

> sound is produced by the actions of the speech production mechanism. The acoustic signal then travels to the ears of the listener and back to the speaker in the form of feedback. The auditory percept (a stretch of speech) is first processed peripherally within the mechanisms of the ear, followed by neurological activation of the 8th cranial nerve and the auditory pathway to the receiving areas in the brain. As increasingly complex cognitive processes are invoked, the stretch of speech under analysis may be described in terms of a number of complex messages. . . . Voice patterns convey information (more or less successfully) about affect, attitude, psychological state, pragmatics, grammatical function, sociological status, and many aspects of personal identity, all of which emerges from this complex enfolding of phonatory, phonetic, and temporal detail.[24]

This passage makes clear that voice, in general and in theatre, cannot be approached as a solely physiological or perceptual concern but needs to be theorized further as a relational phenomenon, dependent upon the social context in which both producers and perceivers of sound participate.

The implication of each of these various elements—the physiological, the perceptual, and the relational—in the larger whole of speech will be essential to understand as I move forward with my analysis of *Vocal Action*. Referring to the work of dialogic linguist Marie-Cécile Bertau, Kreiman and Sidtis make a case for moving beyond studies that focus on one of these elements to the exclusion of the other, stating that

> production and perception are inseparably linked. In this view, a human voice is a concrete, perceivable event that is inseparable from (and thus indexes) the body that produced it, which in turn shapes the sound of the voice. At the same time, voice manifests the speaker's abstract, unobservable consciousness, thus representing the whole person and "underscoring the physicality of psychological self." Further, the speaking person exists in a communicative context that necessarily includes a listener (somewhat reminiscent of the sound made by a tree falling in the woods), and the voice that is produced cannot be separated from the act of listening that provides the context for production. . . . Voice reflects the whole physical and social self and is shaped in part by communicative context.[25]

It is against this backdrop that we must understand the process of vocal production onstage. As I move through this chapter and build an increasingly nuanced understanding of the actor's work with voice, I will demonstrate how it is as impossible and unwise to separate the speaker from the context as it is to separate the voice from the body.

The Embodied Voice

Even when taking into account only the physical processes of vocal sound creation, the whole body must be considered. If, for example, we were simply to focus on the vibration generated by the vocal chords alone, the sound we would hear would be basically unrecognizable and indecipherable. As Kreiman and Sidtis put it, "the sound produced by the vibration of the vocal folds, if it were heard independent of the influence of the rest of the vocal tract, resembles a buzz more than it does what we think of as a human voice." The system of resonators in the body amplifies and transforms that basic buzz into the sound of a full voice. "The process by which the vocal tract interacts with the vocal source to produce the final sound of a voice is called *resonance*," they add. "More generally, resonance is the process whereby acoustic energy is transferred from a source of vibration to another body."[26]

In the scientific terminology, the resonators normally at work in the creation and amplification of the human voice are called "formants," and the central tones associated with those resonators are called "formant frequencies." Altering the active resonators by manipulating the various body parts involved has the effect of changing the formant frequency. A speaker's base-level formant frequency is referred to as F0, and the variations that result from altered resonation are referred to as F1, F2, F3, and so on, depending on which resonators are activated. "Under normal circumstances," state Kreiman and Sidtis, "the fundamental frequency (F0) of an acoustic voice signal is the primary determinant of the perceived pitch of the voice. Listeners are very sensitive to changes in F0, and can reliably detect changes of as little as 2%."[27] They add that "scientists do not completely understand the manner in which F0 is controlled physiologically," which is of particular interest here, because it is precisely the ability to alter and control both F0 and the other formant frequencies that actors must have in order to create the voiced attributes of a role.[28] Of course, it is not necessary to have a scientific understanding of a physical process in order to perform that process; in general, humans are capable of far greater control over their vocal apparatus than they commonly have cause to understand.

The machinery of the voice is incredibly intricate, to an extent that is generally unobservable and unmanaged by the speaker. Kreiman and Sidtis provide a compelling encapsulation of the stunning complexity of voice production:

> Phonatory behavior involves orchestration of respiratory, laryngeal, and vocal tract movements, coordinating over 100 different muscles. To vocalize, we must commandeer an appropriate amount of breath, push a stream of it through the vocal folds (which must be deftly configured and continuously readjusted), and then must work the jaw, tongue, velum, and lips on that moving airstream while simultaneously adjusting the airstream in response to these articulatory movements. This means that speakers can change their voices by altering something about the way air is delivered from the lungs, or by varying something about the way the vocal folds vibrate, and/or by varying the size and shape of the vocal tract above the larynx (including coupling to the nasal tract)—a rather limited number of parameters. However, speakers can vary these things dynamically in an almost infinite number of time-varying patterns.... All these things can vary dynamically over time, into a variety of vocalizations including talking, yelling, singing, sighing, laughing, humming, cursing, and reciting memorized material, among others.[29]

In one sense, *Vocal Action* allows the actor to focus on basic physiological and mechanical elements that underlie voice production. In everyday speech, the human voice expresses the thoughts and intentions of the speaker effectively and without the need for direct, conscious control. As mentioned earlier, the ability to alter the various component parts of vocalization is not a skill that people generally work on developing. If I wish to make someone move out of my way, I may simply say, "Excuse me, I need to get by." In different contexts, that phrase will sound different. For example, if I am on a busy sidewalk and a fire engine is passing by with its siren blaring and I am trying to prevent my child from walking into traffic, I might yell, "Excuse me, I need to get by!" in a register, at a volume, and with an urgency dictated by the circumstances; whereas if I am attempting to get around just one person in an aisle in a library, I might speak the words very softly, but with understated urgency. This process is common practice for the actor, who knows how to analyze the given dramatic circumstances and form the spoken text in accordance with the intention appropriate for the moment. In this basic realistic theatrical scenario, the actor builds upon a preexisting ability to allow the voice to respond to context.

It is useful, however, if not essential, to be able to use and work with the elements of vocalization as expressive material. *Vocal Action* allows the actor to explore the possibilities of voice beyond the usual dependence upon verbal meaning and social context. This is why it is important in preparing the text for use in the exercise not to focus on the meaning of the words. It is, of course, virtually impossible to say a word that one understands without connecting in some way to its meaning, which is why I said earlier that it is useful to have a text with poetic qualities; if one is going to be saying words without focusing mainly on their denotational meaning, it can be helpful for them to be associatively multivalent and sonically rich. It is possible, in fact, to focus so much on the sounds of the words that the meaning ceases to determine fully the mode of their articulation.[30] Additionally, the method of sound production in *Vocal Action* referred to previously as the "river of sound" further prevents the sense of the words from controlling the sound, since the cadences that normally result from the grammatical structure and its concomitant meaning are interrupted and replaced by a more or less constant, chant-like stream of vocal sound. When the locus of vocal production control is taken away from the meaning, the focus can shift to an exploration of the physiological components that normally occupy a subsidiary role in the awareness of the speaker.

It is important to note that actors engaged with *Vocal Action* are not focusing simply on the activation of the various resonators in an antiseptic sense. In fact, after actors become acclimated to the basic requirements of the exercise, it generally becomes useful to employ a host of associations and images to engage the resonators more fully. What is more, the level of affective response brought about by the "technical" manipulation of resonators is a crucial element of the training experience connected to the exercise. For example, regardless of the words being vocalized, it is often the case that moving the vibration from the facial mask to the crown of the head can bring about a sensation connected to a feeling of crying, and during this, actors can experience feelings of extreme sadness. Likewise, moving the vibration to the nasal cavity, especially if the face is placed into a posture of smiling, can activate uplifting feelings in the doer. Linklater, in a pedagogical style that, as I mentioned earlier, allows for a degree of terminological looseness, refers frequently to affective responses in resonator exploration, explaining that "you may experience different energy or emotional content in each area, particularly when you are playing with colors, and there are intrinsically different energies that come with changes of pitch."[31] The various feelings elicited by the movement of vibration through the body are generally not simple, though, and actors tend to experience a complex stream of affect along with the river of sound.

Beyond the placement and location of the vibration, actors experience emotional reactions to other qualities of the sound they produce. Vocalizing loudly can elicit feelings of anger or alarm, for instance, while producing a soft voice can feel soothing and calm. The whole gamut of emotions, which are so intimately connected to the function of the voice in everyday life can be activated by the manipulation of various qualities of vibration, even if the meaning of the words being spoken in a given moment runs completely counter to the feeling being experienced. The value of this lesson for the actor-in-training is difficult to miss. As alluded to earlier, in everyday life the ways in which people say words are rarely dictated solely by the denotational meanings of the individual words in and of themselves. Rather, it is as if there are always at least two tracks operating simultaneously in the speaker. Of course, on the one hand, meaning is most certainly carried by the words. If I say, "hand me that shovel," it should generally be clear exactly what object I would like the person to whom I am speaking to pick up and give to me. On the other hand, though, there is a world of less literal meaning running along simultaneously with the way I form the command, namely through *intonation*. According to philosopher Mladen Dolar, "intonation is another way in which we can be aware of the voice, for the particular tone of the voice, its particular melody and modulation, its cadence and inflection, can decide the meaning. Intonation can turn the meaning of a sentence upside down; it can transform it into its opposite."[32] If I am filling in a grave at a funeral, the words can carry sadness, whereas if I am rushing to fend off an attacking dog, the words carry that sense of panic and determination and fear along with their literal meaning, but there is obviously no direct semantic link between the word "shovel" and any of these emotions.

The Components of Prosody

The aspect of speech that relies on what we have been calling *voice quality*, and which allows for variation of intonation, is generally referred to as *prosody*. Since one of the primary benefits of *Vocal Action* is that it permits actors to focus on the development of the prosodic elements of vocalization, the field of its study is extraordinarily useful for my current investigation. While I refer to a number of prosody scholars as this chapter progresses, I find that Kreiman and Sidtis provide perhaps the best basic definition. "Speech prosody," they explain, is

> an area of intensive study in speech science, psycholinguistics, and neuropsychology. Prosody traditionally encompasses average pitch and pitch variability (or the mean and variability of fundamental frequency), loudness (or intensity) mean and variation, the large array of temporal factors that determine perceived speech rate and rhythm, and voice quality narrowly defined (for example, creakiness and breathiness, which function subtly—and sometimes not so subtly—in everyday speech to communicate meaning).

Put more succinctly, there are "four primary components of prosody—pitch, loudness, timing, and voice quality."[33] In daily life these prosodic elements are activated and altered spontaneously and generally without conscious awareness. They are at the very heart of how we communicate with others, and, as Kreiman and Sidtis point out, "the attitudes and intentions communicated in a verbal utterance are at least as important as the words themselves and in some instances, they carry more weight."[34] Exercises like *Vocal Action* that encourage the exploration of vocal tone, rhythm, intensity, and the like provide actors with an opportunity to develop the psychophysical systems that determine voice quality and, therefore, expand the expressive potential for speech prosody as an element of artistic craft.

In the late 1970s scientists studying the human voice began to formulate what is now referred to as the "'dual-pathway model' of human acoustic communication."[35] Over time, developments in the field of neuroscience have allowed researchers to expand their understanding of exactly how the human voice operates, even if there does still exist a good deal of disagreement regarding how to interpret the scientific data. In a recent article on the subject of speech evolution in humans, neurologists Hermann Ackermann, Steffen R. Hage, and Wolfram Ziegler rely heavily on this model, according to which "two separate neuroanatomic 'channels' with different phylogenetic histories appear to participate in human acoustic communication, supporting nonverbal affective vocalizations and articulate speech, respectively."[36] The evolutionary puzzle presented by this dual-pathway model is that one system of vocalization, which is connected to "articulate" or propositional speech, seems to have become superimposed, as it were, on top of another, apparently much older, system, which is more directly connected to emotion and affect. The neural pathways of each of these systems are distinct; however, they operate upon the physiological system of phonation simultaneously and in concert. As Ackermann et al. explain,

> most importantly, activity of the same set of vocal tract muscles and a single speech wave simultaneously convey both the propositional and emotional contents of spoken language. Hence, two information sources seated in separate brain networks and creating fundamentally different data structures (analogue versus digital) contribute simultaneously to the formation of the speech signal. Therefore, the two channels must coordinate at some level of the central nervous system.[37]

For the purposes of the current investigation, the fact that there are two separate channels is as important as the fact that they function in coordination with one another. This dichotomy may explain how it is possible in *Vocal Action* to separate out the prosodic elements of speech from the propositional.

As I have already noted, the way something is said is intimately—and usually unconsciously—connected to what is said, even if those two components of speech are not alike (see the "shovel" example). As Ackermann et al. point out, "often these implicit aspects of acoustic communication—*how* we say something—are more relevant to a listener than propositional content, that is, *what* we say."[38] Moreover, as Kreimann and Sidtis observe, vocal characteristics active in prosody which behave "normally" in everyday usage can be altered through practice. "Controlling these aspects separately is possible," they write, "but normally requires vocal training."[39] Actors and singers can develop the ability to manipulate the four main components of prosody—pitch, loudness, timing, and voice quality—discretely from one another. For example, while the authors note that "loudness variation usually tracks with pitch changes, such that greater loudness follows higher pitch," they also make clear that "it is possible to control these aspects of voice separately. In their training singers learn to uncouple pitch and loudness, and can increase pitch softly and lower pitch loudly."[40] Through training actors can learn, as I have already shown, how to bring under conscious control the normally unconscious functions of voice that affect prosody.

In *Vocal Action* not only do volume and pitch become two distinct and independently controlled vocal functions but normal breathing groups, which generally respond to formation of phrases into meaningful units, are also disrupted by the decentering of meaning in relation to the vocalization of the text. The directive in the exercise to keep the "river of sound" flowing does not simply effect the extension of vowel sounds through increased temporal limits and resonating locations. The doers are also encouraged to follow each breath until the end and, when it is fully expired, to stop wherever they are—even if it is in the middle of a word—breathe, and then begin again from where the text ended prior to inhalation. Beginners often become short of breath and also stop short of the full usage of each breath, as it feels "unnatural" to breathe in a way that is not connected to any logical semantic break or pause. Breathing, as Kreiman and Sidtis note, "is ordinarily autonomically controlled, but is co-opted during speech to form intonational phrases or 'breath groups.'"[41] If the everyday voice is accustomed to a lifetime of connecting to prosodic elements in one way, it takes effort to allow those elements to change.

One way of doing this is to address those functions that are susceptible to conscious control and to increase the amount of conscious control exerted on those functions. Breath is one of these, and as we just noted, the connection of volume to pitch is another. Another is the connection of pitch to resonator. Still another is the habitual relationship of certain emotions and even images to certain words, which becomes immediately apparent when, say, an actor encounters a new script and then, after a predictable "first reading," begins to explore other, more nuanced ways of saying the lines. Exercises such as *Vocal Action* allow actors not only to work the prosodic elements in isolation from each other but also to work the affective channel in a way disconnected from the propositional channel of speech production. Again, the fact that the affective channel normally functions without conscious control does not imply that it cannot be influenced consciously. The decoupling of the prosodic apparatus of voice from the impulse to communicate propositional meaning allows actors to explore phonatory possibilities in their training that will ultimately cycle back into expressive use in performance.

It is important to be clear that the operation of the dual-pathway model should not be taken to comprise the entirety of the process of speech production. As Kreiman and Sidtis stress,

> Producing a voice takes a whole person. . . . Subcortical (including limbic) systems of the brain generate the attitudes, moods, and emotions that find expression in our voices. Temporal and parietal lobes accumulate memories and facts leading to beliefs, assumptions and opinions, which also influence pitch contours and accent, speaking rate, loudness, and other vocal attributes.

Intentions, goals and motor programs are managed by frontal lobe systems in circuitry with the subcortical nuclei that contribute to every vocal effort.... All of these are "heard" along with personal identity in the voice.[42]

In addition, as Marc Bornstein and Gianluca Esposito point out in their critical challenge to Ackermann et al.'s article, it would be a mistake to think of the system of speech production in a simplistic, dyadic way:

> Language—*in toto*, comprehension and expression of phonology, morphology, semantics, syntactics, and pragmatics, at least—has such a multilevel organization, extending as it does from the anatomy of the vocal tract through brain-based motor effectors to interpersonal dynamics and on to cultural experience. By focusing on one level of analysis, Ackermann et al.'s hypothesis misses the essential multilevel and developmental nature of vocal production. Bidirectional influences operate across these multiple levels as biological and cognitive systems are nested within individuals, and individuals are nested within complex social and verbal environments.

While this critique does not succeed in dismantling the dual-pathway model, it does compel us, as we consider its functioning, to take into account the complex of social situation, interpersonal communication, "higher-order components of mental functioning," and "social language learning," without which the systems and processes of speech production would not exist as they do.[43]

Listening

To address the entire role played by sociality in the mechanisms of speech production is an enormous task well beyond the scope of this book. However, it will serve the current exploration of *Vocal Action* to attend to the faculty of audition, which is a function constantly performed by both the speaker and listener in every instance of verbal communication. Of primary importance is the fact that all of the aforementioned voice qualities or prosodic elements exist not in the physical production of the sound per se but actually in the listener. They are heard. "It is important to remember," Kreiman and Sidtis remind us, "that pitch, loudness, and quality are psychological characteristics, and as such they represent the impact of physical signals on human ears"; it is impossible to consider the act of speech and sound production without taking into consideration sociality and intersubjectivity.[44] This is true in the sense of the physics of the speaker/listener relationship, and it is also true in the fact that all impulses to phonate are hardwired with the impulse to communicate to a listener.

Also, beyond the fact that it is impossible for a single subject to produce clearly phonated speech in the absence of accurate auditory feedback via self-monitoring, there is also a constant process of autoregulation of the various aspects of prosody that relies on the speaker's ability to gauge and vary vocal sounds accurately.[45] This is, importantly, another way in which the whole brain is in use during the various processes involved in vocal production. However, as Kreiman and Sidtis admit, there is still much research to be done on the subject of self-monitoring in speech. "Information flowing back from numerous sites and levels of sensory and motor activity is obviously an important aspect of vocalization," they write, "but the role and value of self-monitoring during vocal production is not fully understood."[46] They also acknowledge that "although speakers regulate vocal loudness without much thought or effort, much more research is required to fully explicate the manner in which they accomplish this."[47] These reservations aside, the importance of self-monitoring in speech is clear, if not entirely understood.

Turning back again to the exercise of *Vocal Action*, one fairly common direction to the doer is to pay conscious auditory attention during vocalization not to the sound "inside the head" but, rather, to the sound that bounces back to the ears from the acoustical space of studio. This technique obviously does not bypass the built-in process of self-monitoring that occurs inside the head, but it allows the actor to "turn up the volume" of the portion of sound that others can hear. Grotowski observed that hearing "the echo" of one's own voice in the space made possible a turning of attention away from the self and "towards the outside."[48] This generally leads to a greater precision of pitch and an ability to control one's volume more effectively and subtly. As Slowiak and Cuesta comment, Grotowski "determined that the voice must always be seeking contact, directed toward a precise place in the space, and listening for feedback, in order to adjust and make new contact."[49] Importantly, this element of the exercise is not intended to create actors who are always paying attention to the sound of their own voices in the space. Lessac rightly stresses, in his description of what he calls "'overriding the outer ear' . . . , the primacy of innate control through hearing what you feel neurophysically inside the body's environment, rather than waiting to listen to your voice via air conduction."[50] While it is possible that Lessac and Grotowski might simply have two diverging views on the subject, I contend that, in *Vocal Action*, the "echo," used in the context of an ongoing training, develops an ability to attend aurally to one's surroundings while vocalizing; through practice, this comes to operate on an unconscious level, so that it eventually functions even when it is not being directly worked, without interfering with the actor's ability to self-monitor "neurophysically."

The tonal precision achieved through this process of self-monitoring functions in much the same way as "staying on pitch" while singing. As a matter of fact, someone listening to an actor working on *Vocal Action* might be reminded more of song or chant than of speaking, since the focus is more on the tonal, vibratory elements of language than on the semantic or propositional, as I have discussed. A connection between the neural processes involved in singing and tonal appreciation (the "affective" branch of the dual-pathway model, which incorporates the limbic system) and the ability to process prosody has been demonstrated through a number of experiments in psychology. In one series of such experiments, led by William Forde Thompson, E. Glenn Schellenberg, and Gabriela Husain, it was observed that "musical training is associated with enhanced sensitivity to emotions conveyed by prosody," in languages both native and foreign to the participants.[51] In another, actual vocal training exercises from theatre were found to improve markedly the ability of Turkish students to "experiment with the prosodic aspects of the target language" (which in this case was English), whereby "at the end of the three theatre based voice training sessions there was a significant increase in the vocal skills performance of Turkish learners."[52] According to Ackermann et al., the "'limbic communication system' of the brain of nonhuman primates support[s] the production of affective vocalizations such as laughing, crying, and moaning in our species. In addition, this network might engage in the emotive-prosodic modulation of spoken language."[53] Again, while these hypotheses remain somewhat under-researched, the evidence points to a strong connection between the parts of the brain activated in music processing and those involved in both the production and perception of prosody in speech.

Listening, beyond its role in an actor's ability to speak and hear effectively, is also an action that reads onstage. The act of speaking with a partner onstage is performed not only by the vocalizer but by the listener, as well. In order to be "in sync" with a scene partner, for example, one must be able to activate the whole apparatus of listening. One important difference between listening in everyday life and in the theatre is that, as I have remarked many times already in previous chapters, in everyday life we normally do not know what a person is going to say, whereas onstage we frequently do. So, how can we train actors to behave as if they are hearing something for the first time, even though the dialogue is scripted? Since the faculty of listening is so intimately tied to speech, it stands to reason that vocal training can be used to train listening, as well. In fact, *Vocal Action*, as it allows for more conscious control of the involuntary pathway (emotional, limbic) and more affective resonance in the voluntary pathway (cortical, propositional, "higher functions"), expands the ability "to listen carefully" to more than just the meaning of the words, which are repeated in theatre. When one develops the ability to listen for the prosodic (through work on producing vocal prosody), it becomes clear that an utterance can never truly be repeated without subtle but important variation. As Kreiman and Sidtis observe, "even without conscious manipulation, no speaker ever produces an utterance in exactly the same way twice. Differences within a single speaker in vocal quality (whether intentionally or incidentally produced) across occasions and utterances are called *intraspeaker variability*."[54]

Regardless of intraspeaker variability, voices of particular people are identifiable to an extraordinary degree of accuracy among listeners. In fact, it has been shown experimentally that listeners attend to speakers in wholly different ways depending on the level of familiarity of the voice. "For the most part," explain Kreiman and Sidtis, "unfamiliar voices are simply an unattended part of the background of noise that surrounds us, out of which a familiar voice 'pops,' for example if a friend passes audibly nearby."[55] Not only does a different neural pathway become activated by familiar voices, but also

> typical concomitant mental experiences . . . arise on hearing a familiar voice: focused attention, affective impressions, associated memories, motivation or desire (to remain, to escape), and, not to be minimized, a feeling of familiarity or personal relevance. . . . Familiar voices naturally capture attention in ways that unfamiliar voices do not and familiar voice recognition involves a process that is highly associated with images, properties, emotions, episodes, impressions, and so on. . . . The role of quantity of exposure in acquiring a new personally familiar voice in normal settings is not known. . . . It is likely that a lasting representation of the voice can be and usually is rapidly established.[56]

Judging from the results of studies that show, for instance, how readily listeners can identify the voices of celebrities, it is a fairly safe assumption that, in the course of attending a theatrical performance, the audience engages in a process of vocal familiarization with the actor/character, and that the processes of affective and imagistic association connected with familiar voice processing are fully active.[57] Once the relatively rapid process of vocal familiarization is complete, an expansive realm of reception and processing opens up in the listener, including trust, compassion, etc. As Kreiman and Sidtis elaborate, "it takes a whole brain to produce a voice, and it takes a whole brain to recognize a voice."[58]

It is also true that listeners can gauge a whole set of information about a speaker's physical characteristics from the prosodic elements of speech. "Listeners often treat voice quality as a cue to a speaker's physical characteristics," write Kreiman and Sidtis, "and make judgments about physical size, sex, age, health, appearance, racial group, or ethnic background, based on the sound of a voice."[59] The connection between vocal choices and character in theatre is obvious, and through exercises like *Vocal Action*, actors can experiment with all sorts of possible combinations of sounds, in order to create what eventually will be a character whose vocal patterns can be accepted by the audience, who is able to track even the smallest variations in F0, for example, given the formal conventions of the given performance. Often, "new" voices are discovered by the actor-explorer during the *Vocal Action* exercise, which otherwise would likely never have been found, because the conscious control of the propositional has been temporarily ceded to the limbic, affective branch of the dual-pathway model. In this way, *Vocal Action* is not only useful for a general expansion of the actor's abilities, but it is also a tool for generating performance material. In fact, it often happens that an actor will "find a voice" and label it with a name that will aid in later recall, so that it can be handily revisited and potentially developed further in conjunction with a different text entirely.

Gesture and Speech, Connected

Until now I have referred to voice and speech almost synonymously. I have yet to incorporate into my analysis the extremely important element of gesture, which works hand in hand with the voice in all moments of human communication, and which is always a dynamic component of the *Vocal Action* exercise. In my exploration of gesture, I primarily refer to the trajectory of scholarship begun initially by Adam Kendon in the 1960s and 1970s and elaborated further over time by David McNeill and other important linguists, including Kendon himself. Cornelia Müller and a group of leading linguists and communication scientists, in their expansive volume, *Body - Language - Communication: An International Handbook on Multimodality in Human Interaction*, provide perhaps the most in-depth and contemporary collection of analyses of gesture currently available in the field. According to the detailed overview of the historical development of gesture studies offered by Müller and her team, Kendon's pioneering work marked the first time that a language scientist observed that "communicative bodily actions are highly structured, meaningful and closely integrated with speech." While this seems fairly commonplace now, at the time Kendon's study represented "the first systematic micro-analysis of gestural and vocal units of expression," as most linguistic studies at the time involving gesture focused on the physical movements themselves as elements of "*non*verbal communication," rather than as components of speech.[60]

In 1988, Kendon assembled a series of descriptions of various types of gestures, and in his "landmark book," *Hand and Mind: What Gestures Reveal about Thought*, McNeill puts them in the following order: Gesticulation—Language-like gestures—Pantomimes—Emblems—Sign Languages, calling them "Kendon's Continuum."[61] As linguist Tim Wharton explains, "The idea is that as we move from left to right on the continuum, the gestures become less natural, take on more 'language-like' properties and depend less and less on the co-presence of language itself." Wharton provides some succinct descriptions of McNeill's version of Kendon's categories, which I reproduce here, as they will prove helpful as I explore the relationship between gesture and speech in my analysis of *Vocal Action*:

- Those movements classified as "gesticulation" in the continuum are the spontaneous movements of the arms and hands that accompany speech: what McNeill describes as "the unwitting accompaniments of speech."
- "Language-like" gestures are similar to gesticulations but are "integrated" into a linguistic string in the sense that they must occur at a certain point and contribute to the interpretation of the string as a whole; so Jack might utter "the dental examination was OK, but when he started [*gesture to represent drilling*] it was agony."
- "Pantomimes" are those movements that depict objects or actions; accompanying speech is no longer obligatory—"there may be either silence or just inarticulate onomatopoetic [*sic*] sound effects ('whoops!,' 'click!,' etc.)."
- "Emblems" are those cultural-dependent symbolic gestures used to convey a wide range of both positive and negative meanings: the British "thumbs up" signal and the two-fingered insult are two examples.
- Finally, "Sign Languages" are, of course, languages proper, with their own syntactic, semantic, and phonological rules.[62]

Depending on the instance of speaking, the gesturing body is engaged in various ways, and so an average speaker will run the gamut of this continuum quickly, spontaneously, unpredictably, and often in ways that elude conscious awareness, both on the part of the speaker and the listener. As Müller points out, "Gestures may replace information, illustrate and emphasize what is being uttered verbally, soften or slightly modify the meaning expressed in speech or even create a discrepancy between the gestural and verbal meaning."[63] The speaker is never simply phonating and is always dynamically engaged at the limit of his or her bodily ability. Interestingly, as linguist Susan Goldin-Meadow notes, "Even congenitally blind speakers who have never seen anyone gesture move their hands when they speak. Although the gestures that accompany speech might, at times, appear to be meaningless movements, they are not mere handwaving. Gestures are synchronized, both semantically and temporally, with the words they accompany and, in this sense, form an integrated system with speech."[64] The gestural impulse is hardwired into the act of speech; Kendon's Continuum is illustrative of how one does not exist absent the other in spoken language.

McNeill succeeded in turning the attention of language scientists away from their primary focus on those elements of gesture that are nonspeech dependent toward gesticulations, "of which," elucidates Wharton, "communicators are either unaware or, at best, only marginally aware."[65] Kendon's Continuum focuses on the specific relationships to speech inherent in each type of gesture, and McNeill theorizes the concept of the "Growth Point" (GP) as "the minimal gesture-speech unit," which is made up of a dynamic, yet oppositional synthesis of "language" (speech) and "imagery" (gesture).[66] Speech, in this usage, is comprised of the stable semiotic sign of the spoken word, containing a largely consistent array of fixed meanings across speakers, while gesture is abstract and idiosyncratic. As they occur together in the speaker, particular meaning expressed in context through language is the result.

As I attempt to assemble a useful picture of the various processes at play during vocalization, both in general and in *Vocal Action*, the formulation of a conceptual separation and practical union between speech and gesture is extremely helpful. Müller notes that McNeill "proposes that gesture and speech are different but integrated facets of language," which "reside on two different modes of thought: one imagistic—the other one propositional, and McNeill considers the dialectic tension between the two modes of thought as propelling thought and communication."[67] For McNeill, the two are combined in an effort on the part of the speaker to communicate, to allow another to receive the contents of thought via perceptual modalities. Quoting McNeill's formulation, Müller proposes that "both speech and gesture are outcomes of 'the moment-by-moment thinking that takes place as one speaks,' whereby different modes of thinking are reflected in both modalities—imagistic thinking in gestures and analytic and categorical thinking in language."[68] Meaning emerges through a combination of gesture and speech that unfolds during verbal discourse, which must be seen as a process (rather than as an instance) of thinking-in-action.

The similarity between the gesture-speech relationship and the prosody-voice relationship should be obvious. Not only do both gesture and prosody act simultaneously and in concert with verbal utterance in order to create moments of meaningful communication, they also latch on to similar aspects of expressivity and experience. Referring back to the dual-pathway model discussed earlier, one notices that the defining characteristics of prosody, attributed to the neurological channel that incorporates the limbic system, are in this model given over to gesture. As noted by Marcus Perlman and Raymond W. Gibbs Jr., linguists researching gesture and its relation to cognitive processes, "various studies demonstrate that gesture is highly correlated with communication about imagery-laden topics that span a range of motor, visual, and spatial imagery," and that "these findings are not at all surprising as one considers the highly imagistic nature of gestures themselves, which are inherently visible, spatially-oriented motor actions."[69] It is easy to see how gestures, which work with speech to color it with supplementary (and essential) expressive information, are working with the elemental components of prosody discussed earlier.

Of course, it would be overly simplistic (and empirically insupportable) to assert an equivalence between the two. The literature on the neurological connection between gesture and prosody is extremely limited; however, it is clear that they are connected, if only even intuitively and phenomenologically. Indeed, Perlman and Gibbs note a strong connection between prosodic elements of speech and gesture in their discussion of the literature on phenomena known as "vocal gestures" and "co-speech vocalizations." Vocal gestures and co-speech vocalizations mobilize all four of the components of prosody—pitch, loudness, timing, and voice quality—in order to express elements of meaning connected to descriptive qualities of the subject matter being discussed. As Perlman and Gibbs put it, "When people talk, they commonly pattern their voice in a variety of ways to iconically depict an aspect of their subject matter. Many times these iconic correspondences are created within the domain of sound, with the sounds of our voice imitating the sounds of our environment." Some examples of vocal gestures could be the imitation of "certain characteristics of [a] person's voice, such as their emotional state, accent, and tonal quality," or the imitation of the sounds of animals (e.g., yapping dogs) or of inanimate objects (e.g., the clanking of a machine). Co-speech vocalizations might include, say, a description of "'a *looong* snake'" or "'a *quicklittlebug*.'"[70] In each of these examples, we can see how there is no clear line to be drawn between the gestural components and the prosodic components of the utterances.

Just as Perlman and Gibbs insist that "co-speech vocalizations are, in fact, the same qualitative sort of behavior as manual gestures," we can just as accurately assert that vocal gestures are the same qualitative sort of behavior as prosody.[71] In fact, linguist Dwight Bollinger called early attention to the strong connection between intonation and gesture in his 1986 book, *Intonation and Its Parts: Melody in Spoken English*, stating that intonation was "part of a gestural complex whose primitive and still surviving function is the signaling of emotion."[72] The similarity between his view and the positions taken by the neuroscientists interested in the evolutionary development of the dual-pathway model discussed earlier is noteworthy. However, for the purposes of my current exploration, it is enough to take note of the fact that gesture is connected functionally to prosody, and that both gesture and prosody are connected to the affective and imagistic components of speech production.

In this light, *Vocal Action* can be seen as a theatre laboratory experiment, in which we are able to observe how the very same aspects of bodily consciousness (imagination, emotion, musicality, spatial indication, etc.) are activated by the two interrelated domains of gesture and prosody. In fact, it is almost impossible to perform the exercise effectively without engaging bodily with the faculty of imagination. For example, as I have already touched upon in passing, a task as simple as moving the center of resonation from the mouth to the nose can be managed in a number of ways. The least effective way to accomplish it well is by calling upon pure motor feedback. In other words, attempting to move the vibration in a purely mechanical way will yield mechanical-sounding results. Of course, it is accurate to say that calling to mind a picture of the inside of the vocal apparatus and the facial mask is, in fact, an activation of the imaginative function, and it is hard to conceive of consciously activating the body schema without the aid of this sort of imagining, but even so, the superficial image will, in the end, yield a thin outcome. The vibration may move as directed, but the resultant sound will be stiff, shrill, and piercing; what is more, the action being performed will read to an onlooker as little more than physical effort to perform an anatomical self-manipulation. Grotowski (and Molik later on) noticed this tendency in his work with resonators, and eventually he found it more effective to focus on finding resonance as a result of associative play rather than through mechanical placement of vibration in the body.[73] While this might prove useful as a purely physical warm-up for the actor, its use as a training exercise will be limited to just that.

However, if the actor were, for example, to imagine transforming into an evil, green witch with a long, gnarled nose, the vibration might not only move to the desired location, but the rest of the body engaging in the action would be filled with micro-actions that contribute to the full-body physicalization of the actor's living mental image. Another way to move the vibration successfully would be to conjure as detailed a mental image as possible to correspond to the action, such as a thin, white satin ribbon being pulled from the nose, or the expulsion from the nose of bursts of steam, etc. In my experience both as a doer and more importantly as a leader and observer of the *Vocal Action* exercise, these image-laden actions yield a far richer and more nuanced result. The sound produced by actors working in this way emerges as a fully embodied action in space and time, and as such has all the qualities of spontaneity normally associated with life itself. It is dynamic, unpredictable, and it challenges the limits of comprehension, rather than being monotonous, mechanical, or cliché. These "lifelike" qualities associated with prosody come into being through the unconscious physical reaction to imaginative cues. The body responds in unexpected ways, for example, to the prompt of "becoming a witch." The variations in vibrations go hand in hand with a series of obvious and subtle gestures that occupy the whole body in the task of affective vocal expression and exploration, existing on a separate channel from the propositional components of the words being spoken, as I have discussed.

Simulation and Vocal Production

Before continuing my analysis of how *Vocal Action* provides a vehicle for actors to explore gesture as a nonpropositional component of vocalization, it will be useful to discuss briefly the concept of *mental simulation* as it pertains to speech. Recent studies in both linguistics and psychology that acknowledge that language, composed of speech and gesture, is a bodily process make frequent use of the growing literature on EC in their research. In Müller's words, "cognitive processes and conceptual knowledge are deeply rooted in the body's interactions with the world."[74] In particular, the field of enactive perception, explored in some detail in the previous chapter, has had a growing influence on the field of gesture studies. Since McNeill, Müller, and others have managed to orient the conversation in linguistics toward the complex interrelation between speech and gesture, an opening has been created for theories that help to understand language as an embodied phenomenon. One such theory makes use of the concept of *mental simulation*, whereby the creation and understanding of gestures is accomplished through an activation of neurological, and thereby physical, activations in the bodies of the communicating subjects.

Understandings of this process range from the neurological to the conceptual. Scientists such as Tyler Marghetis and Benjamin K. Bergen focus on the evidence that seems to support the notion of simulation as activation of sensorimotor neural pathways. According to their thesis,

> meaning is embodied internally when we create embodied simulations, co-opting brain areas specialized for perception or action to create dynamic mental representations, rich in sensorimotor detail. Thinking of petting a kitten, for instance, might include visual simulation of its appearance and motor simulation of the act of petting—all in brain areas typically used to see and touch kittens. At the same time, meaning is embodied externally in representational gestures, actions of the hands and body that represent objects, actions, and ideas. . . . The neural activity supporting language comprehension and production relies on brain areas that are repurposed from perception and action—that is, "embodied" brain areas—and these areas coordinate during comprehension to create "embodied simulations" of linguistic content.[75]

As a counterpoint to this view, some scientists, such as Pierre Feyereisen, are more measured in their reliance on neuroscientific imaging for their theorization of simulation. He insists that the

> close proximity of brain areas involved in speech and gesture processing is only a weak evidence for the interdependence of language and action. If the claim is that connections exist between these two domains, it is trivial, and if the claim is that sensorimotor mechanisms constitute the cerebral basis for language, it is disputable on the basis of the empirical evidence. Rather than attempting to "localize" broad mental functions like language and gesture, neuropsychological studies aim at describing more precisely a functional architecture in which different parts of the brain support different processes.[76]

In my view, Feyereisen harbors a healthy skepticism toward the faddish reliance on functional magnetic resonance imaging (fMRI) and related imaging technologies in cognitive science, and so he is less interested in proving the equivalence of language and gesture and more inclined to examine the complex interplay between the various brain areas involved in mental simulation.

All of these views hold that the online function of mental cognition is not one of storage but of action, in this case, active simulation of the concepts that arise in the course of discourse. It is through the simulation of "embodied possibilities" that the body-mind interacts meaningfully with the world. Put another way, by psychologist Rolf Zwaan, "comprehension is not the manipulation of abstract, arbitrary and amodal symbols, a language of thought. Rather, comprehension is the generation of vicarious experiences making up the comprehender's experiential repertoire."[77]

The degree of simulation associated with gesture has been shown to correlate directly with the degree of imagery and emotion contained in the subject matter being processed through language, and according to Perlman and Gibbs, "studies also suggest that sensorimotor simulations during language comprehension can be shaped by emotion."[78] Once again, we encounter the inescapable connection between gesture, speech, and affect. I have already discussed how this functions in the context of *Vocal Action* with regard to the implementation of image as a method of directing resonator activation in and by the actor. Advanced practitioners of the exercise move beyond the "one resonator at a time rule" to an exploration of more or less freely flowing associations. The "river of sound" opens up into a steady flow of action, guided by the voice as it moves through and from the body in space. Given the physical, dynamic, spatial, and temporal components of the exercise, it is understandably difficult to explain via the written word exactly how this all transpires in the realm of actual studio work. That being said, I will provide a short description to help clarify the elements currently under examination.

As I mentioned earlier, *Vocal Action* begins with the actor walking slowly through space while activating the river of sound. In actors new to the exercise, the attention is directed toward the movement of the sound to and through the various resonators, one at a time. As the doer gains proficiency and comfort, however, what begins as slow walking gradually transforms into full-body engagement. The center of gravity is generally lowered, the arms are raised to an actively ready state, somewhere midway between limp and tense, and the directional flow and placement of the resonators is "opened up," so that the voice can travel in a way undirected by conscious control. The engagement of the whole body brought about by the lowering of the center and activation of the arms serves to jump-start the flow of impulses to the body, as it were. The unrestricted, but still somewhat controlled, movement of the body parts (the limbs do not flail but are permitted to follow where the impulse leads) has the effect of freeing the vibration as it travels through the body, and the freedom of the voice activates the physical imagination (which, in turn, stimulates new movements of the body in space, which leads to activation of different resonators, etc.—the process is autopoietic, in this regard). Sometimes, the actions of the body can be pantomimic, as the actor imagines the surrounding space and exists inside it, in relation to it. Other times, the body seems to move entirely of its own accord. Sometimes this results from the imagery at play in the conscious mind of the actor, and other times it is truly "out of control," responding to the flow of unconscious associations unleashed by the process, which builds in intensity both over the course of a single work session and according to the degree of experience the doer has gained over many sessions of exploration. In all cases, though, the rhythmic, melodic, and spatial components of the voice are never disconnected from the gestures being produced as part of the vocalizing process. Both voice and gesture are unified by their connection to and reliance upon the "inner life" of the embodied mind of the actor, hence the reason behind naming the exercise *Vocal Action*.

As Perlman and Gibbs make clear, "speech and gesture are integrated together as they manifest from the same simulative processes," not to mention that "the embodied representations that arise during these simulative processes are profoundly multimodal."[79] It is even well established that there is a demonstrable connection between the activation of the various parts of the body and the processes of mental simulation and prosody. Perlman and Gibbs point to the connection between gesture and the types of image-schematic mechanisms mentioned in Chapter 1 of this book. "Various concepts," they state, "such as those related to speed, manner of movement, size, and verticality, are spontaneously embodied in the movements of our hands and also in the movements of our vocal tract, and indeed, in the right context, body parts ranging across much of our anatomy."[80] Experiments by Zhaojun Yang and Srikanth Narayanan investigating the relationship between the body and gesture have also revealed that a "tight coupling between speech and lower-body motion, as well as their significant inter-emotion difference, suggest the possibility of synthesizing emotional lower-body gesture driven by speech."[81] This may shed some light on why it is that engaging the lower body in *Vocal Action* has the effect of stimulating associative flow in the body-mind of the actor. What is more, as linguist Dan Loehr points out, "Many parts of the body take part in the relationship with prosody, including the hands, arms, head, torso, legs, eyebrows, eyelids, and other facial muscles. . . . Speech is a fundamentally embodied phenomenon."[82] The relationship between voice quality and gesture is impossible to ignore, once one begins to look in that direction.

Indeed, the turn toward the body in linguistics is crucial to understanding the processes taking place in the course of speech. As noted at the beginning of this chapter, the colloquial understanding of speech, both in the theatre and in everyday life, treats it as if it is a disembodied something, acting in the world as an ethereal carrier of abstract meaning between minds designed to receive and decode sonic vibrations into sense. This view is, of course, nonsense. Part of the reason it has been so slow to be replaced relates directly to the complexity of gesture production and its inherently idiosyncratic composition. Perlman and Gibbs explain the lag in gesture theory as follows:

> Language, through the imaginative processes of simulation, is deeply grounded in movement and the senses, which form the basis for the construction of linguistic meaning. Yet, ironically, as evidence has accumulated for this view on language, empirical research on gesture has been slow to adopt a distinctly simulation perspective, despite its intuitive appeal. One reason for this imbalance may be found in the asymmetry between different approaches to studying meaning in language compared to gesture. While language researchers interested in meaning have tended to focus on comprehension, gesture researchers have tended to pay more attention to production, which does not so easily lend itself to the traditional dependent measure used to examine the online processes involved in meaningful communication.[83]

The focus on communication here is essential. Let us also recall that it was not until McNeill's research in 1992 that the difficult-to-notate function of gesticulation, rather than the more conventionalized forms of gesture, such as emblem and sign language, received any substantial theoretical attention.

The Embodied Voice and Sociality

McNeill ushered in a "new framework," in the words of Perlman, that posits gesture and language on a continuum between the "idiosyncratic, iconic, and analog," not to mention ungovernable by syntactic rules or semiotic components, on one side, and the "conventional system of discrete, arbitrary forms that are strung together by the phonological and syntactic rules" on the other.[84] Likewise, the current trend in language research shifts the focus from the insubstantial and the individual to the physical and the social. The point of bringing the subject of gesture into a chapter on voice is that voice simply never exists on its own, regardless of how commonly it is seen as some sort of disembodied force, rather than a physical process of the whole body. As I stated at the outset of this chapter, voice must be retheorized as a component of embodiment, and so any analysis of voice or vocal training needs to be grounded in an understanding of voice as an embodied process. It follows that any formulation of voice must also be conceived of in its relationship to a community of speaking and gesturing bodies, engaging in a complex array of interactive practices of sociality, language, and other practices that rely on the relational generation of shared meaning and experience.

To this end, I should note that the simulation being discussed earlier is taking place not only in the body of the speaker but also in that of the listener, as well. It is essential to our understanding of how gesture functions in relation to speech that we acknowledge the degree to which communication is inherently social. As Marghetis and Bergen observe, "meaning-making is seldom solitary, and the prototypical linguistic encounter involves multiple interacting agents working together to negotiate shared meaning."[85] The notion that language is fundamentally a social phenomenon is not new; however, recent research in the field of linguistics encourages us not simply to see how language has evolved as a way for humans to interact but, rather, to formulate speech as a mode of thinking-together-in-action, bodily and neurologically.

Perlman and Gibbs make a clear connection between the online simulations that occur during the act of speech and the fact of deep linguistic sociality: "One implication of this work is that people do not just access passively encoded conceptual metaphors from long-term memory during online metaphor understanding, but perform online simulations of what these actions may be like to create detailed understandings of speakers' metaphorical messages."[86] The process of mental simulation takes place, as I have already noted, in both the speaker and the listener. Going a step further, they explain that "one's ability to interpret both speech and gesture as being specifically meaningful in context includes partly simulating what others must be doing by their use of speech gesture," and that "considerable evidence shows that perception of phonemes is accomplished not simply by analysis of physical acoustic patterns but through their articulatory events, such as movements of whelp, tongue, and so on. People hear speech sounds by imagining producing the stimuli they hear."[87] On this view, it can be said that people speak in order to listen, and they simulate the actions contained in the gestures and the prosodic meaning of the speaker's language in order to understand what is being communicated, all within a particular social, cultural, and locational context.

In support of this view of interactive mental simulation, Loehr refers to the early work of psychologist William Condon and his research into the "rhythmic relation between gesture and prosody." He states that Condon noticed a "wavelike" pattern of connection between gesture and small segments of speech, following changes of prosodic quality. "The relationship of gesture and speech Condon termed *self-synchrony*," Loehr explains, "and he suspected it was due to a common neurological basis of both. In addition, Condon also made the 'surprising and unexpected observation that [. . .] the listener moves in synchrony with the speaker's speech almost as well as the speaker does.' Condon termed this *interactional synchrony*, and noticed it in infants as young as 20 minutes old."[88] Expanding upon Condon's discoveries in the 1970s, Loehr demonstrates in his own experiments on interactional synchrony "a rich rhythmic relationship among the hands, legs, head, and voice." He even notes that "eye blinks also took part in interactional synchrony, as listeners blinked in rhythm with the speaker's speech."[89] The research points clearly to the fact that speech is embodied and interactive and simulative. The listener and the speaker dance together through language.

Linguists Anders R. Hougaard and Gitte Rasmussen have developed a system whereby we can fully implement an understanding of the deep ways in which bodies act together to communicate in socially determined contexts. They have developed what they call the "Fused Bodies approach to sense-making in social interaction."[90] Hougaard and Rasmussen take the notion of interactional synchrony and combine it with the type of situational linguistics promoted by researchers such as Jürgen Streeck. "Streeck," explains Müller, "conceives of the meaning of gestures in terms of particular situational settings, e.g. 'gesture ecologies.'"[91] These two combined approaches, in conversation with a number of other emergent theories in the field, lead Hougaard and Rasmussen to the assertion that "all our knowledge as individuals is not individual but acquired in and through social interaction with and about the world we are a part of. . . . Thus, cognition is social and so is the human mind."[92] The notion that cognition and the human mind are irreducibly social takes the idea of mental simulation a crucial step further. "Social interaction," they say, "fuses bodies—in time and space and through sound, vision, coordination, touch, smell, temperature, and more—and through this fusion social interaction becomes possible and sociality becomes a fundamental fact of our lives."[93] They explain further that "the Fused Bodies approach . . . understands social actions as being inherently social and cognitive, or rather socio-cognitive. . . . Social actions carry out understanding."[94]

The formulation of their proposal as a project with a brand name may raise some suspicion concerning the purity of their scientific motives; however, style of academic presentation aside, their approach makes good sense, and it helps us to understand with even more clarity what exactly is happening between and among bodies as they participate in what Wittgenstein would call "language games" (see Chapter 1). The Fused Bodies approach proposed by Hougaard and Rasmussen "follows a more recent line of research which embeds language as an integral part of the embodied, interactional making of sense.... 'Language' itself, its production and understanding, is a visible bodily doing on a par with gaze, gesture, head movements and movements of parts of the face (e.g., eye brows), body posture, object manipulation, and non-verbal sounds."[95] The Fused Bodies approach allows us to see all of the various components of gesture, prosody, and speech as they function with and among each other in the real context of social interaction in time and space.

Until now, I have attended to the variants of *Vocal Action* that can be done by a single actor, alone in the space. Of course, given what I am currently discussing, I need to acknowledge that even a person speaking alone in a room is engaging in a practice that is never limited to a single body moving in empty space. All aspects of voice and gesture emerge out of life-long encounters and are shaped by the interactive social environment in which they emerge. That being said, there is a version of the *Vocal Action* exercise that makes use of a partner, and now that I have begun my discussion of simulation and interactional synchrony, I am in a better position to examine what is operating inside of it.

In this form of the exercise, two participants are involved. One actor is the *vocalizer* and the other is the *responder*. Before getting started, the responder stands in front of the vocalizer but faces away, so that the vocalizer is looking at the responder's back. The responder's role is to move in reaction to the river of sound produced by the vocalizer. When the vocalizer begins to phonate, the responder's task is to move with as little thinking and hesitation as possible, without looking directly at the vocalizer. The vocalizer, to begin, is generally encouraged to keep the sounds fairly simple and constant, avoiding fast or erratic changes of volume, pitch, or resonation, in order to form an initial "connection" with the responder. Once the responder is reacting without too much interference, the vocalizer mentally chooses an action that the responder should be led to perform and uses the river of sound to bring about the desired result. For instance, the vocalizer might wish for the responder to jump up and down and over the course of vocalizing can explore different options, until the responder does, in fact, jump up and down. I recall one session, for example, when the vocalizer, without even so much as a moment of visual contact between the two, managed to get the responder to cross to the far corner of the room and climb up on the radiator. During another session the responder managed to fulfill the task of the vocalizer by picking up an eraser from a chalkboard that was in the room.

When looking at the vocalizer, one sees a very active body, exerting extreme effort in conjunction with the voice. It is as if the prosodic elements of voice are being distilled and channeled through the gestural channels of the body and flung toward the responder. The body of the responder is also fully engaged, as it prepares itself to be ready to react to the nonverbal indications of the vocalizer. Exactly by what means this exercise functions is unresolved. One explanation is that a system of common signals is developed in a very short amount of time between the two participants. In the beginning moments of the exercise, the elements are developed, tested, and agreed upon, and once that happens, the rest is easily enough accomplished. In other words, it is very likely that, on some level at least, in those first moments, the vocalizer and responder come to some sort of agreement that high pitches mean "move up," low pitches mean "move down," loud means "go forward," soft means "move backward," and so on. Even if the mechanism were that simple, it would still reveal the impressive degree to which we are primed to react to the prosodic elements of voice, completely absent the significance of the propositional word. Feyereisen speaks about this very thing when he says that "the knowledge that the speakers can assume in their partners plays an important role in the use of gestures."[96]

One gets the sense, however, while watching and/or doing this version of *Vocal Action* that something more is at play. Drawing from the subject of the previous section, I can postulate that the responder is engaged in an act of simulation during this exercise, and because this is taking place in a theatre studio, rather than in an everyday situation, the degree of permissible gestural engagement is much greater. Those traces of invisible simulation that take place during normal listening are allowed and encouraged to expand. If this is so, then it is also true that the exercise is helping to develop the capacity of interactional synchrony, not to mention the ability of the vocalizer to fine tune the prosodic and gestural components of speech through a focused session of trial and error through a vocal signal and feedback response loop. It is also the case, however, that not everyone is as adept at decoding and responding to prosodic cues as everyone else. As evidenced earlier by the experiments that observed a connection between music training and prosodic ability, receptivity to prosody, and in this case prosody in conjunction with gesture, is a skill that can be developed. On a crucial level, this is one important aspect of what this version of *Vocal Action* accomplishes. It is important to remember that, even when one is not engaged in the vocalizer/responder dyad of this version of the exercise, all of the elements of simulation, interactional synchrony, prosodic attunement, gestural relation to vocal intention, etc., are still active in the vocalizing subject, both during the exercise, onstage, and to a lesser degree, even in everyday life.

Of crucial significance is the fact that these gestural processes exist as part of the language game of the everyday. In the theatre these practices, which have been developed mostly unconsciously over the course of a lifetime, must be drawn upon and recreated, assembled into new forms to serve the fictive realities of particular stages at particular times in particular places. They must be crafted through improvisation and rehearsal into final, repeatable forms that are able to communicate the intentions of the scene, meaningfully and artfully. Onstage, gestures cannot be arbitrary. They must be chosen, and even if the actor is not thinking about these choices, the director is ultimately using the gestures as material, often in direct relation to textual meaning, depending on the style of performance. If a moment onstage is not working, for example, the director will work with the actor, making adjustments to the combination of voice and gesture as needed until an acceptable solution is found. As I have repeated throughout this study, theatrical convention will ultimately guide the final forms of these creations, but regardless of style, the actor's task always requires a mobilization of real bodies in active relation to fictive circumstances. Even the "Invisible Theatre" of Augusto Boal, for example, in which the audience may never even realize that they have witnessed a performance, requires actors to find a way to speak and gesture that fits the conventions of the form and makes it possible for the desired content to be presented believably and effectively to the unsuspecting audience.

Vocal Action is only one tool out of many at the disposal of actors to aid them in their preparation to accomplish this difficult task; training schools make use of a countless variety of exercises that explore bodily processes of vocalization. All speech onstage (even if there is no actual "stage") is comprised of voices, and each of those voices is unique to each actor, containing qualities that set it apart from every other voice on the planet. We have seen that the qualities that make this uniqueness possible are fully embodied. The prosodic elements of voice live in, through, and among bodies, just as the gestural components do. All actors have one primary tool, namely their bodies, which is also the medium of their craft, and these actual bodies are inseparable from the actual lives they lead. Streeck defines "craft" as "a set of physical skills acquired by individuals over a lifetime, involving routines, devices, methods, and standards that are shared with others at the same time as they are inalienable properties of the individual bodies that have acquired them."[97] This formulation nicely summarizes the approach to the craft of acting put forth in this book, and it applies equally well to the way *Vocal Action* acts as an accomplice to actors developing the craft of their embodied voices.

Theatre theorist Erika Fischer-Lichte, whose work appears alongside many of the linguists and psychologists in the volumes cited in this chapter, provides a useful way for us to make a connection between Streeck's way of thinking and the theatre:

> Actors usually have to undergo some training in order to acquire body techniques different from those they employ in everyday life. On the basis of the *habitus* they acquired within a particular culture they have to adopt a new one, which depends on specific aesthetic norms, rules, or simply preferences. It is meant to enable the actor to represent different dramatic characters—or, as in the Italian commedia dell'arte, the Japanese Noh or the Indian Kathakali—one particular type. . . . Unlike the learning processes in which children acquire body techniques that might be typical of their culture, and also unlike the life-long learning processes undergone by actors in particular traditional theater forms, workshop training will not result in the shaping of a particular *habitus*. It will lead to different results for each participant depending on their expectations or the kind and number of other workshops they attended before.[98]

I would add to this that the results also depend upon the rigor of the workshop training encountered by the participant. Nevertheless, Fischer-Lichte calls for a high degree of cultural specificity as we formulate our theories about actors, regarding both their lives and the theatrical forms with which they engage.

Theatre as a Site of Engagement

In theorizing the voice it is of the utmost importance, as I have emphasized, to keep in mind constantly the various forces that are always at play. We are never dealing with bodies "in general." All bodies are bodies that were born and have grown up at a specific time, with unique inborn traits and abilities, under the influence of the various social forces with which they have learned to interact in particular ways. Streeck talks eloquently about the importance of understanding bodies as always enculturated. "Practice theorists," he notes,

> insist on the culturally constituted character of the body and its experiences in the world: it is the real body with its culturally specific sensibilities and skills that our conceptual systems draw upon . . . not the products of our anatomical bodies, but of our concrete *dwelling* in the world, that is, the habitual experiences and skills that living bodies acquire in their daily immersion in a specific, culturally shaped world.[99]

He adds that "human hands are *enculturated hands*. But the practice of gesturing also enculturates them."[100] This way of thinking helps us see clearly how the body is actively engaged in meaning-making; in fact, it is not only involved in the process, but it is itself the very medium of the process. For Streeck, "understanding, thus, does not come from shared rules of grammar or a shared lexicon, but rather from sufficiently shared practices."[101]

As we consider the questions at the heart of this book, we always need to remind ourselves not to fall into the unwitting trap of universalization. When theorizing speech and gesture, for instance, we have seen how a tradition of conceiving of voices and minds as disembodied, individual, and asocial can lead to a theoretical slippage of an extremely unfortunate kind. As cognitive scientists Elena Cuffari and Thomas Jensen warn, "when 'embodied experience' is undertheorized and left to its own conceptual devices, implicit folk ideas about what a body is take hold. . . . Actual living bodies, with their idiosyncrasies, in their historical, geographical, social-cultural performances, communicating and communing, are lost; only mysteries about intentions and others [sic] minds remain."[102] Such unstable theoretical formulations undermine not only our efforts to frame language according to its interactional qualities, but it also run the risk of decomposing human bodies into something biologically generic and devoid of social influence.

Of course, the approach presented throughout this book could not be further from that notion. The difficulty of maintaining theoretical rigor on these matters is no easy task, especially since I am talking about bodies, and these bodies often have certain physical characteristics that they seem to share in common. Cuffari and Jensen understand this bind well and offer the following way of thinking, perhaps as a means to smooth the apparent friction between the old notions that have taken hold in the folk and the new revelations of contemporary research. "We are not denying that human bodies in general share physical processes and features of universal character," they explain. "Instead, we are arguing that when academics theorize about embodiment they tend to use an idealization, a standard—an implicit mental image or representation, if you will—of 'the human body,' rather than real bodies. In this way the notion of embodiment is often undetermined and can wind up being reductive, even if unintentionally so."[103]

With this in mind, I would like to call upon a helpful term coined by linguist Ron Scollon: "sites of engagement." Scollon's term elegantly takes into account the various elements of sociality, context, and temporal flow that are always active, not only in everyday situations of intersubjective communication but also onstage. It acts as a shorthand that allows us to remember, at each instance of its use, the various elements involved in the scenic moment without running the risk of calcification that can easily accompany the static analyses of living processes. According to linguist Sigrid Norris,

> Scollon theorised that an action occurs at a site of engagement, which is the window opened up by the social actor(s) and the mediational means when an action is being performed. A site of engagement is not a place, but does include a spatial element; it is not a time, but does include a temporal element as well; it is not the cultural tools, but does include the particularities of cultural tools that are being used; it is not the social actors, but includes the psychological and physical makeup of the social actors performing the action. A site of engagement emphasises the one-time occurrence of actions and thus moves opposite to any possibility of reification.[104]

In a perfect world, we would not need such a term. We could simply refer to bodies and events with the implicit understanding that they must be considered together with the various aspects of situatedness, enculturation, and difference that are part and parcel of their very existence. However, until such time, perhaps we might make use of terms such as "sites of engagement" to remind ourselves that these forces are always importantly at play and must be considered if we are to avoid the detrimental effects of outmoded ways of thinking about bodies.

Concluding Thoughts

Throughout this chapter I have endeavored to present a clear picture of both the elements of the *Vocal Action* exercise and also the ways in which it functions to build the components of technique necessary for the development of the actor's voice in performance practice. Although I spend quite a bit of time writing about "the body" and "the voice," I hope to have made clear that, as I stated in the Overview, I am more concerned with the abilities of the bodies in question than with the biophysical structures that allow for the development of such techniques. Along with researchers such as Cuffari and Jensen, I am optimistic about the prospect of a shift away from reductive approaches toward enculturated bodies in scientifically rigorous academic disciplines. They are happy to report that "two developing paradigms in cognitive science—distributed cognition and enactive cognition—begin from this new starting place, thus offering avenues to re-thinking the role of 'embodiment' in language, communication, thinking, and meaning."[105] They predict, in fact, that "the unit of analysis in cognitive science may shift from the body, and its EC, as a well-defined isolated phenomenon, to the inter-relation between bodies and environmental structures that make up an extended ecology."[106] In line with this theoretical orientation, I have aimed in this chapter to piece together a way of approaching voice and speech in the theatre that takes into account the complex of forces acting in, upon, and between actors as they engage in their craft. It is my hope that, by considering the *Vocal Action* exercise, we can begin to see how speech functions in tandem with gesture to form language writ large, and furthermore, how actors must function if they are going to be able to achieve fluency in their craft, or using Wittgenstein's phrase, to learn "how to go on" in the very particular *site of engagement* that we call theatre.

Afterthinking

Introduction

I began this book with the intentionally open-ended pronouncement that acting is a mysterious craft. In my opinion, the biggest danger for any systematic analysis of acting is that it lead to a reification of theatrical practice. This is not to say that nothing good will come of rigorous theoretical explorations of praxis; on the contrary, I would hope that I have not wasted my time in doing just that. However, the impulse to engage in this investigation springs from my ongoing personal fascination with the ineffability of the theatrical experience, and in some very real way, I believe this quality to be irreducible. In other words, no matter how much I dissect it or put it under the scientific or philosophical microscope, live theatre will always remain bewildering and magical at its core. I will never entirely apprehend it in the same way that I can never really say that I will fully understand life itself. I would consider it a failing on my part, therefore, if the reader were to come away from this with the sense that I have somehow diminished the work of the actor by laying it bare on the page. My own assessment of this exegesis of practice is that it has not closed off but rather opened up avenues of thinking about the art form, which can only be fully explored if one starts with the presupposition that the actor's craft is always dynamic and relational, and in its very essence, deeply enigmatic.

Each of the preceding chapters centers on an investigation of one particular exercise, with its own set of defining characteristics, taken from my experience working in the training studio over the course of my theatrical career. With each exercise I choose to focus on one particular set of theoretical explorations, always remembering that the exercises are designed to serve many pedagogical objectives, not solely the ones that I isolate in my analyses. In Chapter 1 I present the *plastiques* and center my analysis primarily on the concept of action, which is at both the etymological and practical root of acting. In Chapter 2 I look at *The 3 Layers* exercise, basing my discussion around the ways in which perception and proprioception function inside the actor's craft. In Chapter 3 I enter the realm of voice with the *Vocal Action* exercise, examining the relationship between voice,

voice quality, prosody, and gesture in the actor's approach to creating meaningful and evocative theatrical experiences. Throughout all of this I attempt, first, to present the exercises in a way that would make sense even to someone who has never experienced anything like them and, second, to peel back the layers of the work, one at a time, to reveal what is going on inside and underneath the formal components of the embodied structures. As I reiterate many times over the course of this book, in order to understand the tools, we have to be able to envision their application in the context of the larger craft, and at the same time, the big picture of theatre as an art form can be brought into focus by detailed study of the minutiae of technique.

Of course, however much one grounds an exploration in the details of a starting point, there are always going to be elements that one misses as the perspective widens into the larger field. Not everything will fit into the flow of articulation, and some questions will tempt from the periphery but will ultimately remain unaddressed, because attending to them would take us too far afield to be productive within the limits of the current undertaking. For instance, I speak frequently about *emotion* and its relation to voice and to acting in general, but what exactly is emotion? I also employ the term "imagination" fairly liberally throughout the book, but again, what precisely do I mean by it? The philosophical literature in each of these areas is vast, and the history is long, and there is very little agreement on how each term should be understood and defined. For this reason I tend to rely on the colloquial usage of these terms, rather than turning my attention toward a prolonged attempt at providing the final word on the subject. However, it would be beneficial at least to provide some indication of how some of the recent thinking about emotion and imagination factors into, and can even help to clarify, the considerations of actor training with which I have been engaging here. I would like to use this concluding section to touch upon these points, to examine in a bit more detail some potential limitations of my approach, and also to raise some questions for future exploration.

An Enactive Theory of Emotion

Emotion is generally considered to be a central component of the theatrical experience across genres, for the actor and also for the audience. Especially in the realm of contemporary realism, the degree to which the actor seems to embody a believable and apparently "complete" emotional life is considered by many to be the sign by which a successful role can be measured. Beyond the famous paradox, elucidated by Diderot and a host of other theorists of theatre (which I will not tackle here anymore than I have already), that the actor can simultaneously possess and be possessed by the emotional life of the character, we are still left with the question of what emotion actually is, and further, how it figures into the ways in which actors approach their craft.[1] That emotions rise and fall in actors as they engage with the various exercises I have described seems obvious. Sometimes they know exactly why they are experiencing certain emotions, and sometimes the emotion overtakes them in inexplicable ways, at times quite powerfully, and at other times more subtly. Can we be more precise, though, in this observation?

As I point out in my discussion of Joseph Roach's *The Player's Passion*, the history of theorizing emotion in the actor's craft is as long as history itself. Roach discusses emotion, or *pathos*, as it appears in the ancient texts of Quintillian, and before that, he says, the term was "worn threadbare by Aristotle, Horace and Cicero."[2] In fact, the word "emotion" does not enter common usage until the mid-sixteenth century, but even then, as Roach points out, emotion is conceived of as a system of bodily fluids that literally *moves through* (*emovere*) the body, resulting in the activation of certain moods and feelings.[3] According to Ruth Padel, in her groundbreaking study of embodied mind in fifth-century BCE Greece, the innards, or *splanchna*, made up of the actual non-metaphoric heart (*kardia* or *kēr* or *ētor*, depending on gender and usage), liver (*hēpar*), and the less easily identifiable *thumos* (sometimes translated as "spirit"), were the determining agents of consciousness and affect.[4] In general, throughout the majority of history, emotions are seen more as bodily substances and their effects than as the psychological forces they are formulated as today. Even in the contemporary field of affect studies, there is serious disagreement not only as to how emotion, affect, and feelings are to be defined but also regarding the disciplinary lens through which they are to be analyzed.[5] How, then, can we theorize emotion in a way that takes into account the contemporary scientific considerations and claims of embodiment I take pains to elaborate in this book?

The theory of emotion proposed by philosopher Jesse Prinz in his book *Gut Feelings* is particularly appealing as I put together a picture of the actor's work that takes into account the research and perspectives I rely upon in this text. Prinz grounds his "perceptual theory of emotion" in the work of pragmatist philosopher William James and Danish physician Carl Lange, who in the late nineteenth century famously proposed that physiological activity was the instigator of and precursor to emotion, rather than the reverse, which was commonly understood to be the case at the time. Prinz combines this "somatic feeling theory" with a theory put forth by contemporary neuroscientist, Antonio Damasio, who expands the notion of physiological activity to include both chemical and hormonal changes in the body and also neurological changes in the brain.[6] Prinz's theory, which is at once simple and radical, is not only that emotions track "how we are faring in the world" but also that "emotions are perceptions, and they are used to perceive our relationship to the world."[7]

Rather than conceiving of emotions as precursors to bodily activity, he sees them as resulting from changes in the body that are reactions to "core relational themes," which help us to situate ourselves as we move through our environment. "A core relational theme," he explains, "is a relation that pertains to well-being."[8] The core relational theme of "facing an immediate, concrete, and overwhelming physical danger," for example, gives rise to fright, whereas the core relational theme of "making reasonable progress toward the realization of a goal" connects to the emotion of happiness. According to Prinz, core relational themes "capture the basic situations that emotions are designed to discriminate."[9] When one is confronted by a poisonous snake or a barking dog, for example, one's bodily processes change quite immediately and dramatically, and this change registers as an emotional experience. The same applies to seeing a friend or a loved one, or to encountering something literally or metaphorically indigestible, or even to seeing something that is difficult to identify for whatever reason. The body undergoes an immediate series of reactions in relation to the various stimuli, and the resulting experience is called emotion. If nothing changes, there is no emotion.

Formulating emotion as perception is highly appropriate to the philosophical principles supported by the research I present here, especially with regard to the earlier conversation in Chapter 2 regarding enactive perception and its application to the work of the actor. If emotion is the perceptual modality by which one senses and evaluates how one is faring in the world, and if perception is co-constitutive of action, then it would seem to follow logically that emotion is also co-constitutive of action. Prinz does not take this extra step (and even views enactivism with a certain amount of contempt), but he does clearly note the strong connection between emotion and action, arguing that emotions "instigate the search for appropriate actions. They beg for action without demanding it. . . . They are . . . perceptions of the body's preparation for action."[10] He adds that they "goad us to select a response that is appropriate for perpetuating or ending the situations that induce them. The link between emotion and action is thus strong but indirect. Emotions compel us to act, but they are not action tendencies" (in that, "at this point in processing, no action has been selected, no strategy has been determined, no plan has been conceived").[11] For Prinz, emotions point the way toward action but need not result in that action being committed in order to fulfill their role as evaluators of core relational themes.

For my part, I suggest that an enactivist approach would release Prinz from the trap of "the dichotomy between input and output systems" in which he finds himself.[12] Noë claims that vision is co-constitutive with action, as is hearing, smell, and touch, smell, and taste as well. Adding emotion to this process of acting in the world not only creates no philosophical problem, but it also reinforces Prinz's notion that emotion participates in action. Prinz supports a view of emotion that functions according to the following process: the world changes; it is input perceptually; then the body undergoes changes, which register as emotion; the concomitant action in the world is the output; and so on in a continuous and overlapping cyclical flow. This input/output view can productively be superseded by the more processual and interactionist model held up by enactivism. People know how to see because they have seen in action, and they know how to feel for the same reason. They feel their way through the world, and their bodily reactions are not *to* the world but *with* the world as it is being made with their *feeling through* it. If we accept that, to employ Noë's formulation, "perception and perceptual consciousness are types of thoughtful, knowledgeable activity," then emotion, as formulated by Prinz, is part of our action in the world in much the same way that any perceptual modality is.[13] Emotion, then, is just another form of "sensorimotor know-how."

I note frequently that actors develop the ability to mobilize behaviors for the fictive stage environment based on those that they have learned for application in everyday life. Actors create a performative body schema for the stage; they expand the breadth and sensitivity of voice to allow new voice qualities and formant frequency assemblages to enter into existence for the stage; and they open channels of gesture based upon interactive synchrony and simulation that correspond to the fictive environment of the stage. In these ways the body is engaged in a series of actions and perceptions that function to create a believable scenic presence appropriate to the stylistic conventions in a given theatrical circumstance. Among these actions and perceptions, we can include emotion, which, instead of evaluating the real-world scenarios and relationships of everyday life, is responding primarily to imaginary scenarios and relationships. These fictive circumstances achieve a level of reality through the full-body engagements of action and perception just mentioned. The essential practical component of emotion in the theatre, of course, is not whether or not a particular emotion is being felt by an actor, but whether or not the physical presence of the actor is able to convey to and arouse in the audience a particular emotion. The particularities of how, precisely, this is accomplished vary according to style and formal convention, but the ability to play effectively in this way relies first and foremost upon the actor's ability to act and perceive, as I have already discussed.

One way that the audience perceives the emotionality of an actor is by perceiving the alterations of their physiognomy in the process of their own experiencing of a particular emotion, or at least the stylized semblance of that emotion. As cognitive neuroscientists Marco Tamietto and Beatrice de Gelder observe, the perception of emotion in another is a complex process, made up more of nonconscious reception and processing than conscious, and that emotional information is received from a variety of stimuli. In fact, they report that "recent findings suggest that not just a person's face but their whole body posture can trigger non-conscious perception of the person's emotions in an observer."[14] Elsewhere, de Gelder partners with Jean Vroomen to show the connection between these emotional signs and tone of voice, noting that, in one experiment, "identification of the emotion in the face is biased in the direction of the simultaneously presented tone of voice."[15] Furthermore, the audience relies upon the complex of voice and gesture, which includes all the various elements of prosody discussed in Chapter 3, acting in relation to the meaning of the words being spoken and in relation to the unfolding plot of the drama.

Emotion in the theatre, just as all of the other elements of action and perception I have discussed, is part and parcel of the shared know-how of a particular community of bodies participating in an ecology. Viewing emotion in this way helps us to understand that, far from being a mercurial and invisible substance that acts at the whim of unpredictable and uncontrollable forces, it is actually just as connected to the body (and to bodies) as voice—another invisible component of the actor's craft, also frequently misunderstood to be a disembodied substance. When we take a moment to look more closely, we see that emotion, like voice, seems to be embodied through and through, and even though there is still a great deal of debate on the subject, theorizing it in this manner enables us to come a step closer to understanding its place in the theatre and its utility in the toolkit of the actor.[16]

Imagination as an Embodied Process

I just now mentioned in passing that emotion onstage exists in relation to "imaginary scenarios and relationships," but what does that mean? What is imagination? Is it a mental picture, as Hume would have it, or should we think of imagination along the lines of Kant's formulation of it as a power of contemplation freed from the material constraints of the real perceptual world?[17] Is imagination like perception, like seeing in the mind? Is it more related to belief, or perhaps to desire? Perhaps imagination is, as Ryle asserts, pretending?[18] When actors working the *plastiques*, for example, experience what we call "associations," is that imagination? And if they seem to have them, but they are not connected with an image in the mind, then what are they? Motor imaginings? And are they called upon or do they just happen, and why? On top of that, there also seems to be a strong connection between imagination and emotion. There are many views on these questions, and while it would be unrealistic to expect a simple answer to these questions to materialize at this point in my discussion, it would be helpful as we think about what the actor does in the studio to have a better sense of what we might mean when we talk casually about imagination. It will have one implication for how we understand the actor's process if we accept the view that imagination is perception-like and another if we understand it to be more connected to, say, a desire or a belief, or to pretense, for that matter. The more clarity we can gain in theory, the more effective can be the exercise as it is approached by both actor and teacher. A clearer view of imagination and how it functions may also shed some light upon the experience of the audience and how it relates to the imaginary circumstances of the fictive world encountered in the theatrical setting.

Not only are the accepted views regarding imagination far from settled, it is also the case that philosophical approaches to imagination are often somewhat inapplicable to our experience of it in everyday life, to say nothing of their relevance to the practical realm of the theatre. As Gregory Currie and Ian Ravenscroft point out, "philosophers have made ambitious claims for the imagination. Hume used it to account for our belief in enduring objects; for Kant it explained how we unite concepts with sensory experience. These claims take us a long way from imagination as understood by the rest of us."[19] However, to arrive at a working understanding of imagination, it can be useful to approach the concept through philosophy and to see which views can be made to line up with the known practical elements of theatrical craft.

Once again, as with the subject of emotion, there is a strong argument to be made for the rootedness of imagination in embodied experience. In *Imagining Bodies* James B. Steeves presents a compelling argument for the grounding of imagination in the body by calling upon the philosophy of Merleau-Ponty, whose work not only has been experiencing a resurgence of late but was also instrumental to the feminist theory of Elizabeth Grosz and other theatre theorists of the body in the 1990s, as I discuss in the Overview. In fact, many of the thinkers referred to in this book can trace significant aspects of their theories back to his phenomenological innovations. Steeves shows how for Merleau-Ponty the perceiving body is formulated not as a "passive agent that receives sense data," as "the traditional theory of perception treats the body," but as an active participant in the environment in which it exists, along the lines of enactivists such as Noë, whose work builds very directly upon Merleau-Ponty's.[20] With regard to the question of imagination, the body, as an active agent in the world, has the capacity not only to sense itself from the inside through the proprioceptive functioning of the body schema but also to sense itself as a "virtual body," which can run through a series of potential courses of action as it navigates and responds to the environment. These courses of action consist not only in what might be called "motor functions" but also in the intricate network of perceptions with which the subject engages with and in the world. The body schema works together with the virtual body to form what Steeves calls the "imagining body" in the following manner:

> The body schema and the virtual body actually exist as two poles of a dialectic in which old habits are developed to meet new situations and general bodily structures are applied to consciously, or unconsciously, chosen projects.... They do remain grounded in the world and open to new possibilities, and the body schema and the virtual body as two poles of a dialectic constitute what might be called the imagining body. Two examples of the imaginative capacity of the body, or the imagining body, are the experiences of the body as an image in the mind and as a vehicle for expressive behavior.[21]

Of course, I am concerned here primarily with this latter case—the imagining body as a vehicle for expressive behavior.

In working with the *plastiques*, for instance, the imagination seems to function in predominantly two modes. The first is often referred to as activating "the mind's eye," whereby it is as if there is an overlay between the actual surroundings of the studio and the visual (or recalled) world invented by the actor. The second, the experiencing of "associations," which I have already discussed, is generally not comprised of an assemblage of visual details, as in a film, but rather as something less perceptually discernible and more like a stirring of only just barely conscious sensations that arise through the activation of the actions and perceptions of the body at work in the course of the exercise.

The appearance of these two modes varies from moment to moment and from actor to actor. Some actors are very "visual" and seem to get lost in the imagined reality that comes to surround them, while others often do not have a clear picture of where they are, but it is as if the processes of the body are no longer under the influence of the actual surroundings but are actively engaged with some other present but invisible environment and set of influencing circumstances.

According to the view of Merleau-Ponty put forth by Steeves, the notion of imagination being like a picture in the head is not supportable. While it may ultimately seem to the actor that "fanciful images," as Steeves calls them, are being formed in and by "the mind's eye," it is actually the functioning of the virtual body as a whole that allows for the possibility of the imagining body to come into being, and this body gains its ability to imagine in the same ways that the actual body is able to perceive, namely through an interactive relationship with environment, the content of which appears in the doing or living of the moment. "It will no longer suffice," says Steeves,

> to describe the fanciful image as being a quasi percept or picture, or to describe the imagination as a quasi perception. Both fancy and perception involve different ways of the body's making space, along a continuum of possibilities of embodiment.... While not being bound to actual experience, fanciful thinking is still bound to the virtual body and its relation to reality, providing the imaginer with the basic orientation and roundedness that are necessary for experiencing an alternative world.[22]

Part of this "basic orientation" concerns the space that is being made by the actor's embodied interaction with the environment, and so faculties of proprioception and the body schema, which are developed through exercises like the *plastiques*, can be said to participate in concert with the virtual body toward the activation of fanciful images.

Associations seem to be different, though. They appear not so much as fanciful images but, rather, as something decidedly less visual in nature. Even so, the view of imagination as an embodied process supports both modes of actor imagination. Steeves clarifies how the virtual body is always acting in relation to the environment to varying degrees as part of one's being-in-the-world. "The context of the perceptual scene," he explains, "or the lifeworld as Merleau-Ponty likes to describe it, is interpreted by the perceiver as offering virtual modes of embodiment."[23] It is as if the phenomenal world exists as an affordance, available for use, and it is partly through the activity of the virtual body that it is navigated and, ultimately, brought into being as phenomenological experience. He goes on to clarify, using the theatrical motif to which he consistently returns throughout the entirety of his text, that

> the virtuality of perception, however, resembles the virtuality of the body because the virtual qualities implied by the actually perceived quality are also modes of virtual embodiment. . . . Just as the actor engages in a virtual body to explore the world of the fictional character, so the perceiver must engage with the virtual modes of embodiment implied by the receding qualities to perceive the focused quality as an instance of a particular structure. Thus to perceive is to engage with virtual qualities that are essentially virtual modes of embodiment.[24]

According to this view, perception is seen as a "creative activity" in which the various qualities of the world come into focus and recede, and so the line between imagination and perception is blurred, supporting the notion that all imagination, regardless of whether it seems more or less visual or associative, is grounded in the embodied processes of creative perception.

Approaching the subject from a different direction, Currie and Ravenscroft theorize what they call the "recreative imagination," a view that ultimately argues for conceiving of the imagination as mimetic, in the sense of Elin Diamond's feminist interpretation of the term as generative and transformative, "tak[ing] the relation to the real as productive, not referential, geared to change, not to reproducing the same."[25] Starting with "what we take to be the obvious function of the imagination: enabling us to project ourselves into another situation and to see, or think about, the world from another perspective," Currie and Ravenscroft offer a systematic critique of the various ways imagination can be theorized.[26] They explain that

> imaginative projection involves the capacity to have, and in good measure to control the having of, states that are not perceptions or beliefs or decisions or experiences of movements of one's own body, but which are in various ways like those states—like them in ways that enable the states possessed through imagination to mimic and, relative to certain purposes, to substitute for perceptions, beliefs, decisions, and experiences of movements. These are what we are calling states of recreative imagination.[27]

While their view, on the whole, is less committed to embodiment than Steeves's, they do spend a good deal of time discerning the phenomenon of motor imagery, whereby the body itself has the capacity for recreative imagination on its own terms. Just as perceptual imagination is creatively mimetic with regard to actual perceptions, motor imagination functions in a similar way with regard to motor functions. Referring to a chronometric study in which the timing of actual hand movements is compared with that of imagined hand movements, Currie and Ravenscroft show that, when it comes to basic movements, there is almost no difference between the internal bodily factors that constrain the two. It is significant that "the discrepancy between real and imagined performance times is significant only for awkward movement," which for them makes sense, since more complex bodily movements can be expected to rely on a series of sensory (mainly visual, in this case) and proprioceptive feedback during action.[28] It should be noted, however, that they ultimately argue that, even though the *contents* of motor images are movements of the body, their relationship to recreative imagination functions on the level of perception.

To explain it another way, Currie and Ravenscroft propose that "motor imagery is imagined perception of action," a formulation that helps to understand more clearly how it is in practice that actors engage with the dual functions of motor activity and imagination.[29] If we take this view as a given, it means that during the *plastiques* exercise, for example, actors move through the space in conversation with the constantly recreative imaginings of perceptual processes, which, as I have already established, are constitutive of the very action with which they are bound up. The phenomenal overflow engendered by this autopoietic process is in keeping with the observation of Currie and Ravenscroft that "while we claim that motor imagery is the simulation of experience, we don't say that motor imagery is always consciously experienced. Imagery in all its modes can occur, we take it, without being conscious, just as perceptual experience can fail to be conscious."[30] While working the *plastiques*, actors are encouraged to leave open the door to the imagination (what I refer to in Chapter 2 as the fourth layer). This small direction is generally enough to activate a flow of motor imagery in connection with the quick succession of actions necessitated by the exercise. In addition, such recreative imaginings can connect to the actor's emotional life, since as Currie and Ravenscroft note, "in action we try to adjust the boundary between how the world is and how we want it to be; emotions give us a phenomenologically rich picture of how things are at various places on the boundary."[31] The actor's work in the studio takes place precisely along this boundary between the world as it is and as it is not yet, and the emotions experienced in reaction to the "fictional characters and imaginary situations" encountered there arise as actors evaluate with virtual bodies how they are faring in that virtual world.[32]

Some Possible Concerns about This Book

Ethnographic Challenges

I have provided a brief theoretical account of emotion and imagination, again, not in a way that I expect is going to settle any ongoing philosophical disputes about the precise nature of either but in a manner that can provide a bit more grounding in the context of the current investigation. Of course, these two points are by no means the only areas of potential concern one might have with my approach. In addition to these, I am cognizant of quite a few more, including problems that may arise as a result of my ethnographic approach, concerns around specificity versus generality, including the ways in which I refer to types of bodies, trainings, and performance forms, questions of ephemerality and subjectivity that come about in relation to studies of theatrical practice, and considerations of the role the audience plays in performance. I take a moment here to address each of these, beginning with the first, which concerns the methodology I have opted to employ in this analytical project, namely that of an ethnographer of theatrical practice.

Gay McAuley, who has spent her career as an ethnographer of rehearsal practice, and whose work I hold up as an inspiration for my own, points to a number of concerns that have arisen over time in the field of ethnography. For instance, much has been said about the role of participant/observers, who share the same space with the group being studied, but whose function is not as a participant in their culture. Referring to the work of Margaret Mead, McAuley explains that "the experience of ethnography is that the participant/observer in the field has to be both vitally enmeshed in the daily experiences of the people being studied and, at the same time, sufficiently distanced to make observations, write notes about what is occurring and find time to write these up in more detail."[33] Such a presence in any circumstance, not just that of a rehearsal room, is certain to effect the subject of observation. One cannot become truly invisible, and even if the ethnographer limits direct interaction with those observed, even that behavior is relational and is sure to have an impact, perhaps even one that cannot be observed by the ethnographer as it transpires.

In this regard, my role in the research connected to this book is complex. During the moments that I am working directly with actors on the training exercises, my attention is mostly focused on doing and saying whatever might be necessary to aid in a performer's, or group of performers', development of technique. I say "mostly" because there is always a part of my thinking that is attending to the analysis of the exercise as it transpires. Especially, but not only, in the moments that I am not speaking, I frequently find myself thinking about how elements of the exercise might be better understood and explained to the actors, in order that I might be a more effective teacher. In the studio my role as director is always already one of participant/observer: first, as I just described, even while leading an exercise (participant) I am analyzing it (observer); second, I frequently participate as a doer for long stretches (again depending on the nature of the actor or group at work), and so even though I am doing what everyone else is doing, I also narrate as we go, which also necessitates that I will be able to observe the others without it derailing the group flow and in a way that allows me to be reactive in every moment to the various turns the exercise is taking all the time. Even when I am not doing the exercise, and I am directing from the sidelines, my participation in the room is partly as an observer by its very nature.

This combined function of participant and observer is, fortuitously, contained in the role of director, in general. As I just remarked, it is always the case that directors observe. Actors simply take it as a given that the director is going to be watching what they do very closely. This is certainly not to say that this observation has no effect on the actor; on the contrary, it does, and some would claim that the impact of the director's gaze upon the actor is an important and even essential component of the creative process. Whether this is the case or not, the fact remains that my role as director could never be other than participant/observer; the director is always both. It could certainly be argued that my participation in this way should disqualify me from being authorized to analyze the event, and I would be open to such a critique, if the event I were analyzing were the dynamic of the room or the cultural forces and power dynamics of the ensemble itself, which is precisely what McAuley is documenting and analyzing in her own work. However, the object of my study is not the system as it figures into the culture as a whole but, rather, the processes at play inside of the exercises and the work of the actors in using the tools of training in order to develop technique, which is exactly what I am attending to in my role as director, anyway, regardless of whether I choose to write about it later or not. An "outside" observer would certainly have a different vantage point and would perhaps "see things that familiarity has rendered unremarkable to the insider," as McAuley observes, but this does not render my position as "insider" invalid.[34]

Epistemological Uncertainty

This question of ethnography brings up a deeper potential cause for concern, which resides on the epistemological level. While I have, over the years, taken copious notes on my experiences as a leader of these exercises, both during sessions and in moments of reflection afterward, the reader will observe that I have not included any of them in this text. My "field notes," as it were, are conspicuously absent, which could give rise to suspicions of, at worst, fraudulence and, at best, overgeneralization. Of course, even if I were to include quotations from my notebooks, there would be no way for anyone to verify their veracity, short of gaining access to the filing cabinet where I keep them, and even then, the observations inscribed in those pages are a far cry from being acceptable evidence of anything other than the fact that I wrote them. In other words, inclusion of my field notes would be proof of nothing and would lend no more weight to my assertions than they hold in the absence of notes. What we are left with is closer to the sort of anecdotal evidence that comprises oral history than to the experimentally based data that might support a sound qualitative analysis.

Can my research be duplicated? Can it be proven? Can it even truly be called research at all? I believe that the answer to all of these questions is yes. In order to determine repeatability, I propose that we would first need to clarify what it is that we might expect to be repeated. Surely, since I am talking about human action and behavior, there is no hope of any aspect of that being repeated without at least some variation. I have already spoken about this regarding performance, particularly in reference to vocal production, and it applies to all aspects of the actor's work. One might base the claim of repeatability on the degree of effectiveness of the exercises. This would perhaps mean that those who practiced them will have, over time, reached a certain high level of performance ability. The trouble with this approach should be obvious, in that there is no way of gauging the degree of a performer's ability on any objective level, and even subjective evaluation would not yield anything close to a result that would be verifiable or even acceptable. All that one needs to do is read a handful of reviews written by a randomly selected assortment of professional critics to see that there can be no grounds for agreement on the matter of a performer's ability.

What we can do, however, is look at those elements of craft that the exercises are designed to develop and see if a case can be made for them as effective tools toward those ends. For example, as I have already established, *Vocal Action* is partly designed to develop the actor's capacities for resonance. It is clear to me that, in this regard, the exercise does what it is supposed to do. After actors work with *Vocal Action* for some time, it is readily apparent that their voices acquire a vibrational depth and breadth well beyond what was present prior to encountering the exercise. The same can be said of the actor's ability to run quickly through the space in silence and without bumping into other actors, which, as I mentioned, usually occurs after prolonged work on *The 3 Layers* exercise. Again, these abilities, which I believe have proven to be repeatably gained in many instances over many years, are not the ultimate aim of the exercises. Rather, they are small components of craft that come together to form the overall technique of the performer. Together, the exercises develop skills that actors need to possess somehow if they are going to be able to perform according to the conventions of a given theatrical form.

The research that takes place in the theatre laboratory is in my view just as valid epistemologically as psychological experiments, such as the "inverting glasses" experiments, in which a person's vision is upended by wearing a pair of goggles that turn the visual world upside down. Through these experiments we can learn from subjects' behavior and self-reporting how, after experiencing a "partial disruption of seeing itself," the wearers' sense of upright vision returns to them; from this, psychological and philosophical inferences can follow.[35] Similarly, in my own research, I fashion my analyses both by observing the behavior of the doers and by listening to their own self-reporting as they learn, all the while engaging with my own cumulative embodied history with the exercises. Acting exercises are living practices guided toward repeated effects, rather than forms that are simply or mechanically repeated. They must alter and develop according to an ever-changing network of pedagogical circumstances, but this should not disqualify them as a basis for knowledge; on the contrary, the liveness of the search is a sign of its ultimate legitimacy.

Other Limitations

Part of the challenge, and the excitement, of engaging with the type of exercises I present here is precisely that they cannot be formally or dogmatically repeated if they are to be effective. Just as we can say that each person's voice is unique, it is also true that all actors are working with a set of tools and abilities completely peculiar to them. This is as true for differing heights and weights as it is for all of the various levels of ability and disability that may exist in an actor. While it may seem at certain points in my presentation of these exercises that they assume a base level of ability on the part of the actor-in-training, this is simply not the case. Each one of these exercises, as I have been stressing, is designed to work in active relation to a given set of individual needs, limitations, desires, etc. Sometimes, an exercise will need to be reoriented in reaction to an actor's inability to turn his or her head sideways, for instance, while walking in a circle, and sometimes, it will need to accommodate an actor who cannot walk at all. I recall working with an actor over a period of many months, for example, who had badly injured his back and so could not move around with the other actors during *The 3 Layers*. My solution in this case was to ask him to sit on a chair, at a different location each session, and to participate in the exercise as well as he could while seated. By evaluating the experience of the actor through observation and through conversation after the training sessions, we worked together to recalibrate the exercise for him over time, and in the end, the fundamental component of perceptual engagement with the changing space was well worked. It became apparent that even though he could not move through the space, the fact that the other actors were moving around him created a space that was always in a state of change. In addition, he was able to focus on what I now might characterize as the functioning of his virtual body and its relationship to both immobility and the changing environment.

The concern about whether these methods are appropriate for different bodies is connected to the question of their applicability to various forms of performance. It is certainly true that these exercises emerge from the Grotowski lineage of laboratory theatre, and that even if they are used in the service of mainstream forms of contemporary psychological realism, they still represent a very particular type of actor training. They seem to have very little in common, for example, with Meisner technique or Strasberg's "Method," but I maintain that these differences are superficial. I am not making a claim that they are designed to do the same things; rather, I am saying that the fact that they are designed to develop technique for application in particular forms of theatre unites them in the same camp. Acting exercises are meant to be effective, and that means that if they are to remain pertinent, they must work toward an actor's ability to create a role in accordance with a given style's demands. In this way, even the exercises of Kathakali that develop a young actor's ability to form the hand gestures, or *mudras*, can be compared to the famous Meisner repetition exercise. Each one makes it possible for the performer to communicate the essentials demanded by the craft. One can learn as much about the necessities inherent to the performance form of Kathakali by studying *mudra* exercises as one can learn about realism by analyzing the component parts of the Meisner exercise.[36]

A key difference between these two training exercises is the context in which they are learned. Erika Fischer-Lichte's distinction between the training required by traditional theatre forms versus what she calls "workshop training," which I speak about in Chapter 3, emphasizes that of the two, only the former will have the capacity to form a new *habitus* on the part of the performer. One very real limitation of workshop training is the short amount of time actors spend on any one aspect of training. This is, of course, another potential objection to the work I am presenting in this study. The training model I discuss in relation to my own work both privileges and is privileged by an abundance of space and time. It can certainly be argued that it is simply not possible to affect the kind of bodily change I am talking about here in the scant amount of time actors generally are able to spend on training at large, much less rehearsing for a particular show.

It is true that actor training in earnest frequently ends when school does, and that short workshops here and there cannot provide the in-depth development that a conservatory MFA program can, for example. Again, while I concede that this is true, I also affirm once again that the exercises discussed in this book are designed to take all of the various experiential and practical obstacles and limitations into account. Of course, just as practicing piano for one hour every week will not do much to turn a novice into an expert, training for the theatre takes time and effort. Without it, aspiring actors are left to rely upon the abilities they have already developed, one way or another. However, it is possible to concentrate the work on these exercises in beneficial ways. A savvy teacher can work with a student for a relatively short amount of time, and if the exercise is distilled and applied correctly, it can be made to develop at least some portion of technique.

One final point I feel the need to address here is the question of audience bodies and their involvement in the theatrical experience, not just as interpreters or observers, but also as participants. As I explain in the section on listening in Chapter 3, the prosodic components of voice are psychological characteristics located in the listener. I have also spoken a great deal about the necessity of seeing individual bodies always in relation to others, and instead of perpetuating the philosophically outmoded concept of the discreet subject, I have consistently argued for formulations that posit ecologies of bodies in meaningful relation to and communication with each other. In this book I have drawn the line, for the most part, between the stage and the audience; however, it must be noted that this is an artificial line, and I readily admit that it is not a helpful one. The field of reception theory has provided theatre theorists with a fertile field of inquiry, taking the role of spectator not as an extraneous component of the theatrical experience but, rather, as an integral part of it. Without the audience there could not be theatre. It is also true that the work of the actor, which is the focus of my project, cannot be fully theorized without taking into account the active role that the audience plays in it. I have, at times, referred to the audience, especially with regard to the actor's process of "doing for" and embodying meaning through image schemas. However, it would be fruitful for future inquiry to analyze in a more focused way how the audience participates through embodiment in the creative act itself, especially given my insistence upon the enactive relationship of perceiving bodies and their role in bringing worlds, both real and imaginary, into being.[37]

Escaping the Dualistic Language Trap

There are also a number of considerations regarding my project overall that, rather than giving rise to concern, raise the prospect of new areas of exploration and discovery. One of the most important ramifications of the analyses presented in this book pertains to the language used in relation to both the exercises themselves and to the work of the actor more generally. Throughout, I have attempted to make a strong case for an approach grounded in the programmatic assumptions of EC. This means that, at a bare minimum, we should conceive of actors not as dualistic beings, made up of bodies that act and minds that process meaning, but rather as body-minds whose cognitive and performative abilities are inextricably bound up with a fully embodied interaction with the environment. As difficult as it is to theorize these questions of language use clearly on paper, it is even harder to break free from the habitual use of outmoded language to talk about the actor's instrument in the practical space of the studio.

In my recent work I have been trying to implement new verbal formulations that stay true to this way of thinking without slippage back to the words and phrases commonly used both in general colloquial settings and in the actor-training process. For example, when leading *The 3 Layers* exercise through verbal narration, I try to link up the actors' movement through the space with the attentional focus on the perceptions of the first layer. I also attempt to emphasize the connection between changes in first layer perceptual focus and the bodily adjustments that occur as part of the second layer, always stressing that these layers are part of a whole experience and cannot be separated out completely. I speak of the connection between the movement of the eyes, for example, and how that affects changes to the overall network of joints in the body from the head all the way down to the feet, as I describe in Chapter 2. On the whole, the effort is to ingrain in the actor an experiential understanding of embodiment.

The problem is not that we use the word "mind" when describing cognition and those processes associated with it. The problem is that, when we say "mind," we generally tend to think of some abstract processing system that operates on a separate level of activity from that of the body. We tend to think that consciousness is connected to the function of the mind, when, in fact, consciousness and mind are fully embodied processes, as I have attempted to show in various ways. Using the word "mind" to speak about propositional thinking and calculations, or even to talk about the imagination, is not entirely inaccurate, as long as we are clear that this "mind" is necessarily embodied. However, the meaning of the word is so entrenched in dualistic models that special attention must be paid to clarify for the actor, both directly and subliminally, that we are working with a new model of thinking-in-action.

The implementation of new work terminology can help with this project. For starters, it would be compelling and productive to offer classes called "action" and "embodiment" in actor-training programs, rather than relying on outmoded course titles like "movement" or "voice" or "character." Also, Scollon's term "site of engagement" could be productively used when speaking to actors about where they are working, as I discuss at the end of Chapter 3. Instead of referring to the actors' bodies, we can use the term "body-mind" in its place, as in "you are a body-mind walking through the space; pay attention to the way you are interacting with the details of this particular site of engagement, made up of the walls, the bodies, this moment in time," or even more simply and loosely, "as you move your hand through the space, feel how your thoughts and your actions are inseparable; use your movements to see the space into being." Of course, using new verbal formulations can feel strange, and even a bit forced, at first, but after some time and some explanation as to why these particular terms are being consciously chosen to replace the old words, their usage will eventually come more naturally. After all, if we can expect to see changes in the ways in which actors move, speak, and activate their various associative faculties through repeated practice in their training overall, there is no reason to think that actors cannot become proficient at using a few newly coined terms of art. If the theoretical rationale for these attempts is grounded in solid understanding, the necessity for the use of new terms will constantly make itself obvious; furthermore, the artistic realm of the theatre studio allows for the sort of fanciful, imagistic, poetic, and playful language that other areas, including academic writing, do not. I readily admit that a complete replacement of terms in our culture is not likely to happen anytime soon. However, one of the great potentialities of theatre has always been the way it allows us to bring into material existence new ways of being, even if the theatre turns out to be one of the few places where such dreams might become real.

The Proficiency Model: Real-life Benefits of Actor Training

Throughout this book I have repeatedly spoken about the reliance of theatrical techniques on their connection to everyday life. In addition to the notion that behaviors onstage reflect analogous daily behaviors on the level of social significance and image-schematic meaning, this interconnection also results from the fact that the actor's instrument is the body. If this body is developed in a certain way for the stage, and if we are claiming that all processes, including "mental" ones, are material and embodied, then there is no way to say that these changes will not carry over into the everyday life of the actor. To see the truth in this, all we need to do is call to mind the very basic example of an actor training for a performance in a way that causes the body to grow muscular, for the purpose of playing a particular character or simply as a byproduct of achieving some other demanding training objectives. It is a simple matter to see that those muscles will be there when the actor goes home at night after rehearsal; the body of the actor is the body of the person, and the same goes for the various embodied faculties to which we have been referring here. At the same time, it should be noted that the performative body schema, which determines actors' relationships to the bodies of their characters, for instance, is able to lie dormant until called upon for use in the performance setting. If this were not the case, actors would have no way of preventing one character's body schema from getting mixed up with that of an entirely separate role, which is patently not the way things work.

By looking at the ways the development of theatrical technique effects the everyday, some new areas of consideration open up to us. I remember one day, for example, walking down the street, and because my mind was occupied by these sorts of thoughts, I became aware that both my visual perception and my proprioceptive reactions were operating in a very different way from the people I was passing on the sidewalk. As a result of my own training, my eyes were moving around quite a bit, from the faces of the oncoming pedestrians to the buildings across the street, even to the sky that is often completely ignored by busy city-dwellers. Of course, I do not claim the ability to read minds, but it isn't difficult to see where the eyes of others are looking, how much tension another body is holding in its neck and shoulders, how repetitious or varied a person's gait is, and so on. My own body was reactive to these stimuli, and there was a host of perceptions going on without my awareness, even after having become aware of more sensory activity than usual. In daily life, such an active array of perceptions is unnecessary. It would mostly be a distraction and result in nothing short of confusion. Actors, however, need to learn to live in excess; first, because their life experience is the stuff of their own creative raw material, and the fuller it is, the more effectively it can contribute to the creative act; and second, because in order to be compelling onstage, the actor must be dynamic—larger-than-life, as it were. As I was walking down the street, I was still perceiving the world incompletely and virtually, to use Noë's terminology, but I was undoubtedly perceiving quantitatively more and qualitatively better than I would have been able to had I never engaged in actor-training exercises like (but certainly not limited to) *The 3 Layers*. I could see more, hear more, feel more, and smell more because I was *doing* more, and because I *knew how* to do more.

Often, neurophilosophers tend to rely on what I call the *deficiency* model of analysis, in which conditions such as optic ataxia, visual agnosia, numbsense, and phantom limbs are used to show how the inability of an organism to function "normally" might reveal the sine qua non of perception and consciousness. The idea runs basically as follows: subject X suffers from numbsense and so cannot feel her body, although if she is touched, she can reach for the exact place she has been touched.[38] The fact that she can react with motor precision to touch with a deficiency of feeling may indicate that motor activity does not rely upon feeling, or it may indicate that feeling (or at least the particular type of feeling that connects to motor activity) does not require conscious awareness of its existence in order to function in cooperation with motor activity. This basic approach allows philosophers and scientists to prove the independence of two or more systems or functions that had previously perhaps been considered to be interdependent. In the example just presented, the systems of tactile awareness and motor activity can be shown to be independent, while tactile processing can be separated out from tactile awareness. Following the deficiency model it is theoretically possible to arrive at an understanding of the basic, minimum components necessary for a particular experience, or what I have referred to as "the minimal supervenience base" of perceptual experience.[39]

While this methodology continues to prove extremely useful toward developing new understandings of the ways in which bodies function, it seems to me that by itself it does not allow for a thorough consideration of the larger picture of human experience and functioning. For instance, the enactive view asserts not just that perception is determined by what we *do* but that it is determined by what we *know how* to do. The early years of habituation are intensely packed full of trial and error and vast amounts of learning, and few will argue that once something is learned, there is hardly any necessity to learn it over and over again. At the most, one might argue that there is some energy required to *maintain* knowledge, but that amount of energy is a far cry from what it would take to relearn constantly. The enactivist could easily claim that in later life there is little need to be as flexible or malleable as in early life, so it would stand to reason that a subject who has, say, lost an arm in an accident would suffer a period of shock and rehabilitation, in which a difficult period of relearning would need to occur. How all of this might relate to the complicated experience of phantom limbs is, at best, exceedingly difficult to ascertain, but the point is that the know-how acquired over the course of training, both in life and in the studio, comes to define who we are and how the world is for us. Our capacities to do things are just as important to consider as our incapacities.

By no means is it my aim here to dispute theories based on the deficiency model, but I would like to propose another avenue of exploration, using what can be called the *proficiency* model. For example, one could transform a deficiency case into one of proficiency by focusing on the ways in which a patient who has experienced an accident learns a new way of acting in the world in order to bypass the debilitating effects of an injury. Another less clinical example would be someone learning a musical instrument. One could observe in such a person the actions taken to manipulate the instrument physically—fingers for the piano keyboard, fingers and mouth for a woodwind, arms and legs for a drum kit, etc.—and could track the development of cross-modal interaction, as the sounds would feed back and alter the subsequent actions of music-making. If we were to take the actor in the training studio as an example, we would have to consider, at a minimum, all the various areas of technique development which I have discussed over the course of this book and observe what they might tell us about the latent potentialities that exist inside the faculties in question.

One of the reasons I find the enactive view so compelling is because it seems to reflect accurately the way I experience the world. Even when faced with the overload of stimuli and physical tasks presented to the actor in the training studio, the system of action-based perception functions. As a matter of fact, it appears to function better the more it is challenged. In the theatre laboratory we can see the process of learning, of acquiring know-how, occur in already "fully-developed" human subjects. It is always tempting to turn to the deficiency model because it leads us toward an understanding of the minimal conditions necessary for a particular experience to exist, but the minimal condition represents only one end of the experiential spectrum. To gain a more robust picture of how humans experience the world, we need to look also to the other end of the spectrum, toward the maximal conditions of perceptual proficiency. As I have mentioned already, in everyday life we generally feel the need to economize our actions in order to bear up under the inexorable routines of the day-to-day, and there is usually no reason to keep developing our perceptual abilities past a certain point. But to use this configuration of human experience as our only starting point is a faulty premise, especially once we see what is possible for perception as it operates toward its maximum potential. If nothing else, observing proficiency scenarios allows us to understand how, in regular daily life, we function at a level far removed from what is possible.

There are many ways in which proficiency is experienced in the context of actor-training exercises, and because of the fact that the actor's body is the person's body, the crossover of these abilities into daily life is worth noting. In addition to noting how well-developed faculties of perception and proprioception carry over into the day-to-day lives of actors, I could also point to all of the various ways actors learn in the studio to be in relation to other bodies. These exercises, because of the ways in which they work bodily interactivity as a focus of craft, develop a whole set of abilities connected to interpersonal relationships. Not only does the ability to move gracefully and meaningfully in reaction to the movement of other bodies affect how we feel and communicate in a wide array of social settings, but also our receptivity to gesture and the prosodic components of voice enables us to function at a higher level of comprehension and sensitivity as we go about our daily activities. In the Introduction to Acting classes that I have taught, I consistently heard from my students at the end of the semester that the sense of freedom and power (physical, vocal, and social) that they developed over the course of engaging with the training exercises had already improved their confidence level in everyday social situations. Similar side effects of actor training include the ability to trust one's partners, to listen well, to initiate and maintain eye contact without a feeling of awkwardness, to focus one's attention on the present time and place without a wandering mind, and to have a general feeling of physical well-being, to name just a few.

I want to conclude by admitting that there is something about all this that makes me somewhat uncomfortable. There seems to be something like a latent, or perhaps not so latent, elitism contained in this notion of the proficiency model used in relation to actor-training techniques. It could be interpreted to imply that "normal" people are just dullards and automata and that actors are akin to superheroes of the senses. While this is absolutely not the claim I am making in this study, there does seem to be a grain of truth to the notion that consistent training along these lines offers a unique, heightened experience for the doer. Perhaps this is one reason why it is so appealing to particular (types of) people. There certainly seems to be an attraction, bordering on addiction, wherein once one has a taste of the experience both of the heightened perception elicited by these training methods, and also of being onstage, one does not wish to return to the more subdued perceptual interactivity of quotidian life. This might go some distance to explain why it is that actors pursue their craft even to the overwhelming detriment of their financial well-being. It seems to me an unavoidable fact that the development of perceptual action ability leads to a richer experience of everyday life, even if that richness in some turns out to be more of a curse than a blessing.

Concluding Thoughts

This concluding section has been focused on issues that arose in the course of the deeper analytical work done in the main chapters but, for one reason or another, were not able to be addressed or developed further at the time. As I noted at the beginning of this chapter, the flow of analysis does not allow for all evidence in support of a developing argument to be present at every moment. As the text unfurls, so does the clarity of the investigation, and this applies to the entirety of this book. I began Chapter 1 by looking at the *plastiques* exercise, learning through a "thick description" of its use in the theatre studio how one might come to understand action in the theatrical context. From there, in Chapter 2, I entered into a detailed analysis of *The 3 Layers* exercise, examining the concepts of perception and proprioception through the lens of EC philosophers and related thinkers. In Chapter 3 I mobilized a thorough analysis of speech and gesture in order to shed light on the *Vocal Action* exercise. Each of these chapters contains conceptual formulations that can (and should, I think) be productively applied to the content in the other chapters as part of the overarching inquiry of the book, namely that examining the work of the actor through the various views developed by EC and connected fields can yield a rich understanding of the actor's craft and how to theorize it as a fully embodied process of interaction with the environment. To this end it would have been helpful, for instance, to have already acquired an understanding of how *enactivism* functions in relation to the actor-in-training before attempting to discuss action, and it would have been useful to have clarified the distinction between the various types of gestures and signs elucidated by Kendon's Continuum prior to addressing the inner workings of intention. Clarifying the concepts of imagination and emotion at the end of the study helps in retrospect, but it would have been preferable for these areas to have been at least somewhat elucidated beforehand. Of course, this would be an entirely unreasonable expectation. The very nature of philosophically oriented analyses such as the one presented here is that they build understanding from one moment to the next. One assertion leads to a new question, which can be answered by the next assertion, and so on. Similar to the process of rehearsing a play, whereby the performance that is ultimately produced is a living assemblage and record of the bodies that have been laboring throughout the process, this text stands as a record of labor—the labor of writing and my work in the studio for decades on end. According to this model of perpetual progress, there can be no true sense of completion. I can only hope that this book, if nothing else, might provide an opening for further investigation into how explorations of actor-training techniques can lead to deeper understandings of human experience, both in theory and in practice.

Notes

Overview

1 Joseph Roach, *The Player's Passion: Studies in the Science of Acting* (Ann Arbor: The University of Michigan, 2011), 39.
2 Ibid., 225.
3 Simon Shepherd, *Theatre, Body and Pleasure* (London; New York: Routledge, 2006), 1.
4 Ibid.
5 Elizabeth Grosz, *Volatile Bodies: Toward a Corporeal Feminism* (Bloomington, IN: Indiana University Press, 1994), x.
6 Ibid., 22.
7 Shepherd, *Theatre, Body and Pleasure*, 2–5.
8 Roach, *Player's Passion*, 11. See also Colette Conroy, *Theatre & the Body* (Basingstoke: Palgrave Macmillan, 2010); Mariam Fraser, *The Body: A Reader* (London: Routledge, 2008); Janet Price and Margrit Shildrick, *Feminist Theory and the Body: A Reader* (New York: Routledge, 1999); Donn Welton, *The Body: Classic and Contemporary Readings* (Malden, MA: Blackwell, 2004).
9 I continue to use the term "Cartesianist" in this text, rather than "Cartesian," because the question of Descartes' actual stance on dualism is actually quite complicated and somewhat unsettled. As philosopher Michael L. Anderson encapsulates nicely, "That Descartes is the thinker most responsible for the theoretical duality of mind and body is one of the things that everybody knows; and like most such common knowledge it is not quite accurate. Descartes' arguments for the separation of body and soul are part of a long legacy of dualistic thinking, in which Plato's discussion of the immateriality of the soul and the Christian metaphysical tradition which adopted and preserved that discussion played a central role. Indeed, Descartes himself always insisted that, although body and soul were conceptually, and therefore *ontologically* distinct, they nevertheless formed an empirical unity. What we *have* inherited from Descartes is a way of thinking about our relation to the world—in particular our *epistemological* relation to the world—which serves to support and strengthen this ontological stance" Michael L.

Anderson, "Embodied Cognition: A Field Guide," *Artificial Intelligence* 149, no. 1 (2003): 92.
10 Lisa Shapiro, *The Correspondence between Princess Elisabeth of Bohemia and René Descartes* (Chicago: University of Chicago Press, 2007).
11 See Mario Bunge, *Matter and Mind: A Philosophical Inquiry* (Dordrecht: Springer Netherlands, 2010); Anthony Dardis, *Mental Causation: The Mind-Body Problem* (New York: Columbia University Press, 2008).
12 See R. Darren Gobert's excellent analysis of Descartes' influence on the theatre R. Darren Gobert, *The Mind-Body Stage: Passion and Interaction in the Cartesian Theater* (Redwood City: Stanford University Press, 2013).
13 Anne L. Fliotsos and Gail S. Medford, *Teaching Theatre Today: Pedagogical Views of Theatre in Higher Education* (New York: Palgrave Macmillan, 2004), 108.
14 Ben Spatz, *What a Body Can Do: Technique as Knowledge, Practice as Research* (London; New York: Routledge, Taylor & Francis Group, 2015), ix.
15 Larry Shapiro, "The Embodied Cognition Research Programme," *Philosophy Compass* 2, no. 2 (2007): 338.
16 Lawrence A. Shapiro, ed., *The Routledge Handbook of Embodied Cognition* (New York: Routledge, Taylor & Francis Group, 2014), 4–5.
17 Margaret Wilson, "Six Views of Embodied Cognition," *Psychonomic Bulletin & Review* 9, no. 4 (2002): 626; Andy Clark, *Being There: Putting Brain, Body, and World Together Again* (Cambridge, MA: MIT Press, 1997), 35.
18 Wilson, "Six Views of Embodied Cognition," 625.
19 Anthony Chemero, *Radical Embodied Cognitive Science* (Cambridge, MA; London: MIT Press, 2009), 29.
20 Ibid., 65.
21 Mark Johnson, *The Meaning of the Body: Aesthetics of Human Understanding* (Chicago: University of Chicago Press, 2007), 113.
22 Ibid., 117.
23 Ibid., 119 (italics in the original).
24 Ibid., 117.
25 Chemero, *Radical Embodied Cognitive Science*, 187; Clark, *Being There*, 149–52.
26 Alva Noë, *Action in Perception* (Cambridge, MA: MIT Press, 2004), 23.
27 Alva Noë, *Varieties of Presence* (Cambridge, MA: Harvard University Press, 2012), 20.
28 Mark Rowlands, *The New Science of the Mind: From Extended Mind to Embodied Phenomenology* (Cambridge, MA: MIT Press, 2010).
29 http://performancephilosophy.ning.com/about (accessed August 27, 2021).
30 John Lutterbie, *Toward a General Theory of Acting: Cognitive Science and Performance* (New York: Palgrave Macmillan, 2011), 13–14.
31 Ibid., 22.
32 Rick Kemp, *Embodied Acting: What Neuroscience Tells Us About Performance* (New York: Routledge, 2012), xv.

33 Ibid., 17–18.
34 Laura Cull Ó Maoilearca and Alice Lagaay, *Encounters in Performance Philosophy* (Germany: Palgrave, 2014), 4.
35 David Krasner and David Z. Saltz, *Staging Philosophy: Intersections of Theater, Performance, and Philosophy* (Ann Arbor: University of Michigan Press, 2006), 8; Cull Ó Maoilearca and Lagaay, *Encounters in Performance Philosophy*, 23.
36 Spatz, *What a Body Can Do*, 1.
37 Ibid., 66.
38 Ibid., 32–3.
39 Konstantin Stanislavski, *An Actor's Work: A Student's Diary*, trans. Jean Benedetti (London; New York: Routledge, 2008), 43–59; Sharon Marie Carnicke, *Stanislavsky in Focus* (London; NY: Routledge, Taylor & Francis Group, 1998), 84.
40 Maurice Merleau-Ponty, *Phenomenology of Perception* (London; New York: Routledge, 2012), 261.
41 Clifford Geertz, *The Interpretation of Cultures Selected Essays* (New York: Basic Books, 1973), 3–30.
42 Ibid., 412–53.
43 Gay McAuley, *Not Magic but Work: An Ethnographic Account of a Rehearsal Process* (Manchester: Manchester University Press, 2015), 9–10.
44 Catherine Malabou, *What Should We Do with Our Brain?* (New York: Fordham University Press, 2008), 32.
45 Brian O'Shaughnessy, "Proprioception and the Body Image," in *The Body and the Self*, ed. José Luis Bermúdez, A. J. Marcel, and Naomi Eilan (Cambridge, MA: MIT Press, 1995), 197.
46 Jody Kreiman and Diana Sidtis, *Foundations of Voice Studies: An Interdisciplinary Approach to Voice Production and Perception* (Malden, MA: Wiley-Blackwell, 2011), 261.

Chapter 1

1 Lisa Wolford and Richard Schechner, *The Grotowski Sourcebook* (London: Routledge, 1997), 37.
2 I cover the subject of gaining expertise in more detail in the following chapter.
3 John Dewey, *Experience and Nature* (New York: Dover Publications, 1958), 338–9.
4 Johnson, *The Meaning of the Body*, 10; Dewey, *Experience and Nature*, 16.
5 Bert O. States, *Great Reckonings in Little Rooms: On the Phenomenology of Theater* (Berkeley, CA: University of California Press, 1985), 46.
6 In addition to States, mentioned earlier, there are a host of other theatre scholars who focus on the analyses of theatrical realities, phenomenological

and otherwise. While I have drawn upon their ideas in the course of developing my thinking in this area, my focus in this chapter's analysis is primarily on understanding the actor's craft as it is developed through the encounter with the *plastiques* exercise. For more detailed accounts of these approaches to how reality appears in the theatre, see Stanton B. Garner, *Bodied Spaces: Phenomenology and Performance in Contemporary Drama* (Ithaca, NY: Cornell University Press, 1994); Daniel Johnston, *Theatre and Phenomenology: Manual Philosophy* (London: Palgrave, 2017); Krasner and Saltz, *Staging Philosophy: Intersections of Theater, Performance, and Philosophy*; Drew Leder, *The Absent Body* (Chicago: University of Chicago Press, 1990); Peggy Phelan, *Unmarked: The Politics of Performance* (London; New York: Routledge, 1993); Alice Rayner, *To Act, to Do, to Perform: Drama and the Phenomenology of Action* (Ann Arbor: University of Michigan Press, 1994); Richard Schechner, *Between Theater and Anthropology* (Philadelphia: University of Pennsylvania Press, 1985); Phillip Zarrilli, "The Actor's Work on Attention, Awareness, and Active Imagination: Between Phenomenology, Cognitive Science, and Practices of Acting," in *Performance and Phenomenology: Traditions and Transformations*, ed. Maaike Bleeker, Jon Foley Sherman, and Eirini Nedelkopoulou (Florence: Taylor and Francis, 2015), 75–96.

7 All parenthetical text references hereafter are to the numbered "remarks" of Ludwig Wittgenstein, *Philosophical Investigations: The English Text of the Third Edition*, ed. G. E. M. Anscombe (Upper Saddle River, NJ: Prentice Hall, 1958).

8 For related explorations of the temporal relationship between thought, will, and action, see Patrick Haggard, "Human Volition: Towards a Neuroscience of Will," *Nature Reviews. Neuroscience* 9, no. 12 (2008): 934–46. The central argument revolves around whether or not volition can be said to be connected to conscious thought, since experimental evidence suggests that in some circumstances, the action centers in the brain activate prior to the activation of the thought. See also Elisabeth Pacherie and Patrick Haggard, *What Are Intentions?* (Oxford: Oxford University Press, 2010). For contemporary thinking on mental causation, or whether or how a mental event can prompt a physical action, see Dardis, *Mental Causation*; Pierre Jacob, "Embodying the Mind by Extending It," *Review of Philosophy and Psychology* 3, no. 1 (2012): 33–51.

9 For a useful taxonomy of intention, see Elisabeth Pacherie, "Towards a Dynamic Theory of Intentions," in *Does Consciousness Cause Behavior?*, ed. Susan Pockett, William P. Banks, and Shaun Gallagher (Cambridge, MA: MIT Press, 2006), 145–67. Note that a distinction is made between the initiation of an action and the process of monitoring and guiding that occurs over the course of the action's life.

10 Wolford and Schechner, *The Grotowski Sourcebook*, 497.

11 Pacherie, "Towards a Dynamic Theory of Intentions," 156.

12 P. M. S. Hacker, *Wittgenstein: Mind and Will* (Oxford, UK; Cambridge, MA: Basil Blackwell, 1996), 542.
13 Johnson, *The Meaning of the Body*, 174.
14 Carnicke, *Stanislavsky in Focus*, 153–6.
15 Eugenio Barba, *Beyond the Floating Islands* (New York: PAJ Publications, 1986); Eugenio Barba and Nicola Savarese, *A Dictionary of Theatre Anthropology: The Secret Art of the Performer* (London: Routledge, 2006).
16 Johnson, both on his own and in his collaborative work with linguist George Lakoff, places a great deal of attention on how our embodied relationship to the world shows up through verbal metaphor. This work is instructive in the current investigation, but it does not require recapitulation here. See George Lakoff and Mark Johnson, *Philosophy in the Flesh: The Embodied Mind and Its Challenge to Western Thought* (New York: Basic Books, 1999); *Metaphors We Live By* (Chicago: University of Chicago Press, 2003).
17 Marcus Perlman and Raymond W. Gibbs, "Sensorimotor Simulation in Speaking, Gesturing, and Understanding," in *Body - Language - Communication: An International Handbook on Multimodality in Human Interaction*, ed. Cornelia Müller, et al. (Berlin; Boston: De Gruyter, 2013), 520; Susan Goldin-Meadow, "How Our Gestures Help Us Learn," ibid., 799.
18 Mark Johnson, *The Body in the Mind: The Bodily Basis of Meaning, Imagination, and Reason* (Chicago: University of Chicago Press, 1987), 73.
19 Ibid., 87.
20 Rudolf Arnheim, *Art and Visual Perception: A Psychology of the Creative Eye* (Berkeley: University of California Press, 1974). Quoted in Johnson, *The Body in the Mind*, 76.
21 Johnson, *The Body in the Mind*, 76.
22 Ibid., 73.
23 Ibid., 85.
24 Wolford and Schechner, *The Grotowski Sourcebook*, 45.
25 For one compelling formulation of this widely theorized notion, see Judith Butler, *Undoing Gender* (New York: Routledge, 2004), 21: "The body has its invariably public dimension; constituted as a social phenomenon in the public sphere, my body is and is not mine."
26 Another instantiation of this can be seen quite easily by comparing "realistic" films from previous decades to those of today. The acting seems less realistic, but really what appears is a denuding of style at the hands of an outmoded underlying image-schematic structure. A similar phenomenon can be observed by comparing "realistic" contemporary styles of acting between different countries. Here, though, it is not time but space that reveals the different set of image-schematic structures at play across cultures.

27 Stephen Wangh, *An Acrobat of the Heart: A Physical Approach to Acting Inspired by the Work of Jerzy Grotowski* (New York: Vintage Books, 2000), 79–84.
28 Maxine Sheets-Johnstone, *The Primacy of Movement: Expanded Second Edition* (Netherlands: John Benjamins, 2011), xxvii.
29 Ibid., xxvii–xxix.
30 Ibid., xxxi–xxxii.
31 Ibid., 331.
32 Ibid., 332.
33 Johnson, *The Body in the Mind*, 74 (italics in the original).
34 Ibid., 82–3.
35 Ibid., 87.
36 James Slowiak and Jairo Cuesta, *Jerzy Grotowski* (London; New York: Routledge, 2007), 93–4.
37 Sheets-Johnstone, *The Primacy of Movement*, 330.
38 Kemp, *Embodied Acting*, xvii.
39 Sheets-Johnstone might note that it is important that these two subjects are of the same species and can thus mutually imagine themselves in the position of the other.
40 Dewey, *Experience and Nature*, 228.
41 Ibid.

Chapter 2

1 Noë, *Action in Perception*, 1.
2 The enactive view has also been formulated and supported by S. L. Hurley, *Consciousness in Action* (Cambridge, MA: Harvard University Press, 1998); J. Kevin O'Regan and Alva Noë, "A Sensorimotor Account of Vision and Visual Consciousness," *Behavioral and Brain Sciences* 24 (2001): 939–73; Alva Noë, "On What We See," *Pacific Philosophical Quarterly* 83 (2002): 57–80; Evan Thompson, "Sensorimotor Subjectivity and the Enactive Approach to Experience," *Phenomenology and the Cognitive Sciences* 4 (2005): 407–27.
3 Noë, *Action in Perception*, 3; Hurley, *Consciousness in Action*, 4.
4 Noë, *Action in Perception*, 3.
5 See Ned Block, "Action in Perception (Book Review)," *The Journal of Philosophy* 102 (2005): 259–72; Frederique de Vignemont, "A Mosquito Bite against the Enactive Approach to Bodily Experiences," ibid. 108 (2011): 188–204.
6 Block, "Action in Perception (Book Review)," 263. Additionally, Block and others hold a perhaps even more fundamental objection to Noë's view that the world is perceived directly, that there is no need to rely on a theory of mental (or neural) representation for bodily experience. Such representationalist philosophers claim,

against Noë's thesis, that there must be some way in which the material world is represented in the mind, and that the body itself must be represented neurologically in the brain itself. The argument, then, is ultimately between those who believe that the minimal supervenience condition for consciousness is in the brain, and those who believe that consciousness arises from an organism's perceptual interaction with the environment in which it is actively embedded.
7   Noë, *Action in Perception*, 77.
8   Ibid., 73.
9   Ibid., 72.
10 Ned Block, "Overflow, Access, and Attention," *Behavioral and Brain Sciences* 30, no. 5–6 (2007): 530–48. In fact, Block proposes in this article that the neural machinery of cognitive access may be entirely separate from that of phenomenal consciousness.
11 Noë, *Action in Perception*, 52. See also Ronald A. Rensink, J. Kevin O'Regan, and James J. Clark, "To See or Not to See: The Need for Attention to Perceive Changes in Scenes," *Psychological Science* 8, no. 5 (1997): 368–73. Another excellent (and highly amusing) instance of this can be found in the well-known "Selective Attention Test" series of Daniel Simons and Christopher Chabris, in which the viewer of a video is asked to pay attention to the movements of a ball being tossed around by participants while a gorilla moves undetected through the space: https://www.youtube.com/watch?v=vJG698U2Mvo (accessed August 28, 2021).
12 Noë, *Action in Perception*, 19.
13 Noë, *Varieties of Presence*, 18–19 (italics in the original).
14 Noë, *Action in Perception*, 51–5.
15 The component of "as if" in the actor's work is extremely important, and the subject of perception cannot be explored fully without taking into account the role of the imagination (see examples of Stanislavsky's "magic if" in Stanislavski, *An Actor's Work*, 43–59; Carnicke, *Stanislavsky in Focus*, 84). It is my contention that imagination performs an important function in our perceptual experience even in everyday life. While I would argue that a complete understanding of perceptual content is not possible without a thoughtful consideration of this point, a full account of the faculty of imagination is unfortunately beyond the scope of this book. I do, however, address aspects of the imagination as it functions in relation to the voice in Chapter 3 and propose some areas for additional exploration in the final chapter.
16 The terms "focused" and "peripheral" are used commonly and colloquially as general descriptors of two kinds of vision. I would like to propose that they might be applicable to other modalities, as well. For example, we could refer to "focused" hearing for, say, hearing a speaker's words or a bird's call clearly, and to "peripheral" hearing for the sound of the traffic out on the street; similarly, for smell. This may not work for taste, but for touch it does, in that we sometimes "feel" things in a focused

way ("I feel this rough leather football") and sometimes "feel" things peripherally ("I can feel my hair brushing against my neck"). For the area of inquiry addressed in the current investigation, I would like to propose that both the focused and peripheral aspects of each modality should be included in the consideration of active perception.

17 O'Shaughnessy, "Proprioception and the Body Image," 197.
18 Ibid., 245–6.
19 Shaun Gallagher, "A Response: Mapping the Prenoetic Dynamics of Performance," in *Theatre, Performance and Cognition: Languages, Bodies and Ecologies*, ed. Rhonda Blair and Amy Cook (London: Bloomsbury Methuen Drama, 2016), 158–63; "Theory, Practice and Performance," *Connection Science* 29, no. 1 (2017): 106–18. (Also, in the same volume, see Rick Kemp, "The Embodied Performance Pedagogy of Jacques Lecoq," ibid.: 94–105.) For recent references to Gallagher's work in the theatrical literature, see O'Shaughnessy, "Proprioception and the Body Image," 175–204; Naomi Rokotnitz, *Trusting Performance: A Cognitive Approach to Embodiment in Drama* (New York: Palgrave Macmillan, 2016); Lutterbie, *Toward a General Theory of Acting*; Evelyn Tribble, *Early Modern Actors and Shakespeare's Theatre: Thinking with the Body* (London: Bloomsbury Arden Shakespeare, 2017); Phillip B. Zarrilli, Jerri Daboo, and Rebecca Loukes, *Acting: Psychophysical Phenomenon and Process* (Basingstoke: Palgrave Macmillan, 2013).
20 Henry Head et al., eds., *Studies in Neurology*, vol. 2 (London: Henry Frowde, 1920). For a review of the conceptual confusion surrounding these terms, see Shaun Gallagher, "Body Image and Body Schema: A Conceptual Clarification," *The Journal of Mind and Behavior* 7, no. 4 (1986): 541–54.
21 Shaun Gallagher, "Body Schema and Intentionality," in *The Body and the Self*, ed. José Luis Bermúdez, A. J. Marcel, and Naomi Eilan (Cambridge, MA: MIT Press, 1995), 229.
22 Ibid., 228–9.
23 Ibid., 230.
24 This is not meant to imply that the exercise requires that the actor be in conscious control of every movement; *awareness of* a function and *control of* a function must be conceived of as two separate processes.
25 For additional perspective on the phenomenology of bodily absence, see Leder, *The Absent Body*.
26 Gallagher, "Body Schema and Intentionality," 237–41.
27 Gabriele Sofia, "The Effect of Theatre Training on Cognitive Functions," in *Affective Performance and Cognitive Science: Body, Brain, and Being*, ed. Nicola Shaughnessy (London: Bloomsbury, 2013), 177 (italics in the original).
28 Ibid., 177.
29 Gallagher, "Body Schema and Intentionality," 239.
30 Ibid., 233.

31 Ibid., 239–40.
32 Franklin C. Shontz, *Perceptual and Cognitive Aspects of Body Experience* (New York: Academic Press, 1969), 162. Quoted in Gallagher, "Body Schema and Intentionality," 239.
33 Maxine Sheets-Johnstone, "What Are We Naming?," in *Body Image and Body Schema: Interdisciplinary Perspectives on the Body*, ed. Helena De Preester and Veroniek Knockaert (Philadelphia: John Benjamins Publishing Company, 2005), 222 (italics in the original).
34 Ibid., 235.
35 Shaun Gallagher, "Dynamic Models of Body Schematic Processes," ibid., 246–7.
36 Against Richard Schechner's formulation of the concept of "restored behavior," in which "the behavior is separate from those who are behaving," and is somehow "'out there,' distant from 'me,'" I argue that the work of the actor must at all times—from training to rehearsal to performance—be viewed as a process that is actually happening in a live material context. Even if some prior behavior pattern or score is being enacted, that enactment is still occurring in the context of a specific time and place, and in that moment there are a host of essential components—contextual, environmental, phenomenological, neurological, etc.—that need to be considered if we are to understand the actor's craft. In this regard, my approach has more in common with that of Peggy Phelan, who claims unambiguously that "performance's only life is in the present." While Phelan focuses largely on the disappearance of and resistance to reproduction of live performance, I focus my attention in this study on an analysis of what is occurring in those (certainly complex) moments before the present becomes past. Schechner, *Between Theater and Anthropology*, 35–7. Peggy Phelan, *Unmarked: The Politics of Performance* (Florence: Taylor and Francis, 2003), 146.
37 W. C. Howell and E. A. Fleishman, eds., *Human Performance and Productivity: Information Processing and Decision Making* (Hillsdale, NJ: Erlbaum, 1982). Cited in Kemp, *Embodied Acting*, note 214.
38 Kemp, *Embodied Acting*, 32.
39 Gallagher, "Theory, Practice and Performance," 110.
40 John Sutton et al., "Applying Intelligence to the Reflexes: Embodied Skills and Habits between Dreyfus and Descartes," *Journal of the British Society for Phenomenology* 42, no. 1 (2011): 78–103; Barbara Gail Montero, "Thinking in the Zone: The Expert Mind in Action," *Southern Journal of Philosophy* 53 (2015): 126–40. In Gallagher, "Theory, Practice and Performance," 110–12.
41 Gallagher, "Theory, Practice and Performance," 113.
42 In her discussion of Stanislavsky's concept of *perezhivanie*, which I look at more closely later, Sharon Carnicke speaks about this "link between creator and art as especially pronounced in acting where the artist is the medium." Quoting Lee

Strasberg's *Encyclopaedia Britannica* entry for Acting, she notes, "'The actor is at once the piano and the pianist.'" Lee Strasberg, "Acting," in *The New Encyclopædia Britannica*, ed. Philip W. Goetz (Chicago: Encyclopædia Britannica, 1974), 59. Quoted in Carnicke, *Stanislavsky in Focus*, 133.

43   The "founding fathers" of deconstruction and postmodernism discuss presence as, respectively, an impossible proximity to "logos" (see Jacques Derrida, *Of Grammatology*, ed. Gayatri Chakravorty Spivak (Baltimore: Johns Hopkins University Press, 2016)) and as the inherent falsity contained in all representation due to the impossibility of "truth" (see Jean-François Lyotard, *The Postmodern Condition: A Report on Knowledge* (Minneapolis: University of Minnesota Press, 1984); Jean Baudrillard, *Simulacra and Simulation* (Ann Arbor: University of Michigan Press, 1994).). In Theatre studies, the concept was taken up in relation to its connection to the theatrical sense of presence by a number of scholars, from Elinor Fuchs in the 1980s (see Elinor Fuchs, "Presence and the Revenge of Writing: Re-Thinking Theatre after Derrida," *Performing Arts Journal* 9, no. 2/3 (1985): 163–73) to Philip Auslander and Bert O. States (see Philip Auslander, "'Just Be Your Self'": Logocentrism and Difference in Performance Theory," in *Acting (Re)Considered: Theories and Practices*, ed. Phillip B. Zarrilli (London; New York: Routledge, 2002), 53–61; Bert O. States, "The Actor's Presence: Three Phenomenal Modes," ibid., 23–39) to, more recently, Erika Fischer-Lichte (see Erika Fischer-Lichte, "Appearing as Embodied Mind - Defining a Weak, a Strong and a Radical Concept of Presence," in *Archaeologies of Presence*, ed. Gabriella Giannachi, Nick Kaye, and Michael Shanks (Florence: Taylor and Francis, 2012), 103–18). These approaches open up theoretical avenues that call into question some fundamental assumptions about embodiment and how actors themselves become representations. While these questions are not entirely disconnected from the current study, I do not intend to explore them at length. I mention them here mainly because the usage of the term "presence" could arouse confusion were these various registers not addressed or clarified.

44   Depending on the context of practice, "soft" focus is sometimes referred to as "general" focus, as mentioned earlier.

45   Noë, *Action in Perception*, 19. For more on the "two visual system hypothesis," see David Milner et al., *The Visual Brain in Action* (Oxford: Oxford University Press, 2006); B. Bridgeman, "Conscious Vs Unconscious Processes: The Case of Vision," *Theory & Psychology* 2, no. 1 (1992): 73–88; Bruce Bridgeman et al., "Processing Spatial Information in the Sensorimotor Branch of the Visual System," *Vision Research* 40, no. 25 (2000): 3539–52.

46   Daniel C. Richardson, Rick Dale, and Michael J. Spivey, "Eye Movements in Language and Cognition: A Brief Introduction," in *Methods in Cognitive Linguistics*, ed. M. Gonzalez-Marquez et al. (Amsterdam, NL: John Benjamins Publishing Company, 2007), 323–44. Quoted in Kemp, *Embodied Acting*, 29–31.

47   Kemp, *Embodied Acting*, 189 (italics in the original).

48 Tamer Soliman and Arthur M. Glenberg, "The Embodiment of Culture," in *The Routledge Handbook of Embodied Cognition*, ed. Lawrence A. Shapiro (New York: Routledge, Taylor & Francis Group, 2014), 207–19.
49 Dale G. Leathers, *Successful Nonverbal Communication: Principles and Applications* (Boston: Allyn and Bacon, 1997). In Kemp, *Embodied Acting*, 27.
50 I explore this concept in greater detail in Chapter 1.
51 Maxine Sheets-Johnstone, *Insides and Outsides: Interdisciplinary Perspectives on Animate Nature* (Luton, Bedfordshire: Andrews UK, 2016), 346.
52 Ibid., 357.
53 Carnicke, *Stanislavsky in Focus*, 139.
54 Ibid., 146–7.
55 Eugenio Barba, *The Paper Canoe: A Guide to Theatre Anthropology* (New York: Routledge, 1995), 15.

Chapter 3

1 Adriana Cavarero, *For More Than One Voice: Toward a Philosophy of Vocal Expression*, ed. Paul A. Kottman (Stanford, CA: Stanford University Press, 2005), 8.
2 Don Ihde, *Listening and Voice: Phenomenologies of Sound* (Albany: State University of New York Press, 2007), 13 (italics in the original).
3 Nina Sun Eidsheim, *Sensing Sound: Singing & Listening as Vibrational Practice* (Durham: Duke University Press, 2015), 626.
4 Andrew M. Kimbrough, *Dramatic Theories of Voice in the Twentieth Century* (Amherst, NY: Cambria Press, 2011), 41.
5 Ben Macpherson and Konstantinos Thomaidis, *Voice Studies: Critical Approaches to Process, Performance and Experience* (London: Routledge, 2015), 4.
6 Flloyd Kennedy, "The Challenge of Theorizing the Voice in Performance," *Modern Drama* 52, no. 4 (2009): 408. See also Patsy Rodenberg, *The Right to Speak: A Journey through the Voice* (London: Routledge, 1992); Kristin Linklater, *Freeing the Natural Voice: Imagery and Art in the Practice of Voice and Language* (Hollywood, CA: Drama Publishers, 2006); Cicely Berry, *Your Voice and How to Use It Successfully* (London: Virgin, 1990). Linklater, partly because of her published body of work, and partly because of her long-held position as Head of Acting of the Graduate Theatre Division of Columbia University (from which she retired in 2013), is probably the single most well-known figure in contemporary voice studies.
7 Kennedy, "The Challenge of Theorizing the Voice in Performance," 408; Joanna Cazden, "Imagery in Voice Therapy: Neurolinguistic Rationales and Clinical

Guidelines" (paper presented at the American Speech-Language Hearing Association, Annual Conference, San Diego, CA, 2005); Linklater, *Freeing the Natural Voice*. Antonio R. Damasio, *Descartes' Error: Emotion, Reason, and the Human Brain* (New York: Penguin Books, 2005); *The Feeling of What Happens: Body and Emotion in the Making of Consciousness* (New York: Harcourt Brace, 1999).

8 Linklater, *Freeing the Natural Voice*, 31.
9 Arthur Lessac, *The Use and Training of the Human Voice: A Bio-Dynamic Approach to Vocal Life* (Mountain View, CA; London: Mayfield Publishing, 1997), 203.
10 Ibid., 1 (italics in the original).
11 Giuliano Campo, *Zygmunt Molik's Voice and Body Work: The Legacy of Jerzy Grotowski* (New York: Routledge, 2010), 5.
12 Ihde, *Listening and Voice*, 13–14.
13 I should note that Grotowski's position in the pantheon of North American voice training, or for that matter, of actor training in general, is as somewhat of an outlier. When his work is approached in an academic training institution, it is often presented under the heading of "Grotowski work," or some such banner that makes it clear that it is not mainstream enough to be subsumed into a general course on basic voice technique, in the way that, say, Linklater or Catherine Fitzmaurice is. I contend, however, based on my successful experiences using these techniques with beginning theatre students, who have little to no experience with acting, that his approach is not incompatible with a general approach to voice training.
14 James Slowiak and Jairo Cuesta, two of Grotowski's primary assistants during his "Objective Drama" period, based at the University of California at Irvine, describe Grotowski's experimentation with sounds from various languages: "He observed that different languages engage different resonators. The high-pitched sound in certain Chinese dialects emanates from the occipital joint in the nape of the neck. Certain Slavic languages use the stomach as a resonator. Germans utilize the teeth." Slowiak and Cuesta, *Jerzy Grotowski*, 148–9. While I have led *Vocal Action* in non-English speaking countries, my primary experience with the exercise has been in Anglophone settings; therefore, while other languages might reveal new aspects of vocal processes to me, I make no claims to that knowledge here.
15 Ibid., 148; Lessac, *The Use and Training of the Human Voice*, 13.
16 Linklater, *Freeing the Natural Voice*, 33–4.
17 Ibid., 34.
18 This is not to be confused with Stephen Wangh's exercise, called "The Plastique River," which he attributes to Grotowski. Wangh, *An Acrobat of the Heart*.
19 Lessac, *The Use and Training of the Human Voice*, 4.
20 Linklater, *Freeing the Natural Voice*, 217.
21 As Flloyd Kennedy notes, "voices are sound waves creating disturbance in the air, unavailable to our sense of sight; it is tautological, then, to describe a voice as 'invisible.'" Kennedy, "The Challenge of Theorizing the Voice in Performance," 407.

22 Kreiman and Sidtis, *Foundations of Voice Studies*, 5.
23 Ibid., 6. I will explain F0 shortly.
24 Ibid.
25 Ibid., 10. See also Marie-Cécile Bertau, "Voice: A Pathway to Consciousness as 'Social Contact to Oneself,'" *Integrative Psychological and Behavioral Science* 42, no. 1 (2008): 92–113.
26 Kreiman and Sidtis, *Foundations of Voice Studies*, 50.
27 Ibid., 58.
28 Ibid., 59.
29 Ibid., 64–5.
30 It is perhaps this dissociation between "sound and sense" that the Dadaists were playing with in their "sound poems." See Steve McCaffery, "Cacophony, Abstraction, and Potentiality: The Fate of the Dada Sound Poem," in *The Sound of Poetry, the Poetry of Sound*, ed. Marjorie Perloff and Craig Douglas Dworkin (Chicago: University of Chicago Press, 2009), 118–28.
31 Linklater, *Freeing the Natural Voice*, 225.
32 Mladen Dolar, "The Linguistics of the Voice," in *The Sound Studies Reader*, ed. Jonathan Sterne (London; New York: Routledge, 2012), 544.
33 Kreiman and Sidtis, *Foundations of Voice Studies*, 261. Linklater "prefer[s] the simplicity of Wikipedia's definition" to that of Kreiman and Sidtis (which she also references) "because it includes the emotional state and intentionality of the speaker." Kristin Linklater, "The Art and Craft of Voice (and Speech) Training," *Journal of Interdisciplinary Voice Studies* 1, no. 1 (2016): 62. I provide it here, in case the reader might also find it helpful: "In linguistics, prosody is concerned with ... linguistic functions such as intonation, tone, stress, and rhythm. ... Prosody may reflect various features of the speaker or the utterance: the emotional state of the speaker; the form of the utterance (statement, question, or command); the presence of irony or sarcasm; emphasis, contrast, and focus. It may otherwise reflect other elements of language that may not be encoded by grammar or by choice of vocabulary." Wikipedia, "Prosody (Linguistics)," *Wikipedia, The Free Encyclopedia*, https://en.wikipedia.org/w/index.php?title=Prosody_(linguistics)&oldid=811178906 (accessed February 26, 2018).
34 Kreiman and Sidtis, *Foundations of Voice Studies*, 301.
35 R. E. Myers, "Comparative Neurology of Vocalization and Speech: Proof of a Dichotomy," *Annals of the New York Academy of Sciences* 280 (1976): 745–57.
36 Hermann Ackermann, Steffen R. Hage, and Wolfram Ziegler, "Brain Mechanisms of Acoustic Communication in Humans and Nonhuman Primates: An Evolutionary Perspective," *Behavioral and Brain Sciences* 37, no. 6 (2014): 530.
37 Ibid., 531.
38 Ibid.
39 Kreiman and Sidtis, *Foundations of Voice Studies*, 61.

40 Ibid., 274.
41 Ibid., 79.
42 Ibid., 72.
43 Marc H. Bornstein and Gianluca Esposito, "Beyond Cry and Laugh: Toward a Multilevel Model of Language Production," *Behavioral and Brain Sciences* 37, no. 6 (2014): 549.
44 Kreiman and Sidtis, *Foundations of Voice Studies*, 57.
45 Ibid., 190.
46 Ibid., 81.
47 Ibid., 62.
48 Jerzy Grotowski, "La Voix," *Le Theatre* 1 (1971): 119–20. Translated by James Slowiak, quoted in Slowiak and Cuesta, *Jerzy Grotowski*, 149.
49 Slowiak and Cuesta, *Jerzy Grotowski*, 150.
50 Lessac, *The Use and Training of the Human Voice*, 18.
51 William Forde Thompson, E. Glenn Schellenberg, and Gabriela Husain, "Decoding Speech Prosody: Do Music Lessons Help?," *Emotion* 4, no. 1 (2004): 55.
52 Joanne Thirsk and Hilal Gulseker Solak, "Vocal Clarity through Drama Strategy," *Procedia - Social and Behavioral Sciences* 46 (2012): 345. No mention is made in the study of the particular tradition or school of vocal training from which the exercises were drawn.
53 Ackermann, Hage, and Ziegler, "Brain Mechanisms of Acoustic Communication," 535.
54 Kreiman and Sidtis, *Foundations of Voice Studies*, 157.
55 Ibid., 221.
56 Ibid., 222–5.
57 Ibid., 176.
58 Ibid., 189.
59 Ibid., 110.
60 Cornelia Müller, Silva H. Ladewig, and Jana Bressem, "Gestures and Speech from a Linguistic Perspective: A New Field and Its History," in *Body - Language - Communication: An International Handbook on Multimodality in Human Interaction*, ed. Cornelia Müller et al. (Berlin; Boston: De Gruyter, 2013), 58.
61 Ibid., 59.
62 David McNeill, *Hand and Mind: What Gestures Reveal about Thought* (Chicago: University of Chicago Press, 1992), 72; Tim Wharton, *Pragmatics and Non-Verbal Communication* (Cambridge: Cambridge University Press, 2009), 149–51.
63 Müller, Ladewig, and Bressem, "Gestures and Speech," 66.
64 Goldin-Meadow, "How Our Gestures Help Us Learn," 793.
65 Wharton, *Pragmatics and Non-Verbal Communication*, 149.
66 David McNeill, *Why We Gesture: The Surprising Role of Hand Movements in Communication* (New York: Cambridge University Press, 2016), 21.

67 Müller, Ladewig, and Bressem, "Gestures and Speech," 59.
68 Ibid., 69. Based on the context of usage, I believe Müller mistakenly uses here the term "language" instead of "speech," which would make more sense, given the dialectic of "speech and gesture" she is attempting to clarify.
69 Perlman and Gibbs, "Sensorimotor Simulation," 519.
70 Ibid., 521.
71 Ibid. For more on vocal gesture, see Karen Emmorey, "Do Signers Gesture?," in *Gesture, Speech, and Sign*, ed. Lynn S. Messing and Ruth Campbell (Oxford; New York: Oxford University Press, 1999), 133–59; Scott K. Liddell, "Sources of Meaning in Asl Classifier Predicates," in *Perspectives on Classifier Constructions in Sign Languages*, ed. Karen Emmorey (Mahwah, NJ: Lawrence Erlbaum, 2003), 199–219; David McNeill, *Gesture and Thought* (Chicago: University of Chicago Press, 2005); Arika Okrent, "A Modality-Free Notion of Gesture and How It Can Help Us with the Morpheme Vs. Gesture in Question in Sign Language Linguistics," in *Modality and Structure in Signed and Spoken Languages*, ed. Richard P. Meier, Kearsy Cormier, and David Quinto-Pozos (Cambridge: Cambridge University Press, 2002), 175–98.
72 Dwight Le Merton Bolinger, *Intonation and Its Parts: Melody in Spoken English* (Stanford: Stanford University Press, 1986), 195.
73 Slowiak and Cuesta, *Jerzy Grotowski*, 148–52; Campo, *Zygmunt Molik's Voice and Body Work*.
74 Müller, Ladewig, and Bressem, "Gestures and Speech," 69.
75 Tyler Marghetis and Benjamin K. Bergen, "Embodied Meaning, inside and Out: The Coupling of Gesture and Mental Simulation," ibid. (2014), 2000. See also Vittorio Gallese, "Embodied Simulation. Its Bearing on Aesthetic Experience and the Dialogue between Neuroscience and the Humanities," *Gestalt Theory* 41, no. 2 (2019).
76 Pierre Feyereisen, "Gesture and the Neuropsychology of Language," in *Body - Language - Communication: An International Handbook on Multimodality in Human Interaction*, ed. Cornelia Müller et al. (Berlin; Boston: De Gruyter, 2014), 1889–90.
77 Rolf A. Zwaan, "The Immersed Experiencer: Toward an Embodied Theory of Language Comprehension," in *Psychology of Learning and Motivation*, ed. Brian Ross (New York: Academic Press, 2015), 38. I do not believe that Zwaan is here referring directly to Diana Taylor, but there is a distinct similarity between mental simulation, as I am presenting it here, and notions of performance and performativity discussed by Taylor. Along with Judith Butler, J. L. Austin, Victor Turner, and Richard Schechner (to name a few), Taylor's notion of performativity seems to rely on a process similar to mental simulation, in that one's own experience is made up of impulses born from "outside forces," yet incorporated in fully embodied action, which is also generative. See Diana Taylor, *The Archive*

and the Repertoire: Performing Cultural Memory in the Americas (Durham: Duke University Press, 2007), 4–7; Judith Butler, *Excitable Speech: A Politics of the Performative* (New York: Routledge, 1997), 15–20; J. L. Austin, *How to Do Things with Words* (Cambridge, MA: Harvard University Press, 1981), 6; Victor Witter Turner, *The Anthropology of Performance* (New York: PAJ Publications, 1988); Richard Schechner, *By Means of Performance: Intercultural Studies of Theatre and Ritual* (Cambridge; New York: Cambridge University Press, 1990).

78 Perlman and Gibbs, "Sensorimotor Simulation," 516.
79 Ibid., 524–5.
80 Ibid., 525.
81 Zhaojun Yang and Shrikanth Narayanan, "Analysis of Emotional Effect on Speech-Body Gesture Interplay," *INTERSPEECH-2014* (2014): 1937. https://www.isca-speech.org/archive_v0/interspeech_2014/i14_1934.html.
82 Dan Loehr, "Gestures and Prosody," in *Body - Language - Communication: An International Handbook on Multimodality in Human Interaction*, ed. Cornelia Müller et al. (Berlin; Boston: De Gruyter, 2014), 1381.
83 Perlman and Gibbs, "Sensorimotor Simulation," 518.
84 Ibid., 529.
85 Marghetis and Bergen, "Embodied Meaning," 2000.
86 Perlman and Gibbs, "Sensorimotor Simulation," 517; see also Raymond W. Gibbs, "Metaphor Interpretation as Embodied Simulation," *Mind & Language* 21, no. 3 (2006): 434–58.
87 Perlman and Gibbs, "Sensorimotor Simulation," 513, 15.
88 Loehr, "Gestures and Prosody," 1385; William S. Condon, "An Analysis of Behavioral Organization," *Sign Language Studies* 13, no. 1 (1976): 305.
89 Loehr, "Gestures and Prosody," 1385.
90 Anders R. Hougaard and Gitte Rasmussen, "Fused Bodies: On the Interrelatedness of Cognition and Interaction," ibid. (2013), 564.
91 Müller, Ladewig, and Bressem, "Gestures and Speech," 62.
92 Hougaard and Rasmussen, "Fused Bodies," 571.
93 Ibid., 565.
94 Ibid., 566.
95 Ibid.
96 Pierre Feyereisen, "Psycholinguistics of Speech and Gesture: Production, Comprehension, Architecture," ibid., 163.
97 Jürgen Streeck, "Praxeology of Gesture," ibid., 675.
98 Erika Fischer-Lichte, "Gestures in the Theater," ibid. (2014), 1441–2.
99 Streeck, "Praxeology of Gesture," 676.
100 Ibid., 678.
101 Ibid., 679.

102 Elena Clare Cuffari and Thomas Wiben Jensen, "Living Bodies: Co-Enacting Experience," ibid. (2014), 2020.
103 Ibid., 2018.
104 Sigrid Norris, "Multimodal (Inter)Action Analysis: An Integrative Methodology," ibid. (2013), 276; Ron Scollon, *Mediated Discourse: The Nexus of Practice* (New York: Taylor & Francis, 2001).
105 Cuffari and Jensen, "Living Bodies," 2020.
106 Ibid.

Afterthinking

1 Denis Diderot, *The Paradox of Acting*, trans. Walter Herries Pollock (New York: Hill and Wang, 1957).
2 Roach, *Player's Passion*, 24.
3 Ibid., 25–8.
4 Ruth Padel, *In and Out of the Mind: Greek Images of the Tragic Self* (Princeton, NJ: Princeton University Press, 1992), 15–19.
5 For an overview of affect theory, see Melissa Gregg and Gregory J. Seigworth, eds., *The Affect Theory Reader* (Durham, NC: Duke University Press, 2010); Patricia Ticineto Clough and Jean Halley, eds., *The Affective Turn: Theorizing the Social* (Durham, NC: Duke University Press, 2007). For a nice summary of affect in relation to theatre, see Erin Hurley, *Theatre & Feeling* (Basingstoke: Palgrave Macmillan, 2010). See also Teresa Brennan, *The Transmission of Affect* (Ithaca: Cornell University Press, 2004).
6 Jesse J. Prinz, *Gut Reactions: A Perceptual Theory of Emotion* (New York; Oxford: Oxford University Press, 2004), 5; Damasio, *Descartes' Error*.
7 Prinz, *Gut Reactions*, 78, 225.
8 Ibid., 15.
9 Ibid., 16.
10 Ibid., 228.
11 Ibid., 242, 194.
12 Ibid., 229.
13 Noë, *Action in Perception*, 3. To elaborate further the connection between this theory of perceptual emotion and the enactivist view, see also Lawrence Barsalou's concepts of situated emotions and emotion regulation. Christine Wilson-Mendenhall, Lisa Barrett, and Lawrence Barsalou, "Situating Emotional Experience," *Frontiers in Human Neuroscience* 7 (2013): 1–16.
14 Marco Tamietto and Beatrice de Gelder, "Neural Bases of the Non-Conscious Perception of Emotional Signals," *Nature Reviews Neuroscience* 11, no. 10 (2010): 704.

15 Beatrice de Gelder and Jean Vroomen, "The Perception of Emotions by Ear and by Eye," *Cognition and Emotion* 14, no. 3 (2000): 289.
16 For a more thorough overview of contemporary theories of emotion (which contains a thoughtful critique of Prinz's position), see Julien A. Deonna and Fabrice Teroni, *The Emotions: A Philosophical Introduction* (London; New York: Routledge, 2012).
17 David Hume, *A Treatise of Human Nature* (Oxford: Clarendon, 1888), 19; Immanuel Kant, *Critique of Pure Reason*, trans. J. M. D. Meiklejohn (London: Everyman's library, 1991), 119. in James B. Steeves, *Imagining Bodies: Merleau-Ponty's Philosophy of Imagination* (Pittsburgh, PA: Duquesne University Press, 2004), 68–9.
18 Gregory Currie and Ian Ravenscroft, *Recreative Minds* (Oxford; New York: Oxford University Press, 2002), 31. See also Gilbert Ryle, *The Concept of Mind* (New York: Barnes & Noble, 1959).
19 Currie and Ravenscroft, *Recreative Minds*, 1.
20 Steeves, *Imagining Bodies*, 46.
21 Ibid., 26–7.
22 Ibid., 84.
23 Ibid., 43–4.
24 Ibid., 48.
25 Elin Diamond, *Unmaking Mimesis: Essays on Feminism and Theater* (London; New York: Routledge, 1997), xvi.
26 Currie and Ravenscroft, *Recreative Minds*, 1.
27 Ibid., 11.
28 Ibid., 77.
29 Ibid., 87.
30 Ibid., 88, note 25. Andy Clark handles the issue of overflow by proposing a mechanism of "predictive processing" that conceives of "perception, understanding, reason, and imagination as co-emergent," enabling "the embodied and environmentally situated mind" to find its way through the world by evaluating the likelihood of circumstances based on past experience. Andy Clark, *Surfing Uncertainty: Prediction, Action, and the Embodied Mind* (Oxford: Oxford University Press, 2015), 295.
31 Currie and Ravenscroft, *Recreative Minds*, 198.
32 Ibid., 196.
33 McAuley, *Not Magic but Work*, 9.
34 Ibid., 7.
35 Noë, *Action in Perception*, 7–11.
36 The basic format of the Meisner repetition exercise requires one of a pair of actors to verbalize an observation about the other, in response to which the latter responds

by way of repeating the phrase with slight alterations. Here is an example provided by David Krasner: "one actor might begin by saying 'You're looking at me,' and the other actor might reply, 'I'm looking at you.' The essence of the phrase ('looking at') is repeated about a dozen times, all the while each actor 'reads' the other actor's behavior.... As actors gain confidence through repetition, their insight deepens with respect to the other member of the scene. In other words, rather than saying 'you're staring at me,' they begin to address the feelings that lurk behind the stare. Such insight is then reflected in phrases such as 'you're angry with me,' or 'you're laughing at me'. Actors no longer take 'inventory' of the other actor superficially, but observe the scene-partner's emotions, feelings and thoughts." According to Krasner, "the impulses received from the other actor, stimulated through repetition, take on a dynamic based on the continuing real life examination of human give-and-take." David Krasner, "Strasberg, Adler and Meisner: Method Acting," in *Twentieth Century Actor Training*, ed. Alison Hodge (London; New York: Routledge, 2000), 144–6. See also Sanford Meisner and Dennis Longwell, *Sanford Meisner on Acting* (New York: Vintage Books, 1987).

37 For useful scholarship on audience and reception theory, see Adam Alston, *Beyond Immersive Theatre: Aesthetics, Politics and Productive Participation* (London: Palgrave Macmillan, 2016); Susan Bennett, *Theatre Audiences: A Theory of Production and Reception* (London; New York: Routledge, 1998); Erika Fischer-Lichte, *The Transformative Power of Performance: A New Aesthetics* (New York: Routledge, 2008); Helen Freshwater, *Theatre and Audience* (London: Palgrave Macmillan, 2009); Anna Harpin and Helen Nicholson, *Performance and Participation: Practices, Audiences, Politics* (London; New York: Palgrave, 2017); Baz Kershaw, *The Politics of Performance: Radical Theatre as Cultural Intervention* (New York: Routledge, 2002); Josephine Machon, *Immersive Theatres: Intimacy and Immediacy in Contemporary Performance* (Houndmills, Basingstoke, Hampshire: Palgrave Macmillan, 2013); Joanne Whalley, *Between Us: Audiences, Affect and the in-Between* (London: Palgrave Macmillan, 2017).

38 Yves Rossetti, Gilles Rode, and Dominique Boisson, "Numbsense: A Case Study and Implications," in *Out of Mind: Varieties of Unconscious Processes*, ed. Beatrice de Gelder, Edward H. F. De Haan, and Charles A. Heywood (Oxford: Oxford University Press, 2001), 265–92.

39 Block, "Action in Perception (Book Review)," 264.

Bibliography

Ackermann, Hermann, Steffen R. Hage, and Wolfram Ziegler. "Brain Mechanisms of Acoustic Communication in Humans and Nonhuman Primates: An Evolutionary Perspective." *Behavioral and Brain Sciences* 37, no. 6 (2014): 529–46.

Alston, Adam. *Beyond Immersive Theatre: Aesthetics, Politics and Productive Participation*. London: Palgrave Macmillan, 2016.

Anderson, Michael L. "Embodied Cognition: A Field Guide." *Artificial Intelligence* 149, no. 1 (2003): 91–130.

Arnheim, Rudolf. *Art and Visual Perception: A Psychology of the Creative Eye*. Berkeley: University of California Press, 1974.

Auslander, Philip. "'Just Be Your Self': Logocentrism and Difference in Performance Theory." In *Acting (Re)Considered: Theories and Practices*, edited by Phillip B. Zarrilli, 53–61. London; New York: Routledge, 2002.

Austin, J. L. *How to Do Things with Words*. Cambridge, MA: Harvard University Press, 1981.

Barba, Eugenio. *Beyond the Floating Islands*. New York: PAJ Publications, 1986.

Barba, Eugenio. *The Paper Canoe: A Guide to Theatre Anthropology*. New York: Routledge, 1995.

Barba, Eugenio, and Nicola Savarese. *A Dictionary of Theatre Anthropology: The Secret Art of the Performer*. London: Routledge, 2006.

Baudrillard, Jean. *Simulacra and Simulation*. Ann Arbor: University of Michigan Press, 1994.

Bennett, Susan. *Theatre Audiences: A Theory of Production and Reception*. London; New York: Routledge, 1998.

Berry, Cicely. *Your Voice and How to Use It Successfully*. [in English] London: Virgin, 1990.

Bertau, Marie-Cécile. "Voice: A Pathway to Consciousness as 'Social Contact to Oneself.'" *Integrative Psychological and Behavioral Science* 42, no. 1 (2008): 92–113.

Block, Ned. "Action in Perception (Book Review)." *The Journal of Philosophy* 102 (2005): 259–72.

Block, Ned. "Overflow, Access, and Attention." *Behavioral and Brain Sciences* 30, no. 5–6 (2007): 530–48.

Bolinger, Dwight Le Merton. *Intonation and Its Parts: Melody in Spoken English*. Stanford: Stanford University Press, 1986.

Bornstein, Marc H., and Gianluca Esposito. "Beyond Cry and Laugh: Toward a Multilevel Model of Language Production." *Behavioral and Brain Sciences* 37, no. 6 (2014): 548–49.

Brennan, Teresa. *The Transmission of Affect*. Ithaca: Cornell University Press, 2004.

Bridgeman, Bruce. "Conscious Vs Unconscious Processes: The Case of Vision." *Theory & Psychology* 2, no. 1 (1992): 73–88.

Bridgeman, Bruce, Andrea Gemmer, Trish Forsman, and Valerie Huemer. "Processing Spatial Information in the Sensorimotor Branch of the Visual System." *Vision Research* 40, no. 25 (2000): 3539–52.

Bunge, Mario. *Matter and Mind: A Philosophical Inquiry*. Dordrecht: Springer Netherlands, 2010.

Butler, Judith. *Excitable Speech: A Politics of the Performative*. New York: Routledge, 1997.

Butler, Judith. *Undoing Gender*. New York: Routledge, 2004.

Campo, Giuliano. *Zygmunt Molik's Voice and Body Work: The Legacy of Jerzy Grotowski*. [in English] New York: Routledge, 2010.

Carnicke, Sharon Marie. *Stanislavsky in Focus*. London; NY: Routledge, Taylor & Francis Group, 1998.

Cavarero, Adriana. *For More Than One Voice: Toward a Philosophy of Vocal Expression*. Edited by Paul A. Kottman. Stanford, CA: Stanford University Press, 2005.

Cazden, Joanna. "Imagery in Voice Therapy: Neurolinguistic Rationales and Clinical Guidelines." Paper presented at the American Speech-Language Hearing Association, Annual Conference, San Diego, CA, 2005.

Chemero, Anthony. *Radical Embodied Cognitive Science*. Cambridge, MA; London: MIT Press, 2009.

Clark, Andy. *Being There: Putting Brain, Body, and World Together Again*. Cambridge, MA: MIT Press, 1997.

Clark, Andy. *Surfing Uncertainty: Prediction, Action, and the Embodied Mind*. Oxford: Oxford University Press, 2015.

Clough, Patricia Ticineto, and Jean Halley, eds. *The Affective Turn: Theorizing the Social*. Durham, NC: Duke University Press, 2007.

Condon, William S. "An Analysis of Behavioral Organization." *Sign Language Studies* 13, no. 1 (1976): 285–318.

Conroy, Colette. *Theatre & the Body*. [in English] Basingstoke: Palgrave Macmillan, 2010.

Cuffari, Elena Clare, and Thomas Wiben Jensen. "Living Bodies: Co-Enacting Experience." In *Body - Language - Communication: An International Handbook on Multimodality in Human Interaction*, edited by Cornelia Müller, Alan Cienki, Ellen Fricke, Silva Ladewig, David McNeill and Sedinha Tessendorf, 2016–26. Berlin; Boston: De Gruyter, 2014.

Cull Ó Maoilearca, Laura, and Alice Lagaay. *Encounters in Performance Philosophy*. Germany: Palgrave, 2014.

Currie, Gregory, and Ian Ravenscroft. *Recreative Minds*. Oxford; New York: Oxford University Press, 2002.

Damasio, Antonio R. *Descartes' Error: Emotion, Reason, and the Human Brain*. New York: Penguin Books, 2005.
Damasio, Antonio R. *The Feeling of What Happens: Body and Emotion in the Making of Consciousness*. New York: Harcourt Brace, 1999.
Dardis, Anthony. *Mental Causation: The Mind-Body Problem*. New York: Columbia University Press, 2008.
de Gelder, Beatrice, and Jean Vroomen. "The Perception of Emotions by Ear and by Eye." *Cognition and Emotion* 14, no. 3 (2000): 289–311.
de Vignemont, Frederique. "A Mosquito Bite against the Enactive Approach to Bodily Experiences." *The Journal of Philosophy* 108 (2011): 188–204.
Deonna, Julien A., and Fabrice Teroni. *The Emotions: A Philosophical Introduction*. London; New York: Routledge, 2012.
Derrida, Jacques. *Of Grammatology*. Edited by Gayatri Chakravorty Spivak. Baltimore: Johns Hopkins University Press, 2016.
Dewey, John. *Experience and Nature*. New York: Dover Publications, 1958.
Diamond, Elin. *Unmaking Mimesis: Essays on Feminism and Theater*. London; New York: Routledge, 1997.
Diderot, Denis. *The Paradox of Acting*. Translated by Walter Herries Pollock. New York: Hill and Wang, 1957.
Dolar, Mladen. "The Linguistics of the Voice." In *The Sound Studies Reader*, edited by Jonathan Sterne, 539–54. London; New York: Routledge, 2012.
Eidsheim, Nina Sun. *Sensing Sound: Singing & Listening as Vibrational Practice*. Durham: Duke University Press, 2015.
Emmorey, Karen. "Do Signers Gesture?". In *Gesture, Speech, and Sign*, edited by Lynn S. Messing and Ruth Campbell, 133–59. Oxford; New York: Oxford University Press, 1999.
Feyereisen, Pierre. "Gesture and the Neuropsychology of Language." In *Body - Language - Communication: An International Handbook on Multimodality in Human Interaction*, edited by Cornelia Müller, Alan Cienki, Ellen Fricke, Silva Ladewig, David McNeill and Sedinha Tessendorf, 1886–98. Berlin; Boston: De Gruyter, 2014.
Feyereisen, Pierre. "Psycholinguistics of Speech and Gesture: Production, Comprehension, Architecture." In *Body - Language - Communication: An International Handbook on Multimodality in Human Interaction*, edited by Cornelia Müller, Alan Cienki, Ellen Fricke, Silva Ladewig, David McNeill and Sedinha Tessendorf, 156–68. Berlin; Boston: De Gruyter, 2013.
Fischer-Lichte, Erika. "Appearing as Embodied Mind - Defining a Weak, a Strong and a Radical Concept of Presence." In *Archaeologies of Presence*, edited by Gabriella Giannachi, Nick Kaye and Michael Shanks, 103–18. Florence: Taylor and Francis, 2012.
Fischer-Lichte, Erika. "Gestures in the Theater." In *Body - Language - Communication: An International Handbook on Multimodality in Human Interaction*, edited by

Cornelia Müller, Alan Cienki, Ellen Fricke, Silva Ladewig, David McNeill and Sedinha Tessendorf, 1440–53. Berlin; Boston: De Gruyter, 2014.
Fischer-Lichte, Erika. *The Transformative Power of Performance: A New Aesthetics*. New York: Routledge, 2008.
Fliotsos, Anne L., and Gail S. Medford. *Teaching Theatre Today: Pedagogical Views of Theatre in Higher Education*. New York: Palgrave Macmillan, 2004.
Fraser, Mariam. *The Body: A Reader*. [in English] London: Routledge, 2008.
Freshwater, Helen. *Theatre and Audience*. London: Palgrave Macmillan, 2009.
Fuchs, Elinor. "Presence and the Revenge of Writing: Re-Thinking Theatre after Derrida." *Performing Arts Journal* 9, no. 2/3 (1985): 163–73.
Gallagher, Shaun. "Body Image and Body Schema: A Conceptual Clarification." *The Journal of Mind and Behavior* 7, no. 4 (1986): 541–54.
Gallagher, Shaun. "Body Schema and Intentionality." In *The Body and the Self*, edited by José Luis Bermúdez, A. J. Marcel and Naomi Eilan, 225–44. Cambridge, MA: MIT Press, 1995.
Gallagher, Shaun. "Dynamic Models of Body Schematic Processes." In *Body Image and Body Schema: Interdisciplinary Perspectives on the Body*, edited by Helena De Preester and Veroniek Knockaert, 233–50. Philadelphia: John Benjamins Publishing Company, 2005.
Gallagher, Shaun. "A Response: Mapping the Prenoetic Dynamics of Performance." In *Theatre, Performance and Cognition: Languages, Bodies and Ecologies*, edited by Rhonda Blair and Amy Cook, 158–63. London: Bloomsbury Methuen Drama, 2016.
Gallagher, Shaun. "Theory, Practice and Performance." *Connection Science* 29, no. 1 (2017): 106–18.
Gallese, Vittorio. "Embodied Simulation. Its Bearing on Aesthetic Experience and the Dialogue between Neuroscience and the Humanities." *Gestalt Theory* 41, no. 2 (2019): 113–28.
Garner, Stanton B. *Bodied Spaces: Phenomenology and Performance in Contemporary Drama*. Ithaca, NY: Cornell University Press, 1994.
Geertz, Clifford. *The Interpretation of Cultures Selected Essays*. New York: Basic Books, 1973.
Gibbs, Raymond W. "Metaphor Interpretation as Embodied Simulation." *Mind & Language* 21, no. 3 (2006): 434–58.
Gobert, R. Darren. *The Mind-Body Stage: Passion and Interaction in the Cartesian Theater*. Redwood City: Stanford University Press, 2013.
Goldin-Meadow, Susan. "How Our Gestures Help Us Learn." In *Body - Language - Communication: An International Handbook on Multimodality in Human Interaction*, edited by Cornelia Müller, Alan Cienki, Ellen Fricke, Silva Ladewig, David McNeill and Sedinha Tessendorf, 792–804. Berlin; Boston: De Gruyter, 2013.
Gregg, Melissa, and Gregory J. Seigworth, eds. *The Affect Theory Reader*. Durham, NC: Duke University Press, 2010.

Grosz, Elizabeth. *Volatile Bodies: Toward a Corporeal Feminism*. Bloomington: Indiana University Press, 1994.

Grotowski, Jerzy. "La Voix." *Le Théatre* 1 (1971): 87–131.

Hacker, P. M. S. *Wittgenstein: Mind and Will*. Oxford, UK; Cambridge, MA: Basil Blackwell, 1996.

Haggard, Patrick. "Human Volition: Towards a Neuroscience of Will." *Nature reviews. Neuroscience* 9, no. 12 (2008): 934–46.

Harpin, Anna, and Helen Nicholson. *Performance and Participation: Practices, Audiences, Politics*. London; New York: Palgrave, 2017.

Head, Henry, W. H. R. Rivers, James Sherren, Gordon Holmes, Theodore Thompson, and George Riddoch, eds. *Studies in Neurology*. Vol. 2. London: Henry Frowde, 1920.

Hougaard, Anders R., and Gitte Rasmussen. "Fused Bodies: On the Interrelatedness of Cognition and Interaction." In *Body - Language - Communication: An International Handbook on Multimodality in Human Interaction*, edited by Cornelia Müller, Alan Cienki, Ellen Fricke, Silva Ladewig, David McNeill and Sedinha Tessendorf, 564–77. Berlin; Boston: De Gruyter, 2013.

Howell, W. C., and E. A. Fleishman, eds. *Human Performance and Productivity: Information Processing and Decision Making* Hillsdale, NJ: Erlbaum, 1982.

Hume, David. *A Treatise of Human Nature*. Oxford: Clarendon, 1888.

Hurley, Erin. *Theatre & Feeling*. Basingstoke: Palgrave Macmillan, 2010.

Hurley, S. L. *Consciousness in Action*. Cambridge, MA: Harvard University Press, 1998.

Ihde, Don. *Listening and Voice: Phenomenologies of Sound*. Albany: State University of New York Press, 2007.

Jacob, Pierre. "Embodying the Mind by Extending It." *Review of Philosophy and Psychology* 3, no. 1 (2012): 33–51.

Johnson, Mark. *The Body in the Mind: The Bodily Basis of Meaning, Imagination, and Reason*. Chicago: University of Chicago Press, 1987.

Johnson, Mark. *The Meaning of the Body: Aesthetics of Human Understanding*. Chicago: University of Chicago Press, 2007.

Johnston, Daniel. *Theatre and Phenomenology: Manual Philosophy*. [in English] London: Palgrave, 2017.

Kant, Immanuel. *Critique of Pure Reason*. [in English] Translated by J. M. D. Meiklejohn. London: Everyman's library, 1991.

Kemp, Rick. *Embodied Acting: What Neuroscience Tells Us About Performance*. New York: Routledge, 2012.

Kemp, Rick. "The Embodied Performance Pedagogy of Jacques Lecoq." *Connection Science* 29, no. 1 (2017): 94–105.

Kennedy, Flloyd. "The Challenge of Theorizing the Voice in Performance." *Modern Drama* 52, no. 4 (2009): 405–25.

Kershaw, Baz. *The Politics of Performance: Radical Theatre as Cultural Intervention*. New York: Routledge, 2002.

Kimbrough, Andrew M. *Dramatic Theories of Voice in the Twentieth Century*. [in English] Amherst, NY: Cambria Press, 2011.

Krasner, David. "Strasberg, Adler and Meisner: Method Acting." In *Twentieth Century Actor Training*, edited by Alison Hodge, 129–50. London; New York: Routledge, 2000.

Krasner, David, and David Z. Saltz. *Staging Philosophy: Intersections of Theater, Performance, and Philosophy*. Ann Arbor: University of Michigan Press, 2006.

Kreiman, Jody, and Diana Sidtis. *Foundations of Voice Studies: An Interdisciplinary Approach to Voice Production and Perception*. Malden, MA: Wiley-Blackwell, 2011.

Lakoff, George, and Mark Johnson. *Metaphors We Live By*. Chicago: University of Chicago Press, 2003.

Lakoff, George, and Mark Johnson. *Philosophy in the Flesh: The Embodied Mind and Its Challenge to Western Thought*. New York: Basic Books, 1999.

Leathers, Dale G. *Successful Nonverbal Communication: Principles and Applications*. Boston: Allyn and Bacon, 1997.

Leder, Drew. *The Absent Body*. Chicago: University of Chicago Press, 1990.

Lessac, Arthur. *The Use and Training of the Human Voice: A Bio-Dynamic Approach to Vocal Life*. [in English] Mountain View, CA; London: Mayfield Publishing, 1997.

Liddell, Scott K. "Sources of Meaning in Asl Classifier Predicates." In *Perspectives on Classifier Constructions in Sign Languages*, edited by Karen Emmorey, 199–219. Mahwah, NJ: Lawrence Erlbaum, 2003.

Linklater, Kristin. "The Art and Craft of Voice (and Speech) Training." *Journal of Interdisciplinary Voice Studies* 1, no. 1 (2016): 57–70.

Linklater, Kristin. *Freeing the Natural Voice: Imagery and Art in the Practice of Voice and Language*. Hollywood, CA: Drama Publishers, 2006.

Loehr, Dan. "Gestures and Prosody." In *Body - Language - Communication: An International Handbook on Multimodality in Human Interaction*, edited by Cornelia Müller, Alan Cienki, Ellen Fricke, Silva Ladewig, David McNeill and Sedinha Tessendorf, 1381–92. Berlin; Boston: De Gruyter, 2014.

Lutterbie, John. *Toward a General Theory of Acting: Cognitive Science and Performance*. New York: Palgrave Macmillan, 2011.

Lyotard, Jean-François. *The Postmodern Condition: A Report on Knowledge*. Minneapolis: University of Minnesota Press, 1984.

Machon, Josephine. *Immersive Theatres: Intimacy and Immediacy in Contemporary Performance*. Houndmills, Basingstoke, Hampshire: Palgrave Macmillan, 2013.

Macpherson, Ben, and Konstantinos Thomaidis. *Voice Studies: Critical Approaches to Process, Performance and Experience*. [in English] London: Routledge, 2015.

Malabou, Catherine. *What Should We Do with Our Brain?* [in English] New York: Fordham University Press, 2008.

Marghetis, Tyler, and Benjamin K. Bergen. "Embodied Meaning, inside and Out: The Coupling of Gesture and Mental Simulation." In *Body - Language - Communication: An International Handbook on Multimodality in Human Interaction*, edited by

Cornelia Müller, Alan Cienki, Ellen Fricke, Silva Ladewig, David McNeill and Sedinha Tessendorf, 2000–8. Berlin; Boston: De Gruyter, 2014.

McAuley, Gay. *Not Magic but Work: An Ethnographic Account of a Rehearsal Process*. [in English] Manchester: Manchester University Press, 2015.

McCaffery, Steve. "Cacophony, Abstraction, and Potentiality: The Fate of the Dada Sound Poem." In *The Sound of Poetry, the Poetry of Sound*, edited by Marjorie Perloff and Craig Douglas Dworkin, 118–28. Chicago: University of Chicago Press, 2009.

McNeill, David. *Gesture and Thought*. Chicago: University of Chicago Press, 2005.

McNeill, David. *Hand and Mind: What Gestures Reveal About Thought*. Chicago: University of Chicago Press, 1992.

McNeill, David. *Why We Gesture: The Surprising Role of Hand Movements in Communication*. New York: Cambridge University Press, 2016.

Meisner, Sanford, and Dennis Longwell. *Sanford Meisner on Acting*. New York: Vintage Books, 1987.

Merleau-Ponty, Maurice. *Phenomenology of Perception*. [in English] London; New York: Routledge, 2012.

Milner, David, D. Milner, Mel Goodale, and M. Goodale. *The Visual Brain in Action*. Oxford: Oxford University Press, 2006.

Montero, Barbara Gail. "Thinking in the Zone: The Expert Mind in Action." *Southern Journal of Philosophy* 53 (2015): 126–40.

Müller, Cornelia, Silva H. Ladewig, and Jana Bressem. "Gestures and Speech from a Linguistic Perspective: A New Field and Its History." In *Body - Language - Communication: An International Handbook on Multimodality in Human Interaction*, edited by Cornelia Müller, Alan Cienki, Ellen Fricke, Silva Ladewig, David McNeill and Sedinha Tessendorf, 55–82. Berlin; Boston: De Gruyter, 2013.

Myers, R. E. "Comparative Neurology of Vocalization and Speech: Proof of a Dichotomy." *Annals of the New York Academy of Sciences* 280 (1976): 745–57.

Noë, Alva. *Action in Perception*. Cambridge, MA: MIT Press, 2004.

Noë, Alva. "On What We See." *Pacific Philosophical Quarterly* 83 (2002): 57–80.

Noë, Alva. *Varieties of Presence*. Cambridge, MA: Harvard University Press, 2012.

Norris, Sigrid. "Multimodal (Inter)Action Analysis: An Integrative Methodology." In *Body - Language - Communication: An International Handbook on Multimodality in Human Interaction*, edited by Cornelia Müller, Alan Cienki, Ellen Fricke, Silva Ladewig, David McNeill and Sedinha Tessendorf, 275–87. Berlin; Boston: De Gruyter, 2013.

O'Regan, J. Kevin, and Alva Noë. "A Sensorimotor Account of Vision and Visual Consciousness." *Behavioral and Brain Sciences* 24 (2001): 939–73.

O'Shaughnessy, Brian. "Proprioception and the Body Image." In *The Body and the Self*, edited by José Luis Bermúdez, A. J. Marcel and Naomi Eilan, 175–204. Cambridge, MA: MIT Press, 1995.

Okrent, Arika. "A Modality-Free Notion of Gesture and How It Can Help Us with the Morpheme Vs. Gesture in Question in Sign Language Linguistics." In *Modality* and Structure in Signed and Spoken Languages, edited by Richard P. Meier, Kearsy Cormier and David Quinto-Pozos, 175–98. Cambridge: Cambridge University Press, 2002.

Pacherie, Elisabeth. "Towards a Dynamic Theory of Intentions." In *Does Consciousness Cause Behavior?*, edited by Susan Pockett, William P. Banks and Shaun Gallagher, 145–67. Cambridge, MA: MIT Press, 2006.

Pacherie, Elisabeth, and Patrick Haggard. *What Are Intentions?* Oxford: Oxford University Press, 2010.

Padel, Ruth. *In and Out of the Mind: Greek Images of the Tragic Self*. Princeton, NJ: Princeton University Press, 1992.

Perlman, Marcus, and Raymond W. Gibbs. "Sensorimotor Simulation in Speaking, Gesturing, and Understanding." In *Body - Language - Communication: An International Handbook on Multimodality in Human Interaction*, edited by Cornelia Müller, Alan Cienki, Ellen Fricke, Silva Ladewig, David McNeill and Sedinha Tessendorf, 512–33. Berlin; Boston: De Gruyter, 2013.

Phelan, Peggy. *Unmarked: The Politics of Performance*. London; New York: Routledge, 1993.

Phelan, Peggy. *Unmarked: The Politics of Performance*. Florence: Taylor and Francis, 2003.

Price, Janet, and Margrit Shildrick. *Feminist Theory and the Body: A Reader*. [in English] New York: Routledge, 1999.

Prinz, Jesse J. *Gut Reactions: A Perceptual Theory of Emotion*. New York; Oxford: Oxford University Press, 2004.

Rayner, Alice. *To Act, to Do, to Perform: Drama and the Phenomenology of Action*. Ann Arbor: University of Michigan Press, 1994.

Rensink, Ronald A., J. Kevin O'Regan, and James J. Clark. "To See or Not to See: The Need for Attention to Perceive Changes in Scenes." *Psychological Science* 8, no. 5 (1997): 368–73.

Richardson, Daniel C., Rick Dale, and Michael J. Spivey. "Eye Movements in Language and Cognition: A Brief Introduction." In *Methods in Cognitive Linguistics*, edited by M. Gonzalez-Marquez, I. Mittelberg, S. Coulson and M. Spivey, 323–44. Amsterdam, NL: John Benjamins Publishing Company, 2007.

Roach, Joseph. *The Player's Passion: Studies in the Science of Acting*. [in English] Ann Arbor: The University of Michigan, 2011.

Rodenberg, Patsy. *The Right to Speak: A Journey through the Voice*. [in English] London: Routledge, 1992.

Rokotnitz, Naomi. *Trusting Performance: A Cognitive Approach to Embodiment in Drama*. New York: Palgrave Macmillan, 2016.

Rossetti, Yves, Gilles Rode, and Dominique Boisson. "Numbsense: A Case Study and Implications." In *Out of Mind: Varieties of Unconscious Processes*, edited by Beatrice De Gelder, Edward H. F. De Haan and Charles A. Heywood, 265–92. Oxford: Oxford University Press, 2001.

Rowlands, Mark. *The New Science of the Mind: From Extended Mind to Embodied Phenomenology*. Cambridge, MA: MIT Press, 2010.
Ryle, Gilbert. *The Concept of Mind*. New York: Barnes & Noble, 1959.
Schechner, Richard. *Between Theater and Anthropology*. Philadelphia: University of Pennsylvania Press, 1985.
Schechner, Richard. *By Means of Performance: Intercultural Studies of Theatre and Ritual*. Cambridge; New York: Cambridge University Press, 1990.
Scollon, Ron. *Mediated Discourse: The Nexus of Practice*. New York: Taylor & Francis, 2001.
Shapiro, Larry. "The Embodied Cognition Research Programme." *Philosophy Compass* 2, no. 2 (2007): 338–46.
Shapiro, Lawrence A., ed. *The Routledge Handbook of Embodied Cognition*. New York: Routledge, Taylor & Francis Group, 2014.
Shapiro, Lisa. *The Correspondence between Princess Elisabeth of Bohemia and René Descartes*. [in English] Chicago: University of Chicago Press, 2007.
Sheets-Johnstone, Maxine. *Insides and Outsides: Interdisciplinary Perspectives on Animate Nature*. Luton, Bedfordshire: Andrews UK, 2016.
Sheets-Johnstone, Maxine. *The Primacy of Movement: Expanded Second Edition*. Netherlands: John Benjamins, 2011.
Sheets-Johnstone, Maxine. "What Are We Naming?". In *Body Image and Body Schema: Interdisciplinary Perspectives on the Body*, edited by Helena De Preester and Veroniek Knockaert, 211–32. Philadelphia: John Benjamins Publishing Company, 2005.
Shepherd, Simon. *Theatre, Body and Pleasure*. London; New York: Routledge, 2006.
Shontz, Franklin C. *Perceptual and Cognitive Aspects of Body Experience*. New York: Academic Press, 1969.
Slowiak, James, and Jairo Cuesta. *Jerzy Grotowski*. London; New York: Routledge, 2007.
Sofia, Gabriele. "The Effect of Theatre Training on Cognitive Functions." In *Affective Performance and Cognitive Science: Body, Brain, and Being*, edited by Nicola Shaughnessy, 171–80. London: Bloomsbury, 2013.
Soliman, Tamer, and Arthur M. Glenberg. "The Embodiment of Culture." In *The Routledge Handbook of Embodied Cognition*, edited by Lawrence A. Shapiro, 207–19. New York: Routledge, Taylor & Francis Group, 2014.
Spatz, Ben. *What a Body Can Do: Technique as Knowledge, Practice as Research*. London; New York: Routledge, Taylor & Francis Group, 2015.
Stanislavski, Konstantin. *An Actor's Work: A Student's Diary*. Translated by Jean Benedetti. London; New York: Routledge, 2008.
States, Bert O. "The Actor's Presence: Three Phenomenal Modes." In *Acting (Re)Considered: Theories and Practices*, edited by Phillip B. Zarrilli, 23–39. London; New York: Routledge, 2002.
States, Bert O. *Great Reckonings in Little Rooms: On the Phenomenology of Theater*. Berkeley: University of California Press, 1985.

Steeves, James B. *Imagining Bodies: Merleau-Ponty's Philosophy of Imagination.* Pittsburgh, PA: Duquesne University Press, 2004.

Strasberg, Lee. "Acting." In *The New Encyclopædia Britannica*, edited by Philip W. Goetz, 59. Chicago: Encyclopædia Britannica, 1974.

Streeck, Jürgen. "Praxeology of Gesture." In *Body - Language - Communication: An International Handbook on Multimodality in Human Interaction*, edited by Cornelia Müller, Alan Cienki, Ellen Fricke, Silva Ladewig, David McNeill and Sedinha Tessendorf, 674–89. Berlin; Boston: De Gruyter, 2013.

Sutton, John, Doris McIlwain, Wayne Christensen, and Andrew Geeves. "Applying Intelligence to the Reflexes: Embodied Skills and Habits between Dreyfus and Descartes." *Journal of the British Society for Phenomenology* 42, no. 1 (2011): 78–103.

Tamietto, Marco, and Beatrice de Gelder. "Neural Bases of the Non-Conscious Perception of Emotional Signals." *Nature Reviews Neuroscience* 11, no. 10 (2010): 697–709.

Taylor, Diana. *The Archive and the Repertoire: Performing Cultural Memory in the Americas.* [in English] Durham: Duke University Press, 2007.

Thirsk, Joanne, and Hilal Gulseker Solak. "Vocal Clarity through Drama Strategy." *Procedia - Social and Behavioral Sciences* 46 (2012): 343–46.

Thompson, Evan. "Sensorimotor Subjectivity and the Enactive Approach to Experience." *Phenomenology and the Cognitive Sciences* 4 (2005): 407–27.

Thompson, William Forde, E. Glenn Schellenberg, and Gabriela Husain. "Decoding Speech Prosody: Do Music Lessons Help?". *Emotion* 4, no. 1 (2004): 46–64.

Tribble, Evelyn. *Early Modern Actors and Shakespeare's Theatre: Thinking with the Body.* Bloomsbury Publishing, 2017.

Turner, Victor Witter. *The Anthropology of Performance.* New York: PAJ Publications, 1988.

Wangh, Stephen. *An Acrobat of the Heart: A Physical Approach to Acting Inspired by the Work of Jerzy Grotowski.* New York: Vintage Books, 2000.

Welton, Donn. *The Body: Classic and Contemporary Readings.* [in English] Malden, MA: Blackwell, 2004.

Whalley, Joanne. *Between Us: Audiences, Affect and the in-Between.* London: Palgrave Macmillan, 2017.

Wharton, Tim. *Pragmatics and Non-Verbal Communication.* Cambridge: Cambridge University Press, 2009. doi:10.1017/CBO9780511635649.

Wikipedia. "Prosody (Linguistics)." *Wikipedia, The Free Encyclopedia.* https://en.wikipedia.org/w/index.php?title=Prosody_(linguistics)&oldid=811178906 (Accessed February 26, 2018).

Wilson, Margaret. "Six Views of Embodied Cognition." *Psychonomic Bulletin & Review* 9, no. 4 (2002): 625–36.

Wilson-Mendenhall, Christine, Lisa Barrett, and Lawrence Barsalou. "Situating Emotional Experience." [In English]. *Frontiers in Human Neuroscience* 7 (November 26, 2013).

Wittgenstein, Ludwig. *Philosophical Investigations: The English Text of the Third Edition.* Edited by G. E. M. Anscombe. Upper Saddle River, NJ: Prentice Hall, 1958.

Wolford, Lisa, and Richard Schechner. *The Grotowski Sourcebook.* London: Routledge, 1997.

Yang, Zhaojun, and Shrikanth Narayanan. "Analysis of Emotional Effect on Speech-Body Gesture Interplay." *INTERSPEECH-2014* (2014): 1934–38. https://www.isca-speech.org/archive_v0/interspeech_2014/i14_1934.html.

Zarrilli, Phillip. "The Actor's Work on Attention, Awareness, and Active Imagination: Between Phenomenology, Cognitive Science, and Practices of Acting." In *Performance and Phenomenology: Traditions and Transformations*, edited by Maaike Bleeker, Jon Foley Sherman and Eirini Nedelkopoulou, 75–96. Florence: Taylor and Francis, 2015.

Zarrilli, Phillip B., Jerri Daboo, and Rebecca Loukes. *Acting: Psychophysical Phenomenon and Process.* Basingstoke: Palgrave Macmillan, 2013.

Zwaan, Rolf A. "The Immersed Experiencer: Toward an Embodied Theory of Language Comprehension." In *Psychology of Learning and Motivation*, edited by Brian Ross, 35–62. New York: Academic Press, 2015.

Index

abstract knowledge   52
Ackermann, Hermann   123, 124, 126, 128
acting teachers   15
action   33–73; *see also plastiques*
   animate forms   61–3
   cognition for   8
   emotion as   152–3
   image schemas (*see* image schemas)
   intention   44–9
   meaning-making   63–9
   movement *vs.*   62
   perception and   80–4
   rehearsed   45–6
   scenic behavior   49–50
   Wittgenstein's philosophy   39–44
Action in Perception (Noë)   80
action-oriented representations   9
actor-training exercises   1–2
affective memory   68
Altmann, Stuart   68
animation   27, 34, 61–3, 104; *see also* movement
   evolutionary biology   61–2
apprenticeship   104–5
Arnheim, Rudolf   55–7
associations   53–4, 156, 157
   balance image schema   54–9
attention   84–7
   inattentional blindness   84–5
   multi-directional   85
audition   115, 126

balance/balancing
   Barba on   49–50
   bodily   54–6
   extra-daily sense   50
   image schemas   54–9, 63–4, 66
   meaning-making   63–9
   metaphorical extensions   55–6
   space   78–9, 98–9, 103
   visual   55–8

Barba, Eugenio   24, 34, 49, 113
Bell, Charles   88
Bergen, Benjamin K.   136, 140
Berry, Cicely   111
Bertau, Marie-Cecile   118
Block, Ned   81, 84, 180 n.6, 181 n.10
Boal, Augusto   144
bodily balance   54–6; *see also* image schemas; visual balance
bodily knowledge   52
body   2–4
body image   29, 88–94; *see also* body image
   consciousness   90
   defined   89
   reification   93–4
The Body in the Mind (Johnson)   51
Body - Language - Communication (Müller)   130
body schema   29, 88–94, 97–9
   alteration by conscious attention   93
   concept   89
   joint body schema (JBS)   102
   mindless activity   90
   performative   92–3, 102, 104–6, 153, 168
   as prenoetic   90, 92, 93
   reification   93–4
   as subconscious system   89
   virtual body and   156
Bogart, Anne   76
Bollinger, Dwight   134
Bornstein, Marc   126
breathing   125

Carnicke, Sharon   106, 183 n.42
Carreri, Roberta   49, 113
Cartesianism   3, 4, 8–9
Cavarero, Adriana   110
center

Index

balanced body   54–5
  defined   54
  exerting force   55
"The Challenge of Theorizing the Voice in Performance" (Kennedy)   111
challenges to research   160–6
  epistemological uncertainty   162–3
  ethnographic   160–1
Chemero, Anthony   8, 9
childhood and adulthood   37–8
Cieślak, Ryczard   34, 67, 71–2
Clark, Andy   9, 192 n.30
cognition; *see also* Embodied Cognition (EC)
  as action   8–9
  environment and   7–9
  off-loaded into environment   7, 9
  as situated   7
  as time pressured   7
Cole, Jonathan   88
communication   70–2
  intersubjective   71–2
  nonverbal (*see* nonverbal communication)
competency   96–9
comsigns   68
conceptualization   6–7; *see also* Embodied Cognition (EC)
Condon, William   140–1
conscious competency model   96
consciousness   167
conscious reflection   97–8
conscious thought   96–7
The Constant Prince   67, 71–2
conversation   70
  call and response   70
  conscious awareness   70
cooperative action   27–8
core relational theme   152
corporeality   3
corporeal-kinetic intentionality   94; *see also* body image
corporeal-kinetic patterning   94; *see also* body schema
co-speech vocalizations   133–4
Crawley, Tom   44
Cuesta, Jairo   114, 127, 186 n.14
Cuffari, Elena   146, 147
Cull Ó Maoilearca, Laura   10, 12–13
Currie, Gregory   155, 158–9

Daddario, Will   10
Dale, Rick   100
Damasio, Antonio   111, 152
dance   104–5
deficiency model   169–70
de Gelder, Beatrice   154
Descartes, René   4
Dewey, John   13, 27–8, 34, 37–8, 52, 53, 71–2
Diderot, Denis   151
Dolar, Mladen   122
A Doll House (Ibsen)   16–21
dorsal stream   85, 100
dualistic language trap   166–8
dual-pathway model   123–6, 133, 134
Dynamic Systems Theory (DST)   11

Eidsheim, Nina Sun   110
Elisabeth of Bohemia   4
Embodied Acting: What Neuroscience Tells Us about Performance (Kemp)   11–12
Embodied Cognition (EC)   1–2
  Chemero's approach to   8, 9
  Clark's approach to   9
  Johnson's approach to   8–10
  Noë's approach to   9, 10
  Shapiro's approach to   6–8
  Wilson's approach to   7–9
emotion(s)
  as action   152–3
  enactive theory   150–4
  fictive circumstances and   153–4
  as perception   151–3
enactive theory of emotion   150–4
enactivisim (enactive perception)   29, 79–84
Encounters in Performance Philosophy (Cull Ó Maoilearca)   12
environment
  cognition and   7–9
  image schemas and   51, 52
epistemological uncertainty   162–3
Esposito, Gianluca   126
ethnographic challenges   160–1
evolutionary biological perspective of animation   61–2
Experience and Nature (Dewey)   71
eyes   100–1

facial mask resonator   114, 116
Feyereisen, Pierre   136
Fischer-Lichte, Erika   31, 145, 164–5
fluency   34, 44, 63, 105–7
force(s)   54–5, 60; *see also* image schemas
   impulses of counterbalance   54
   symmetrical (or proportional)
      arrangement   54
   as vectors of moving body parts   54
formant frequencies   119–20
formants   119
Foundations of Voice Studies (Kreiman and
      Sidtis)   30, 117
Fowler, Richard   49
full-body-brain-environment system   21
Fused Bodies approach   141–2

Gallagher, Shaun   29, 88–90, 92–4, 96, 97
gaze   77, 79–80, 83, 90, 161
Geertz, Clifford   24
gesticulation   131
gesture   31, 130–5
   Growth Point (GP)   132
   intonation and   134
   mental simulation   135–9
   moment-by-moment thinking
      and   132–3
   prosody and   133–5, 138, 140–4
   sociality/social interaction   139–45
Gibbs, Raymond W., Jr.   133, 134,
      137–40
Glenberg, Arthur M.   102
Goffman, Erving   4
Goldin-Meadow, Susan   132
Grosz, Elizabeth   3, 156
Grotowski, Jerzy   3, 12, 16, 24, 27, 30, 34,
      35, 44, 49, 58, 63, 67, 68, 76, 112–
      14, 127, 134, 164, 186 nn.13–14
Growth Point (GP)   132
Gut Feelings (Prinz)   151

habits   105–7
Hacker, P. M. S.   46
Hage, Steffen R.   123
Hand and Mind (Kendon)   131
hand *plastiques*   36–7, 44
hard focus   100
Head, Henry   89
head *plastiques*   35
hearing   77, 87

Hougaard, Anders R.   141–2
Hume, David   155
Hunter College, NYC   24
Hurley, Susan   80
Husain, Gabriela   128

Ihde, Don   110
image schemas   27, 34, 50–60, 63–8, 72,
      93, 166
   attraction   60
   balance   54–9, 63–4, 66
   blockage   60
   bodily and visual balance   55–8
   concept   51
   counterforce   60
   environment and   51, 52
   force   60
   learning process and   52–3
   resistance   59–60
   restraint removal   60
   scale   51–3
   use   51
imagination   5, 154–9
   modes   156–7
   motor functions   159
   recreative   158–9
   virtual body   156–8
Imagining Bodies (Steeves)   155–6
imagistic thought   132
inattentional blindness   84–5
Indian Kathakali training   15–16
in group   102
input-output picture   80, 81;
      see also perception
intention   27, 33, 43–9
   concept   45
   as inner experience (being
      internal)   46–7
   present-directed   46
interaction
   embodied process   51
   environmental   8, 51, 52
   importance   69–72
   subject-environment context   38–9
interactional synchrony   141
International School of Theatre
      Anthropology (ISTA)   49
intonation   122, 123
   gesture and   134
Intonation and Its Parts (Bollinger)   134

James, William 151
Japanese Noh theatre training 15
Jensen, Thomas 146, 147
Johnson, Mark 8–10, 13, 27, 33–4, 38, 46, 50–60, 73, 93, 179 n.16
joint body schema (JBS) 102
joints 77–8, 90–4; *see also* body image; body schema; proprioception

Kandinsky, Vasily 55
Kant, Immanuel 155
Kemp, Rick 11–12
Kendon, Adam 31, 130–2, 173
Kennedy, Flloyd 111, 112, 186 n.21
Kimbrough, Andrew M. 111
Kinesic communication 102
Krasner, David 12–13
Kreiman, Jody 30, 117–27, 129–30, 187 n.33

Lagaay, Alice 10
Lange, Carl 151
language
 advent/origin of 62
 as an embodied phenomenon 135
 learning through immersion 44
 as social phenomenon 140
 Wittgenstein on 40
language games 39–40, 53, 62, 142
language-like gestures 131
Leathers, Dale 102
Lessac, Arthur 112, 114, 116, 127
Linklater, Kristin 111, 114–16, 122, 187 n.33
listening 126–30
 onstage 128–9
 vocal familiarization 129–30
 vocal training 129
Loehr, Dan 138, 140–1
loudness 123, 124
Lutterbie, John 11

McAuley, Gay 24–5, 160, 161
Macpherson, Ben 111
McNeill, David 31, 130–2, 135, 139
Malabou, Catherine 26
Marghetis, Tyler 136, 140
Mayer, Jerry 44
Mead, Margaret 160

meaning 63–9
 communicating 22–3
 creating/constructing 18–20, 22–3
The Meaning of the Body (Johnson) 51
mental simulation 31, 135–9
Merleau-Ponty, Maurice 20, 83, 96, 155–7
"Method of Physical Actions" 47
mind 9
 body/mind dualism 4–6
 consciousness and 167
 interactionist view 9
 nondualistic, nonrepresentational view 9
Molik, Zygmunt 112
Montero, Barbara Gail 96
mouth resonator 114
movement 61–3
 action *vs.* 62
 intelligence 62
 sense-making 62–3
Müller, Cornelia 130, 132, 135, 141, 189 n.68

Narayanan, Shrikanth 138
nasal resonator 114
Noë, Alva 9, 10, 29, 79–86, 100, 104, 153, 180–1 n.6
nonverbal communication 71
 eyes 100–1
 Kinesic communication 102
 Proxemics 102–4
Norris, Sigrid 147
North American Cultural Laboratory (NACL Theatre) 23

Odin Teatret 24, 34, 49, 113
"ordinary language" philosophy of Wittgenstein 39–44
O'Shaughnessy, Brian 29, 88
Overlie, Mary 76

Pacherie, Elisabeth 46
Padel, Ruth 151
Paillard, Jacques 88
pantomimes 131
pathos; see emotion(s)
pedagogy 15
perceiving 86

perception 75–108; *see also* proprioception
   action and 80–4
   attention 84–7
   as creative activity 158
   emotion as 152
   enactivisim 29, 79–84
   input-output picture 80
   objects and 82–4
   overview 28–30
   presence 85–6, 98
perceptual theory of emotion 151
perezhivanie 106–7
Performance Philosophy 10–13
Performance Philosophy Bibliography 10
performative body schema 92–3, 102, 104–6, 153, 168; *see also* body schema
Perlman, Marcus 133, 134, 137–40
Philosophical Investigations (Wittgenstein) 40, 48
pitch 123–5
plastiques 33–73
   body part isolations 35–6
   challenges 44
   effectiveness 105
   execution in a constant flow 43–4
   as exercises 34–9
   hand 36–7, 44
   head 35
   interaction 69–72
   moves/movement 35–7
   overview 27–8, 33–4
   shoulder 35
   as solo activity 69
The Player's Passion (Roach) 2, 151
practice 14; *see also* technique
preconceptual knowledge 54
prenoetic body schema 90, 92, 93
presence 85–6
   competency and 96–9
Presentation of the Self in Everyday Life (Goffman) 4
The Primacy of Movement (Sheets-Johnstone) 61
principle of continuity 37–8
Prinz, Jesse J. 151–3
proficiency model 168–72
propositional thought 132

proprioception 88–94
   defined 29, 88
prosody 30, 31, 123–6
   autoregulation 127
   components 123
   defined 123
   gesture and 133–5, 138, 140–4
   listening 126–30
Proxemics 102–4
psychological realism 5

Quintillian 151

Rasmussen, Gitte 141–2
Ravenscroft, Ian 155, 158–9
recreative imagination 158–9
rehabituation 95–6, 170
rehearsal process 48
reification 93–4
replacement 7, 8; *see also* Embodied Cognition (EC)
representationalism 9
resistance 59–60; *see also* image schemas
resonance 119
resonators 113–17
   activation 120
   facial mask 114, 116
   formant frequencies 119–20
   technical manipulation 121–2
Richardson, Daniel 100
Roach, Joseph 2, 151
Rodenburg, Patsy 111
Rokem, Freddie 10
Rowlands, Mark 9
Ryle, Gilbert 155

Saltz, David Z. 12–13
scenic behavior 23, 29
   in experimental theatre context 21
   principles 49–50
scenic *bios* 106–7
Schechner, Richard 4
Schellenberg, E. Glenn 128
schooling 103
Scollon, Ron 146–7, 167
second-wave feminism 3
self-consciousness 90, 91

self-monitoring in speech   127–8
self-synchrony   141
sense memory exercises   5
senses   77; *see also* perception; proprioception
sensorimotor knowledge   81–2
sensorimotor tuning   102
Shapiro, Lawrence   6–8
Sheets-Johnstone, Maxine   13, 27, 29, 34, 61–3, 68–9, 93–4, 104
Shepherd, Simon   3
shoulder *plastiques*   35
Sidtis, Diana   30, 117–27, 129–30, 187 n.33
sign languages   131
site of engagement   145–7
Slowiak, James   114, 127, 186 n.14
smell   76
sociality/social interaction   139–45
  Fused Bodies approach to   141–2
socialized bodies   3
socio-physical ecology of theatre   102
soft focus   100
Soliman, Tamer   102
somatic feeling theory   151–2
space   94–105
  balancing   78–9, 98–9, 103
  nonverbal communication   102–3
  schooling   103
spatial indexing   100
Spatz, Ben   5, 13–16
speech prosody; *see* prosody
speech/speech production; *see* voice
Spivey, Michael   100
Staging Philosophy: Intersections of Theater, Performance, and Philosophy (Krasner and Saltz)   12
Stanislavsky   2, 18, 45, 47, 56, 106, 183 n.42
States, Bert O.   39
Steeves, James B.   155–6
Streeck, Jürgen   31, 141, 144–6
Stucky, Nathan   5
Sutton, John   96

tactical deception   68–9
Tamietto, Marco   154
technique   13–23
  acting for audience   18, 20
  activating entire system   20–1
  characteristics   14
  creating/constructing meaning   18–20, 22–3
  defined   13–14
  developing usable skills   15–16
  embodied practice   16–21
  performance contexts/styles   15–21
  transmitting technique pedagogy   15
theatre
  as site of engagement   145–7
  as a strange country   48–9
Theatre, Body and Pleasure (Shepherd)   3
Theatre of Productions phase   34
theory of phenomenal overflow   84
thick description   24, 172
Thomaidis, Konstantinos   111
Thompson, William Forde   128
The 3 Layers   75–108
  joints   77–8, 90–4 (*see also* proprioception)
  senses   77 (*see also* perception)
  space   78–9 (*see also* space)
Tomell-Presto, Jessica   5
touch   76, 82–3
Toward a General Theory of Acting (Lutterbie)   11
"Towards a dynamic theory of intentions" (Pacherie)   46
Tractatus Logico-Philosophicus (Wittgenstein)   40
Turner, Victor   4

ventral stream   85, 100
via negativa   58
virtual body   156–9, 164
vision   77, 80–7, 99–101; *see also* perception
visual art   56–8
visual balance   55–8; *see also* image schemas
Vocal Action   108–48; *see also* voice
vocal chords   113
vocal familiarization   129–30
vocal gestures   133, 134
vocalizer and responder   142–3
vocal resonators; *see* resonators
voice   109–48
  activating muscles   117

definition   118
  as a disembodied entity   117
  and gesture (*see* gesture)
  listening   126–30
  mental simulation   31, 135–9
  prosody   30, 31, 123–6
  resonators (*see* resonators)
  theorizing   110–13
  and voice quality   117–19
Volatile Bodies (Grosz)   3
voluntary *vs.* involuntary action   41–2
Vroomen, Jean   154

Wharton, Tim   131, 132
What a Body Can Do (Spatz)   5

What Should We Do with Our Brain?
   (Malabou)   26
will and action   41–3
Wilson, Margaret   7–9
Wittgenstein, Ludwig   13, 45–9, 56, 62,
   71, 142, 148
   "ordinary language" philosophy
      of   27, 33, 39–44
workshop training   165

Yang, Zhaojun   138

Ziegler, Wolfram   123
Zwaan, Rolf   137

www.ingramcontent.com/pod-product-compliance
Lightning Source LLC
Chambersburg PA
CBHW062227300426
44115CB00012BA/2253